HEALTHY FOOD IN HALF AN HOUR

Jenny Rogers

PENGUIN BOOKS

For Luke, Owen, Emma and Charlotte

Penguin Books Ltd, 27 Wrights Lane, London W8 5TZ (Publishing and Editorial)
and Harmondsworth, Middlesex, England (Distribution and Warehouse)
Viking Penguin Inc., 40 West 23rd Street, New York, New York 10010, USA
Penguin Books Australia Ltd, Ringwood, Victoria, Australia
Penguin Books Canada Ltd, 2801 John Street, Markham, Ontario, Canada L3R 1B4
Penguin Books (NZ) Ltd, 182–190 Wairau Road, Auckland 10, New Zealand

First published 1987

Filmset in Plantin (Linotron 202) by
Rowland Phototypesetting Ltd
Bury St Edmunds, Suffolk

Made and printed in Great Britain by
Cox & Wyman Ltd, Reading, Berks

CONTENTS

INTRODUCTION

This book is aimed at cooks who, like me, want to eat well, cook quickly and live healthily.

It's not always apparent that it is possible to satisfy all three of these demands. At one extreme there's 'healthy haute cuisine', which produces beautiful food where expense is no object and neither is time. The recipes will shamelessly call for Cornish lobster eggs and rare sea vegetables obtainable only at a little greengrocer's in South Kensington. There will be a garnish which will be exquisite: say, sliced truffles tied in little bundles with young leeks, set off with a few out-of-season inch-long mange-tout peas fanned out on a black or red octagonal plate. If I could afford it, I might like to eat out like this. As a style of home cooking it is out of the question.

Straightforwardly traditional vegetarian food does not seem to be the answer either. First, it is often nothing like as 'healthy' as it claims to be, what with all that cheese, eggs and cream. Then, it also seems to demand a life where you can remember both to soak dried beans overnight and to find time to boil them for several hours. The results, too, dare I say it, are often unappetizing: too much leaden wholemeal pastry encasing too many root vegetables in floury cheese sauces.

My own philosophy of cooking and eating is that I simply haven't the time to fiddle about for hours in the kitchen. I love cooking, but equally I want to give time to my husband, my two young sons and a demanding job. I also want us all to eat healthily because I find the evidence irresistibly convincing. So my basic aim is to come home, fling my coat off and have a meal that is both enjoyable and 'healthy' on the table within thirty minutes. This usually has to be accomplished within store-cupboard/refrigerator/freezer limits as, fish apart, we shop only once a week. This book looks at the 'why' and 'how' of living this way.

The first part of the book rehearses some of the evidence for the need to change to a healthier diet, and what this means in terms of equipping and stocking the kitchen, especially when you are short of time. The change in our diet advocated by various medical reports is

7

profound. It means a different kind of shopping and different methods of cooking: spending more, for instance, on fruit and vegetables and less on joints and tins. It may mean putting away the deep-fat frier and perhaps buying a wok and a steamer instead.

The second part of the book is a personal collection of well-tried recipes that meet the triple criteria of being satisfying to eat, healthy and quick. My style of cooking is much influenced by ideas from the Mediterranean, Asia and South America, where, when people have had enough to eat, they have always eaten healthily. Most of the recipes can be made from scratch in about half an hour. The ingredients are neither difficult to find nor expensive.

I have been privileged to work with many talented cooks in the course of my job in television, and all of them have had some influence on the food I cook and serve at home. I must particularly thank Delia Smith, whose scrupulous concern for what 'ordinary people' know and like has been much in my mind while writing this book, Madhur Jaffrey for helping me learn about Indian food, and Claudia Roden for her gentle and scholarly approach to the food of the Middle East. I also owe a debt of gratitude to my former colleague David Cordingley, whose unblinking and penetrating concern for healthier eating in Britain first raised my own level of consciousness about the subject. My friend Clare Brigstocke combines a passionate commitment to good cooking with a thorough knowledge of the principles of good health. Her advice has been invaluable. Thanks, too, to Paula Follin whose expertise with word processors made drafting and re-drafting so much easier. Finally, I must thank my husband Alan, my sons Luke and Owen, and also our friends Chris and David Davey, for eating their way uncomplainingly through so much of this book.

Towards a Healthier Diet

CHANGING HABITS

Many of the most vociferous objections to the evidence on food and health come from the food industry. Changing well-tried methods of production and marketing is expensive; nor is it pleasant to contemplate the idea that your product may be making people ill. Other objections come from people who fancy that at least heart disease is a 'clean way to go', forgetting how often it is quite the reverse – a slow and painful deterioration over many years.

But perhaps the most common popular defence of existing diet comes from people who can cite an aged relation who apparently did all the 'wrong' things, yet lived to a ripe old age. Our postbag at the BBC after our Food and Health campaign was full of 'evidence' of this kind. As one such writer said, 'My uncle is 92, is still running for the bus, and he's eaten chips all his life!'

My own family also seems to provide a perfect example. My mother's father, born in 1877, was driven by poverty to leave his rural home in Dorset. In the 1890s he came to Cardiff and found work loading coal, iron and steel on to ships at the docks, a job which was to last a working lifetime. He spent the last 20 years of his life with us, and certainly tucked into his butter, bacon, lamb, pork, puddings and white bread, just like the rest of us. He liked the occasional pipe, and lived to be 89. Yet looking more closely at his life provides some of the clues to what otherwise might appear to be an exception that proves the rule. In the 1960s, he often told me, marvelling at the plenty we enjoyed, that as a child and a young man there had been little variety or abundance in his diet. 'Bread and scrape' was the staple, with skimmed milk because it was cheaper, potatoes, porridge, and whatever fresh fruit and vegetables you could grow yourself. You had meat once or twice a week, on Sundays and Mondays if you were lucky. No wonder, then, that all his life he was a dedicated and serious allotment gardener, tramping the miles there and back and working flat out hoeing and digging most weekdays, even in his ninetieth year. His life-style was spartan. He never possessed a car and did not enjoy riding in one. He regarded 'proper' shoes as an affectation: for the amount of daily brisk marching he did, boots alone would do. He was not a drinker; the odd pint at weekends was more than enough to satisfy him. His few health problems throughout an intensely active old age were caused, not by diet-induced ~~degenerative diseases, but by~~ the legacies of his work: deafness and an easily cured skin cancer.

So my grandfather's life, far from proving that older generations ate the same as us and survived, in fact suggests the opposite. The diet of his youth, typically boring and restricted as it no doubt was in culinary terms, and possibly short on some minerals and vitamins, was certainly strikingly different from the diet of the British young today, and in most respects a lot healthier. Unrefined carbohydrates formed a huge percentage of his diet: fat played a much smaller part. As a labourer working long hours, exercise came as a normal part of his daily routine: he did not have to seek it out, as I do, in a swimming pool or on a badminton court. Perhaps, too, this abundant hard physical work staved off the effects of a long lifetime of moderate pipe-smoking.

It is odd to reflect that someone born during the depression of the 1870s who was a middle-aged man throughout the depression of the Twenties and Thirties and the later privations of the war years, might in fact have owed his good health to his relative poverty.

One case does not make good epidemiology, but the truth is that where diet is concerned, most of us have short memories and limited vision. We tend to assume that what we eat now is what has always been eaten. The second half of the twentieth century has actually seen a profound upheaval in our eating habits.

HOW OUR DIET HAS CHANGED

• We are eating less, but fat, especially saturated fat, now forms a bigger percentage of our calorie intake.

• Although we are eating less, obesity is now a major health problem, perhaps because we have so much less exercise.

• Far, far more of our food is highly refined. Potatoes are a good example. Potatoes are a perfect 'whole food' and used to be consumed in huge quantities. Now we are eating fewer potatoes, but our consumption of potato crisps has soared. Potato crisps are a refined food, high in fat, salt and mysterious 'flavourings' which come from the laboratory rather than the kitchen.

● Convenience food (not necessarily the same as 'junk food') thrives because 'The Housewife', if she ever existed, has disappeared. Women of my mother's generation were encouraged to think of cooking, housekeeping and childcare as honourable full-time occupations. While my own mother escaped from any feelings of shame about her own need to work outside the home, she still spent about five hours every Sunday in a frenzy of floury activity, producing home-made pies, cakes and biscuits 'to last the week'. Now that far more of us are in paid employment, women have provided a perfect market for manufacturers who are selling time-saving along with their carefully photographed boxes of pizzas, pies and cakes.

● Affluence has meant that meat and butter, previously consumed regularly only by the well-off, are now within everyone's reach. In my grandfather's day, an 'ordinary' family might hope to eat meat a few times a week. Many of us now eat meat three or even four times a *day*.

Eating meat still signifies status and affluence. It has cultural and social resonances beyond the mere culinary, which perhaps explains why so many people resist eating less of it. In a recent poll conducted by MORI for London Weekend Television, people were asked to help the researchers define the standards of living which indicated whether you were above or below the poverty line. Along with not having a warm, dry coat or not being able to afford a holiday came not being able to afford to eat meat or fish at least once every two days. And how many of us, I wonder, still feel a knee-jerk obligation to provide at least one substantial meat course for guests we wish to impress?

● Along with the affluence of the Sixties came a wave of popular interest in '*haute cuisine*'. Looking back through the records of television cookery programmes, it is startling to note that as late as the middle Fifties there were many sober and helpfully meant programmes on making rabbit go further, or offering instructions for making things like 'mock cream'. After a foundation course from Philip Harben on ITV, the way was clear for the 1960s phenomenon of Fanny Craddock. Fanny did not bother with mock cream and was not interested in a hundred ways to make a rabbit go further. She set out to inspire the audience with ambitious dinner-party recipes taken from the classic cookery of Northern France, which, of course, includes lavish use of red meat, butter and cream. The more outrageous were her creations – chocolate swans, spun sugar decorations – the more the audience loved it. It was certainly beyond what most people could achieve, but it helped form people's aspirations. To offer your guests cream of asparagus soup, Steak Diane and a rich 'gateau' was to prove that socially you had arrived. As a young married woman in the middle Sixties I must proudly have cooked this kind of meal many dozens of times. The first cookery book I ever bought was *The Penguin Cordon Bleu Cookery Book* by Rosemary Hume and Muriel Downes, published in the early Sixties and a Bible for devotees of this sort of food.

● Dinner-party eating and supermarket shopping have also been associated with a steep rise in alcohol consumption. In real terms the cost of alcohol has gone down. Going to pubs may be in decline as a pastime, but drinking at home is no longer regarded as the furtive pursuit of the dedicated drinker. Many people now put a few bottles of wine into their shopping trolley as casually as they stock up on detergents.

Fortunately, at the same time, there have been signs of growth in another direction. Foreign travel and the books of Elizabeth David helped, but so did the Italian, Turkish, Indian and Chinese immigrants who opened restaurants and 'take-aways' in every High Street. The astonishing fact was that the stodgy old British were persuaded to buy, to eat and ultimately to wish to cook *spaghetti alle vongole*, lamb kebab with pitta bread, stir-fried vegetables and chicken korma with dhal. In the long term this may prove to have been the most effective means yet of turning the British diet in a 'healthier' direction.

But what, exactly, should this direction be? Is the evidence internally consistent, or will 'They' be changing 'Their' minds again soon?

THE TREND TOWARDS HEALTH

The truth about tobacco was known for many years before the devastating evidence was finally given 'official' endorsement by the

Royal College of Physicians report *Smoking and Health* in 1962. The truth about food has been known for many years too, and some people would say that the evidence for the need for action is even more convincing than it was for smoking in the 1960s.

Nothing much happened in Britain until 1983 when the *Sunday Times* leaked the findings of the National Advisory Committee on Nutrition Education (NACNE). The Report had gone through several drafts over two years but had not so far been published. The reason for the delay was usually given as the need for more 'consultation' in a 'controversial' area. The more cynical interpretation was that the NACNE Report was so devastating in its recommendations that it was an embarrassment to the DHSS ('Why has the Government been allowing us to dig our graves with our mouths for so long?') and a threat to the food and farming industries, which have powerful friends at Westminster.

Once out of the bag, the cat refused to lie down. The alleged cover-up itself was a good story seized with relish by the media. More important in the long term was the realization that here at last was a *British* Committee of eminently cautious and respected medical scientists giving official blessing to findings which were already common currency elsewhere in the world. The Report was itself the result of months of political compromise. Privately, some of NACNE's distinguished members felt it was too timid: too accepting, for instance, of the gargantuan British appetite for sugar. At the same time the Report was attacked by the food industry as being 'too extreme'.

The true importance of the NACNE Report is that it did not just say, 'Cut down a little on this, eat a bit more of that.' It actually set precise targets by showing, for instance, how much fibre, on average, we were currently eating, side by side with a recommendation for the amount to aim for in future.

NACNE's is only one of many such reports world wide. Others have come from the World Health Organization, the McGovern Committee in America and the Committee on Medical Aspects of Food Policy (COMA) in Britain. Although they differ in emphasis and points of detail, the broad sweep of evidence has a remarkable unity. What it tends to show is:

● There is no society in the world consuming large amounts of salt which does not also have a large number of people with high blood pressure.

• All societies consuming a diet high in saturated fat have endemic heart disease which can even begin in childhood.

• Cancer of the colon and other serious intestinal and digestive disorders are common only in countries eating a high-fat, low-fibre diet.

• These problems seem to have nothing to do with ethnic differences. Peasant Africans moving to a more urban life-style begin to show the same health problems as Westerners. Japanese in Japan have little heart disease; Japanese in America have as much as other Americans. Heart disease was virtually unknown in Britain a hundred years ago.

• It is possible to show a direct causal relationship between diet and some of the critical symptoms of 'Western' diseases. It has been shown, for instance, that dramatically reducing salt intake can lower blood pressure and that restricting saturated fat can reduce the level of cholesterol in the blood. (A high blood cholesterol level is an acknowledged risk factor in heart disease.) The effect has also been shown to work in the opposite direction. Professor Anna Ferro-Luzzi worked with a group of Italians who ate the normal 'healthy' southern Italian diet. Their blood cholesterol level was low. When they were persuaded to eat a diet high in saturated fat for six weeks, their cholesterol level rose inexorably to something just below the average British level, which is generally regarded as far too high for health.

Most of the available evidence is drawn from the study of whole populations (epidemiology), so it is not strong on individual predictions. It cannot, for instance, tell you personally that if you eat half a pound of butter a day you will die prematurely of heart disease, only that you may increase the possibility, depending on your heredity, what else you eat and the rest of your life-style. Nor can it guarantee you a long and healthy life if you follow all the 'healthy' guidelines. For instance, there may be a history of heart disease in your family which stacks some of the odds against you. The Wimbledon Champion Arthur Ashe had a heart attack even though he was a young man in peak condition. His father's family, it emerged, had a notable history of severe coronary artery disease. Since we can't be sure what cards our genes have given us, it makes even more sense to be prudent.

However, although the evidence is overpowering, it is not neat. Human beings are not laboratory animals. They cannot be force-fed a high-fat, high-sodium, low-fibre diet for 50 years and then be compared with a control group force-fed a low-fat, low-sodium, high-fibre diet, with their arteries simultaneously dissected to observe the differences. There can also be ethical objections to many pieces of research much less obviously preposterous. For instance, it has proved difficult to devise a trial which would show the relationship between a lack of folic acid (found in green vegetables) and spina bifida pregnancies. After all, if you had the slightest suspicion that you might have a spina bifida baby because you didn't eat enough green vegetables, would you want to be a member of an experimental group deprived of the vitamin? There is more than a suspicion that in some studies, the results have been sabotaged by 'control' groups which in practice did exactly the same as the experimental group.

In practice, too, it is difficult to isolate diet from other aspects of human behaviour. A man who sticks rigorously to a 'prudent' diet may still cling to his 20 cigarettes and four pints a day and go everywhere by car. It is highly likely that smoking, drinking, exercise and stress are all involved in 'Western' disease, and that getting those sorted out as well is important to back up the benefits of a healthier diet.

FAT

A good friend of mine triumphantly informed me recently that all my nagging had finally borne fruit – she had cut out fat! While I was politely murmuring 'oh, good' she went on to explain that the family were now eating Flora with their wholemeal breakfast toast, that sausages had disappeared from the menu, and that the frying pan had been hidden at the back of the deepest cupboard. Even the children's fishfingers were now grilled. While she was speaking, out of the corner of my eye I caught sight of the remains of a family Sunday tea which had included a generous slab of Cheddar cheese, cold ham, several different types of home-made cakes, including a cream-filled sponge, Penguin biscuits and a bottle of gold-top milk.

Banishing butter, sausages and the frying pan was certainly a significant start, but she was very far from 'cutting out fat'. Such confusion is common and is often most skilfully stoked up by the public relations strategies of the food industry. 'A portion of my ice-cream has less fat in it than an avocado,' one manufacturer was reported as saying bitterly, while complaining about the 'antics' of the 'health lobby'. This may well be true, but he did not say that the fat in avocados is polyunsaturated and that the avocado is also a cornucopia of minerals and vitamins, unlike most ice-creams.

Facts on fat

Cutting through this confusion is not difficult. These are the facts:

There is too much of every type of fat in our diets and we should reduce it. At present, fat in food can form up to 40 per cent of our total energy intake. This is too high. The NACNE report recommended that it should be no more than 30 per cent, but many people regard this as too generous. Our actual bodily need for fat is probably extremely small – perhaps as little as ½ oz (12 g) a day.

Eating too much fat can lead to being overweight. As the butter

18

manufacturers have been eager to point out, both butter and margarine have the same number of calories. They do not say how high this is: ½ lb (225 g) of butter or margarine has 1,680 calories. Over-consumption of fat is likely to lead to being overweight, in itself a risk factor in many diseases, notably heart disease and diabetes.

Excessive saturated fat intake makes heart disease much more likely. We should reduce our intake of saturated fat. The evidence strongly suggests that it is saturated fat which is the main villain. It probably leads to a raised level of blood cholesterol which is a risk factor in heart disease.

Saturated fat is mostly of animal origin and is found in meat, milk, lard, cheese, cream and eggs. It is also present in some vegetables (for instance coconut and palm). Some margarines, usually the hard ones, are high in saturated fat.

Unsaturated fat is present in fish and food which is of plant origin: vegetables, fruit, seeds and nuts.

Polyunsaturated fats are thought to be especially valuable in a healthy diet. As a source of linoleic acid they help us maintain body cells, and they are also thought actually to help reduce the level of blood cholesterol. Oily fish, offal, and some soft margarines are high in polyunsaturates.

Monounsaturated fats are thought to be neutral in their effects on blood cholesterol. The best known is olive oil. This is fortunate for cooks, as olive oil must be the best all-purpose cooking and salad oil in the world.

Eating less saturated fat generally is more important than cutting down on foods containing cholesterol. Here is another rich source of confusion. Just as 'healthy food' is often confused with 'Health Food' and vegetarianism, so 'healthy eating' is often confused with 'low-cholesterol' food. Some margarines still flourish the words 'low cholesterol' on their labels as an inducement to buy, though in fact cholesterol is not found in any food of vegetable origin.

A high level of cholesterol in the blood is known to predispose to heart disease. It seemed logical, therefore, to identify foods which contained cholesterol (for instance liver, eggs, shellfish) and to restrict them. However, more recent thinking has suggested that the food we eat which contains cholesterol makes a trivial contribution to the level in the blood. A high level of blood cholesterol seems to be triggered by the body's response to a diet high in saturated fat. This is the current British view, but it is the case that some physicians still suggest a low-cholesterol diet for people with certain kinds of heart disease.

Much of the fat we eat is 'hidden' in the manufacturing process. It is best to cut down on these high-fat foods. Fat, like sugar, helps to prolong the shelf life of food. It is also a cheap ingredient, so it adds to profit. Unfortunately, it's not always as easy to spot as those tell-tale white specks in a pork pie or the yellow layer at the top of a pint of gold-top milk. There is a high fat content in most biscuits, pastry, chocolate, cakes, mayonnaise, crisps, ice-cream, sausages and 'made-up meats' like corned beef, luncheon meat and salami. Avoid these foods as far as possible.

Check-list on cutting down fat

Shopping

Milk. Drink skimmed or semi-skimmed milk rather than gold or silver top. Avoid condensed and evaporated milk and coffee whiteners.

Cheese. Avoid large quantities of hard cheese – eat it moderately. Use Edam, Gouda, Camembert, Brie or low-fat Cheddars instead. Use cottage cheese for snacks.

Cream. Keep cream for special occasions only. Try thickened yoghurt or fromage blanc (see page 70) for everyday use.

Butter. Use it sparingly. Keeping butter softened makes it easier to spread it thinly. Substitute polyunsaturated low-fat spreads for everyday use. Use all these spreads thinly on bread. Bread served with soup does not need a spread at all. Sandwiches with moist fillings (e.g., tuna) don't need butter, nor do toasted snacks like baked beans.

Cooking fats and oils. Use all oils sparingly. Choose olive, corn, soya, walnut, sunflower, peanut or safflower. Avoid: palm, coconut and 'blended vegetable' oils; lard; hard margarines that do not say they are 'high in polyunsaturates'.

Meat. Mince beef yourself after cutting off the fat or buy 'best' mince, which has less fat. White meat is less fatty than red meat, ham and bacon. Trim all visible fat from joints and chops. Buy leaner cuts in smaller quantities. Tenderloin is leaner than belly of pork; leg of lamb is leaner than breast. Buy chicken, turkey, rabbit and fish more often. Remove the skin from chicken and turkey, as this is the fattiest part.

Pies and sausages. Lower-fat sausages are creeping on to the market. If you are addicted to sausages buy these occasionally and grill them slowly so that as much fat as possible runs out. In general, however, it is best to avoid sausages, salami, pork pies, and pressed meats, as their fat content is so high.

Eggs. Egg yolks are fatty. About 4 to 5 eggs a week is the recommended 'safe' level. Adding a little skimmed milk to scrambled eggs and cooking them in a microwave or non-stick pan makes them go further.

Cakes, pastry, biscuits, chocolate, mayonnaise, salad cream. Once in a while as a treat is fine, but these should not be part of your daily diet. Don't buy them, then you won't be tempted.

Cooking

- Grill or oven-bake more frequently.

- Never *pour* oil into a pan – brush or wipe it out evenly with oil instead.

- Use heavy non-stick pans – they need very little fat.

- Never add fat to mince – put it in the pan under a medium heat until the fat runs out, when you can pour it off or blot it up with kitchen paper.

- 'Stretch' meat by adding pulses or vegetables rather than making the meat the centrepiece of the dish.

- Roast meat on a rack – don't baste with added fat.

- Let stock and casseroles cool completely in a refrigerator – that way the fat will solidify and can easily be skimmed off. Most casseroles taste better for reheating.

Some food can only be cooked successfully by adding a little more fat than is desirable; in these cases pat the food with kitchen paper before serving it.

VITAMINS AND MINERALS

I know one heavy consumer of alcohol who, along with his over-generous weekly ration of gin, also buys a bottle of 'vitamin B complex'. He says it helps restore the vitamin balance which alcohol destroys. Dr Linus Pauling has claimed that 'megadoses' of vitamin C can help stave off many illnesses. Both calcium and potassium are now thought to have a possible role in preventing high blood pressure. Yet the official advice is that vitamin and mineral supplements are unnecessary: eating a 'balanced diet' will provide all we need.

It is clear, however, that the vitamin and mineral story is still incomplete and that current research may yet spring a few surprises. Certainly there is little cause for complacency. One recent study of the diet of 3,000 British schoolchildren showed how shockingly deficient in these nutrients many children are. For instance, over 90 per cent of the younger girls were below the DHSS minimum recommendation for iron intake, more than half the girls were below the desirable level of calcium, and a quarter of all the children were not receiving enough thiamin.

Another piece of research in 1980 revealed that as few as 15 per cent of British adults were eating food whose vitamin content matched up to the probably quite modest minimum standards recommended by the DHSS. A large American study showed that 6 per cent of patients attending a dental hospital had no vitamin C in their blood at all. In Britain rickets has reappeared in some children because of vitamin D deficiency. The cause of spina bifida is now strongly suspected to be deficiency in folic acid: the condition is markedly more common in areas where leafy vegetables figure little in the diet and where they are typically boiled in bicarbonate of soda. Osteoporosis (brittle bones) is more common now than it used to be, and is probably caused by lack of calcium. Iron deficiency is common in Britain, especially in women. Even so, self-dosing in tablet form does not seem to be the answer. It does not necessarily follow that because a nutrient is a good thing in small doses, it must be an even better thing in large doses. In fact large doses of both vitamin A and vitamin D can be toxic because the body cannot easily get rid of them.

Where vitamin C is concerned, the debate continues. The minimum recommended dose is small – one tomato or orange a day would meet it. Yet there are scientists who argue that this amount is far too small and that there is a good case for supposing that vitamin C plays a vital role both in reducing the risk of cancer and in lowering blood cholesterol levels.

The sensible posture seems to be not to rush out and buy huge doses of a mineral or vitamin – yet. However mineral and vitamin deficiency is probably far more widespread than we like to think. The old idea of a 'balanced' diet with its division of food into fat, protein and carbohydrate is especially unhelpful here. A *widely varied* diet is a much more useful notion, together with some sensible procedures in the kitchen.

Check-list on vitamins and minerals

<u>Shopping</u>

• Increase the amount of fruit and vegetables you buy: perhaps a third of your weekly food bill might be spent this way.

• Deliberately seek out variety in colour, texture and taste – does your list include red, green, yellow, white and orange fruit and vegetables?

• Wholemeal bread is an important source of minerals and vitamins. Try to eat at least 4 slices a day.

• Reject fruit and vegetables that look tired and limp. Nutrients are lost from the moment of picking. Frozen vegetables may be preferable in some instances.

• Try to eat kidneys or liver once a week. They are good sources of iron and A and B vitamins.

• Buy 'whole' foods wherever possible. They contain more minerals and vitamins than their more processed counterparts. Whole lentils are better than the split variety; brown rice is better than white and wholemeal bread better than white bread.

Storing and cooking

● Light and warmth destroy vitamins – store fruit and vegetables in dark, cool conditions where possible.

● Wherever possible leave the skin on fruit and vegetables, as this is where the greatest concentrations of minerals and vitamins occur.

● Eat fruit and vegetables raw whenever possible. All cooking results in some vitamin loss.

● Cutting and chopping leads to vitamin loss. Delay it until the last moment when you are ready to cook or eat.

● Never soak vegetables before cooking them – many vitamins are soluble in water.

● Never add bicarbonate of soda to vegetables.

● Put vegetables into boiling water: don't start them from cold.

● Use as little water as possible to boil vegetables. Even potatoes will cook under low heat in as little as ½ inch (1 cm) of water if the pan has a tight-fitting lid.

● Save vegetable cooking liquid for stocks, as it will contain many useful nutrients.

● Keep vegetable cooking time as brief as possible. Stir-frying is an excellent method of preserving vitamins and minerals as it is so swift.

● Beware of removing dairy products from your diet: milk and cheese are important sources of calcium, essential for strong bones. Drink at least ½ pint (300 ml) of skimmed milk daily; skimmed milk contains as much calcium as full-fat milk.

FIBRE

I was once at a conference on 'healthy' eating where the star speaker was Dr Denis Burkitt. At lunch, we were just raising our forks when he held the assembled company riveted with the following question, delivered with his usual enormous relish:

'Who can tell me what the average daily weight of stool of an African is compared with an American?'

No one knew the answer, which was that the typical African output is over three times as heavy. This did not prevent us tucking into our wholemeal tuna flans, baked potatoes and cold chicken with yoghurt and cucumber sauce – in fact quite the reverse. We enjoyed it all the more for having had its virtue pointed out to us. It was, of course, Dr Burkitt who was one of the first to see that the diseases of the gut which plague us in the West were rare in Africa and to make the link between diet and intestinal health. Since Dr Burkitt has a pronounced taste for the mischievous, he may also have been the pioneer of the phrase 'sinkers and floaters'. 'Sinkers' are unhealthy hard stools, 'floaters' are the product of a digestive system in good order.

Sadly, 'sinkers' are all too common in Britain. Constipation is a national preoccupation; sales of laxatives are high. It is assumed that everyone will understand the joke implied in a roll of lavatory paper printed as a continuous crossword and intended to make an amusing gift. Cancer of the colon is not amusing and nor are diverticulitis, appendicitis and diabetes, all of them associated with lack of fibre, and almost certainly all preventable by increasing the amount of fibre in the diet. Fibre is the best treatment for constipation and may also be much more important than was previously thought in the prevention of heart disease.

The most helpful way to identify fibre is to think of it as the natural skeleton of plant material – for instance, the skin and membranes of fruit, the hard cell walls which keep seeds and grains firm to the touch, or the ribby basic structure of a leafy vegetable which stops it falling over in the breeze. It cannot be broken down completely by the digestive system, but passes through it. For this reason it was dismissed for many years as 'roughage' – of no dietary value and even to be avoided. Children and invalids would be offered peeled fruit, patients with diverticulitis were advised to eat a fibre-free diet – the exact opposite of what was in fact needed. A low-fibre diet has also been traditionally associated with affluence. Even in Chaucer's day it was a mark of social status to eat white bread.

Today, the pendulum has swung the other way. 'Sliced white' has become a term of abuse. How many of us who pride ourselves on being up to date would publicly admit to buying it? 'Real bread' has become as modish as 'real ale'.

The enshrinement of fibre has come about as it has gradually been realized what its intestinal functions are. First of all it increases the weight, bulk and softness of stools and stimulates the natural muscular urge of the bowel to get rid of them. Secondly, fibre encourages the swift passage of food through the body. Western food takes perhaps three times as long to pass right through the digestive system as is really necessary: 100 hours in the typical Westerner compared with 35 hours in the typical African. Medically this is important because faeces lingering in the colon have more time to produce the toxic materials which might lead to diverticulitis and cancer. High-fibre diets have also been shown to be effective in treating diabetics, many of whom were previously put on a low-carbohydrate (and therefore by implication often a high-fat) diet. Some diabetics have even been able to give up insulin treatment, so successful has the high-fibre diet been. Work in America has shown that fibre from oats and pulses may be useful in reducing blood cholesterol levels and in helping the body restrict its absorption of fats.

How much fibre?

The NACNE Report recommended a 50-per-cent increase in the amount of fibre typically eaten by the average Briton. You would reach this ideal of 30 g a day by eating any of these combinations of food as part of your daily diet.

Bowl of muesli
4 slices wholemeal bread
1 serving dried fruit salad

2 apples
1 helping peas
1 jacket potato

or

1 bowl Allbran
2 slices wholemeal bread
wholemeal spaghetti with broccoli
   and tomato sauce
1 orange

Bowl of raspberries
1 helping leeks
1 helping fruit cake made with
   wholemeal flour

or

5 slices wholemeal bread
1 helping baked beans
packet fruit and nuts

1 helping sprouts
1 potato boiled in its skin

These lists show that only modest consumption of fibre is needed to reach the NACNE recommendations. Some people, however, regard NACNE as too modest, and think that fibre could be increased to a much higher level with beneficial results. Some physicians will even say, and they are only half joking, that the bulk, weight and texture of the human stool is a better predictor of long-term health than blood cholesterol and blood pressure tests.

What kind of fibre?

There are plenty of health food shops still selling bran and even 'bran tablets'. Bran will certainly work to relieve constipation, but it is not the most desirable way to consume fibre. Horses may find bran a delicacy but it is unpalatably like sawdust to the human mouth. Furthermore, sprinkling bran into, for instance, a fatty steak pie is a bit like Denis Healey's description of being attacked by Sir Geoffrey Howe. It felt, he said, 'like being savaged by a dead sheep'. Adding fibre to food that is already unhealthy is a limp way to deal with the problem: it is the balance of the diet that needs to be changed. Eating whole foods will mean that you are getting their minerals and vitamins as well as their fibre.

In fact, eating more fibre is easy if you have already grasped one of the main principles of healthy eating, which is that food of plant origin should greatly predominate over food of animal origin. If you are cutting down on fat you will inevitably be eating less 'animal' food. Since you will not wish to feel hungry, you will probably quite naturally be taking a much larger percentage of your food from plant sources: cereals, fruit and vegetables, pulses, nuts and grains.

Cereal fibre has certainly taken the starring role in the fibre story, and there is no doubt that wholemeal bread, brown rice and wholemeal pastas are critically important to digestive health. However, they are by no means the only sources of fibre and the actions and benefits of other types of fibre may become clearer as they are studied in greater depth. In the meantime it is certain that it is wise to eat fibre from all the main plant sources and not just cereals.

Eating a high-fibre diet has one other effect: it fills you up more quickly. My former colleague David Cordingley, who has successfully produced so many of the BBC's programmes in the health area, has a

27

theory that anyone wishing to lose weight has only to follow his unique plan. This is startlingly simple: you absolutely must consume 7 or 8 thick slices of wholemeal bread a day. You can eat anything else you like. His theory is based on the assumption that eating so much wholemeal bread will fill you so quickly that you will simply not be able to consume enough calories to stay fat. The hypothesis has already been borne out in the cases of several of our chubbier colleagues who have followed his advice!

The same thought is behind the F-Plan Diet. It certainly seems to be true that on a high-fibre diet some people actually find it hard to over-eat. This is a bonus if you are overweight, but it may be a disadvantage for people who are underweight.

Finally, since the plant world offers us so much delightfully palatable fibre, there is no need to worry if you find some of the traditional icons of healthy eating unpleasing. Personally, I adore wholemeal bread and eat a lot of it (especially if it is home-made), but I am not a fan of wholemeal pasta. As my diet is far higher in fibre even than the NACNE recommendations, it doesn't bother me that the pasta I normally cook is white. Plenty of people find wholemeal bread heavy going. They may be better off with a traditionally made unbleached white or wheatmeal loaf, while looking to brown rice, brown spaghetti, fruit and vegetables for the rest of the fibre in their diets.

Check-list on fibre

● Step up fibre intake gradually. Sudden increases lead to abdominal discomfort.

● Have plenty to drink.

● Try to eat plenty of whole-grain cereal daily: oats, brown rice, brown pasta and wholemeal bread, pittas or chapatis. Have bread on the table at every meal.

● Choose a high-fibre breakfast cereal: muesli, Weetabix, Shredded Wheat or Allbran.

●. Make use of pulses in dips, soups and casseroles.

- Use nuts and dried fruit as snacks and in cooking.

- Leave skins on fruit and vegetables wherever possible. Scrub them rather than peeling them. Use the sieve sparingly for soups.

- Aim to eat fresh fruit at least 3 times daily.

- Aim to eat at least 3 servings of salads or vegetables daily.

- Increase the quantities of vegetables in sauces and casseroles.

SALT

Some years ago I was preparing to film an interview with a woman who very kindly offered a simple lunch to the hungry crew. I remember it was home-made soup, bread, cheese and fruit. As we sat down, she shyly explained that there was no salt in the soup because her toddler was having it too. She had stuck to the principle of cooking salt-free food for her child and now preferred it that way herself. The salt pot was put on the table. Everyone politely started their soup without adding salt, then one by one we reached for it. Not one of us could eat the soup without adding salt: I remember the sound recordist adding a whole teaspoon of the stuff.

Today, my own attitude and practice are very different. I rarely add salt in cooking and never at the table. I often find restaurant and canteen food intolerably briny. And I have to confess that some of my own guests, unconverted to healthy eating, can often be seen furtively reaching for the salt pot too.

Old habits die hard where salt is concerned, particularly in the catering business. Many chefs simply cannot believe that food will be palatable without salt. At a lunch given to launch one well-known cook's healthy-eating book, the carefully prepared food (all recipes from the book) was truly spoilt by a heavily over-salted soup which must have had most of the guests drinking pints of water for the rest of the day, though there was no salt in the recipe itself.

Medically, salt is linked with high blood pressure, a risk factor in cardio-vascular disease. It looks as if some people, possibly as many as one in five of us, may be 'salt-sensitive', but at present there is no way of identifying in advance who they are. This is why the advice is for everyone to reduce their salt intake.

Like all links between diet and disease, the salt story is complicated. It could well be that it is a disturbed balance between sodium (salt), potassium and calcium that is the cause of hypertension (high blood pressure), rather than simply too much salt. It will certainly do you no harm to increase your potassium intake by eating a generous quantity of the fruit and vegetables which are high in potassium, while at the same time consuming less salt.

Cutting down drastically on salt has been shown by several studies to be beneficial to hypertensive patients, though the salt restriction has to be severe and it does not work for everyone. Perhaps this is because high blood pressure, like all serious and slow-developing conditions, is unlikely to have a single cause. Smoking, drinking, overweight, lack of exercise, heredity, stress and taking the contraceptive pill are all probably contributory factors.

How much salt?

All the sodium we actually need – about 1 g a day – occurs naturally in food. Everything else is literally a matter of taste. Many of us are consuming at least 10 times and often 20 or 30 times that amount. The NACNE Report recommended that we cut our average salt intake by half, to 2 g of sodium a day. This is about a teaspoonful, which perhaps sounds generous until you remember that about three quarters of the salt typically eaten in Britain is already in manufactured food, including some of the food, such as bread, that is desirable on health grounds.

In general, however, the foods highest in salt tend also to be the ones high in fat and sugar and low in vitamins and minerals: foods we should be avoiding anyway. By and large these are the highly refined processed convenience foods: many breakfast cereals, crisps, salted nuts, packet soups and sauces, bottled sauces, bacon, pies, salami, sausages and ham, tinned vegetables and soups. There is salt in most bought biscuits, pastries and cakes.

Many manufacturers are now producing salt-free or reduced-salt products. For instance, my local supermarket stocks low-salt water biscuits, salt-free muesli, unsalted polyunsaturated margarine and several reduced-salt tinned vegetables. This is a beginning, but there is a long way to go.

Making the change

Don't impose a salt-free regime suddenly. Food will taste bland and if you are cooking for others it may be rejected altogether. Make the change gradually. A good way to begin is to stop adding salt to vegetables: cooked briefly in steam or minimal water, they really don't need it. From this you could progress to not putting salt on the table, then not adding it to pasta and rice.

Many people find that it is surprisingly easy to give up salt. Within a few weeks their taste-buds are completely adapted. Food tastes better because it tastes of the food and not the salt. Others find they cannot manage the change. A low-sodium substitute may be the answer here. These salts are usually either potassium chloride or potassium mixed with sodium chloride. They are expensive and can leave a slightly bitter after-taste when sprinkled straight on to food. In cooked food the difference is much harder to detect. These products are useful for the transitional stage and for people who simply can't do without salt. In the long term, however, re-educating the palate is probably better.

Check-list on salt

● Read the labels on food. 'Sodium', 'brine', 'kippered', 'mono-sodium glutamate', 'sodium polyphosphate', 'sodium bicarbonate', 'sea salt', 'rock salt', 'soda', or the chemical symbol 'Na' all indicate salt. Buy salt-free products wherever you can – that way even if you have to add salt, *you* know how much has gone in.

● Use herbs, spices and other flavourings to add zest to food instead of salt. Ground coriander and lemon juice are particularly useful in this respect.

● Soy sauce is salty – use it sparingly. Most tomato purées have added salt, so be cautious about their use.

● Bottled sauces and dressings are high in salt. It is simple to make your own instead.

● Avoid stock cubes unless you can find one without added salt. Make your own stock instead and freeze it in batches.

● Avoid salty snacks like crisps, cheese biscuits and salted peanuts.

• Prefer fresh or frozen vegetables to tinned, or look for tinned produce in 'natural' juice. Rinse tinned pulses in a colander under a running cold tap.

• Smoked food is salty. Eat smoked fish, bacon and ham only occasionally. Soaking and rinsing food first gets rid of some salt: soak a ham in several changes of water before cooking it.

• Steam or microwave vegetables – they retain their flavour better than boiled vegetables and can therefore be eaten without salt.

• Eat plenty of potassium-rich fruit and vegetables: bananas, potatoes, apples, apricots, dates, grapefruit, oranges, prunes, raisins, beans, sprouts, cabbage, corn, peppers. Whole-grain cereals are also rich in potassium.

• Don't put salt on the table: this reduces the urge to add it out of habit. Put whole spices into an extra pepper grinder on the table instead: coriander, mustard and dried chillies are good this way.

• Start babies and young children on a salt-free diet. They may then be able to continue in the same way.

SUGAR

As a young child and teenager in the Forties and Fifties I spent my pocket money freely on sweets. 'Penny twists' could be full of delightful surprises culled from the broken bits at the bottoms of the sweet jars, then there were liquorice strips, chocolate bon-bons or, if you were really flush, whole fruit and nut bars. My mother was a good cook and we ate cake every day. It is not surprising, perhaps, that another vivid childhood memory is of fairly frequent toothache. Even now I don't like the smell of cloves. It brings back the memory of all those nights when my father tenderly handed me wads of cotton wool soaked in oil of cloves to soothe the raging pain. By the time I left home I had had several teeth extracted, and most of those remaining were heavily filled.

I feel no resentment at my parents for allowing these ravages to occur: they simply did not know of the relationship between sugar and dental caries. If they had, I doubt that a single sweet would ever have passed my lips.

When I was a new parent myself, I vowed that my children would not be allowed sweets. This was fine for the first year or so. Offered a Smartie by the health centre nurse for being a 'good boy' during a vaccination, my older son simply stared at it in bafflement, poked it and refused thereafter to touch it. Where did the rot set in? Was it doting relatives slipping him the odd chocolate bar as a parting present? Was it the sweets brought into the school which by tradition the whole class shares on someone's birthday? Was it my own desperate bribing with biscuits when faced with a child apparently determined to starve himself to death? Whatever the reason, I have not been successful in my ambition to rear sugar-free children, though, interestingly, my younger son has no real taste for refined sugar: offer him a choice between a slab of chocolate and a slice of fresh juicy pineapple and he would choose the pineapple without any hesitation. The problem is that whatever the individual sweet tooth, we live in a sugar-sodden food culture. There is sugar in ketchup, baked beans, breakfast cereal, savoury biscuits and pickles, as well as in the more obviously sweet products like colas, jams, cakes, packet desserts and confectionery. It is a cheap ingredient, an excellent preservative and makes food taste pleasant, so food manufacturers use it a lot.

Facts on sugar

There are various problems with sugar. One is its strong association with dental decay. Teeth must be cleaned within a few minutes of eating sugar to prevent the onslaught of the acids that attack the enamel. Another is its link with obesity. Sugar slips down all too readily, especially when it is dissolved in liquid. Many people might jib at eating seven actual spoonfuls of sugar, but the same amount in a glass of cola is very easy to drink.

Sugar has no nutritional value at all. It is calories and nothing else. There are traces of minerals in some 'unrefined' sugars, but basically all sugars are the same: empty calories. Brown sugar, honey, glucose, molasses, malt, maltose, golden syrup, treacle, sucrose, fructose and dextrose – their tastes vary, but they are all sugars and nutritionally empty.

Sugar is found naturally in unrefined form in all fruit and vegetables. Some are much sweeter than others – e.g., carrots, dried fruit and mango – and can be used to provide natural sweetness while also offering fibre, vitamins and minerals.

How much sugar?

On average, we consume the enormous amount of 2 lb per head a week. NACNE recommended halving this, which would reduce it to the equivalent of about ten teaspoons a day. This, of course, includes the sugar 'hidden' in manufactured foods. To some people this seems over-generous, since physiologically we don't actually need any sugar at all. The NACNE Committee regarded it as a realistic beginning.

My own feeling is that to banish sugar altogether would be ridiculous. Sugar is a most useful seasoning – in its place. If you do not add it to tea or coffee, never eat cakes, sweets, packet soups or fizzy drinks, then the odd teaspoon added to a home-made tomato sauce is not going to do you any harm. I use it in my recipes – but discreetly.

Check-list on sugar

● Read the labels – look out for sugar in the form of 'glucose', 'sucrose', 'fructose' and 'maltose'.

● Choose sugar-free products where you can: look for fruit canned in its own juice, baked beans labelled 'reduced sugar', sugar-free jams, and so on.

● Avoid obviously sugar-coated breakfast cereals. Make your own muesli (see recipes on page 229) or buy low-sugar manufactured cereals – e.g., Weetabix, Shredded Wheat. Don't add sugar to breakfast cereals that already have a lot.

● Avoid fizzy drinks, squash and 'fruit drinks' (which often have a lot of added sugar). Buy natural fruit juice instead.

● Buy dried fruit and nuts as snacks for children instead of sweets and cakes.

● If your children can't give up sweets completely – and few can – make sweets a once-weekly treat.

● Put sugar in a sprinkler rather than keeping it loose in a bowl. That way you will use less.

● Give up sugar in tea or coffee. Use an artificial sweetener as a transition if you still need the sweet taste.

● Stick to simple fruit-based puddings rather than cooking pies and tarts. Raw fresh fruit rarely needs sugar; cooked fruit usually tastes sharper, so there is more of a temptation to reach for the sugar bowl.

ADDITIVES

In 1981 I was working with Madhur Jaffrey on a television cookery series. We were rehearsing a sequence in which she was to demonstrate how to make tandoori chicken. As she came to the end of the practice run she told us, worried and puzzled, that her lips felt 'odd'. As we watched, her bottom lip swelled up dramatically, looking as if it had been stung by a bee. We immediately consulted a dermatologist – the programme was due in the studio only two days later. His first question was, 'Have you been handling yellow food colouring?' The answer, of course, was 'yes'. Somehow the yellow and red food colouring we were using to add traditional Indian cosmetic glamour to the tandoori chicken must have been transferred from Madhur's hand to her mouth, and the reaction was immediate, painful and disfiguring. I now know that the colouring we were using in all innocence was tartrazine, or E102, a notorious member of the group of 'azo' dyes, and one of the most common and suspect additives permitted in Britain. It is widely used, for instance, in the manufacture of orange squash. As well as being a common cause of skin reactions, it is also suspected to be a cause of hyperactivity in some young children.

It is, however, important not to be swept away by anti-additive hysteria. In attacking additives many people make wild assertions about 'chemicals', forgetting that both 'natural' and 'manufactured' substances are 'chemicals' and that many 'natural' ingredients can also be toxic. For instance, it would not be a wise idea to drink 5 pints of carrot juice a day, nor to eat huge quantities of spinach (which contains oxalic acid): both could make you ill. Sensitive people can also be allergic to perfectly pleasant and wholesome food such as strawberries or citrus fruit. The food industry defends additives on the grounds that we need them to make food safe. For instance, they say that without nitrates and nitrites, ham, bacon or pâtés might develop the bacteria which cause the highly dangerous food poisoning botulism. Anti-oxidants protect the fat in biscuits and cakes from rancidity, thus prolonging their shelf-life. Without them, it is claimed, it would be impossible to mass-produce food at reasonable prices.

The food industry also accuses consumers of boycotting food that is without its cosmetic coating of 'sunset yellow' or 'cochineal red'. At the moment this is difficult to judge. Most people never get the chance to choose a kipper without Brown FK154 on it, or to buy the pale creamy haddock that is free of E102.

Concern about additives, though sometimes stated over-stridently, is nonetheless soundly based. While it is true that 'everything is a chemical', this does not prove that additives in food are all right. A chemical that is perfectly safe in its natural context may behave quite differently when added to *other* chemicals in large doses. Also, although many 'natural' foods may be toxic or may be known allergens, this is actually a good reason for being additionally cautious with extra ingredients known to be hazardous.

There are also serious questions to be asked about the safety standards applied to additives. Many additives widely used in Britain are banned in other countries. For instance, FK154 (the FK means 'For Kippers') is not allowed anywhere else in the EEC. In Britain it is widely used not just on kippers but in crisps, sausages, gravy granules and sweets.

Much of the evidence about additives has been gathered by manufacturers and is not open to public scrutiny. Many of the tests have been conducted on animals and may or may not be relevant to the very different biology of human beings. Some additives have never been subjected to any systematic testing. Where they have been tested it has been as single substances. In practice, however, most additives are used in conjunction with others: several colourings, preservatives and anti-oxidants, for instance, in the same product. The long-term impact of these 'additive cocktails' is only guess-work at the moment.

It is true that in some ways today's food is 'safer'. It is not possible, as it was in the nineteenth century, for manufacturers to sell dust and sweepings as 'tea leaves', to put chalk in bread or ground-up acorns in beer. It is true, too, that the general environment is cleaner: we have efficient sewers, clean water and better housing. Nonetheless it is possible to argue that our total environment is just as polluted, though in different ways. Our cities are tainted with lead from car exhausts, our rural environment with agricultural chemicals. Radioactive material from nuclear power stations has been linked with high rates of cancer in local children; the existence of the Health and Safety Executive has not put an end to diseases like asbestosis associated mainly with poor control of industrial processing. Our animals are now routinely fed drugs during the fattening period and again before slaughter. Kept unexercised and overcrowded, they are often as unhealthy as the people upon whose tables they are eventually served. All these are major changes since the last century, and this is the background against which concern about additives must be set. One food colouring occasionally consumed on its own may be of no significance at all. It is much more likely, however, that this food colouring will be one among many, consumed in a meal which also contains hormones, emulsifiers, modified starches, preservatives and flavourings, by a diner already bombarded by environmental pollutants of one kind or another. It is the cumulative effects, and the possible chain reactions, that are worrying.

The long-term effects of additives are quite unknown, as no previous generations have consumed such enormous quantities. There must be particular concern about their effects on children. Children have a smaller body-weight, and their immune systems are more vulnerable. Yet it is in 'children's' food that additives are especially noticeable: fish fingers, fruit squash, instant puddings, hamburgers, sausages, cakes, biscuits, chocolate and sweets.

As well as all these sound scientific reasons for caution about additives, there is another, much simpler reason to avoid them wherever possible: food 'constructed' out of additives is usually inalienably altered and damaged, and tastes awful. I was recently 'treated' by a well-meaning friend to a filled, sweet pancake in a motorway restaurant. Sometime in its past the filling had begun life as a pineapple. Since then, someone had added a lot of sugar and water, and then, to take away a little of the cloyingly sweet taste, something tart (possibly E513, sulphuric acid) had been added. To make it bulkier than it was there was an emulsifier – possibly carrageenan (E407). The garish green-yellow colour bore no resemblance to the natural glow of the real fruit. At a guess I should say that it was E104, one of the azo dyes. The pancake itself, perhaps mercifully, had no taste, but no doubt it came from a packet of 'ready-mix' with all the usual anti-oxidants and stabilizers. It was truly one of the most memorably disgusting dishes I have ever attempted to eat. Fortunately I did not have to fake polite appreciation – my friend's 'morello cherry delight' was just as bad.

Some, but not all, additives are given 'E' numbers – the 'E' refers to the EEC. Concern has focused on a few additives in particular:

E249–E252   Nitrates and nitrites, used on meat. Thought to be potentially carcinogens.

E320–E321   Anti-oxidants. Suspected of causing hyperactivity in children and of raising blood cholesterol levels.

E102–E155   Most (though not all) of these numbers are synthetic derivatives from coal tar, also known as azo dyes. Widely used on fish, in soft drinks, sweets, packet breadcrumbs and many convenience foods such as ice-cream, cake mixes and custard powder. Claimed to be associated with hyperactivity in children, asthmatic attacks in sensitive people, and blurred vision.

E621   Monosodium glutamate, a salty 'flavour enhancer' found in soy sauce, 'meat seasonings' and many convenience foods. Used widely in Chinese food, it has been linked with 'Chinese Restaurant Syndrome' – headaches, palpitations and giddiness.

Check-list on additives

It is impossible to avoid additives altogether. However, many of the most questionable additives are found in food that it is wiser to avoid on other grounds.

● Read the labels on food. Support manufacturers who are making the effort to offer products free of suspect additives (but be prepared for food to look different – usually paler).

● Don't buy food colourings, especially the reds, yellows and browns. Use turmeric (sparingly, because it has a powerful taste) or saffron (if you can afford it) for savoury yellow rice; avoid 'tandoori mixes' if they have the suspect pinky-red glow that comes from E 124. Use paprika if you want a red colouring.

● Use soy sauce sparingly: as well as containing MSG it is salty, another reason for moderation.

● Ham, bacon, pies, mince – prime sources of nitrites and nitrates – have only a limited place in a healthy diet anyway: buy them only very occasionally and in small quantities.

● Buy natural fruit juices rather than fruit squash.

● Support the shop or fishmonger's that will sell you undyed fish, but remember that smoked fish is also salty, so should be eaten in moderation.

● Crisps often contain many dubious additives. Try to persuade children away from them as a snack. They are also fatty and salty, so should be avoided where possible anyway.

● Convenience food: look for the steadily increasing number of products which are 'fresh-chilled' and intended to have a short shelf-life. The best of them copy home-cooking techniques and are without suspect additives (look on the label). They may be a little more expensive.

● Home-made jams, sauces and pickles will usually be infinitely better than the typical manufactured product. Jam made from glucose syrup, gelling agent, E 124 and strawberries is never going to taste as good as home-made strawberry jam.

THE HEALTHY KITCHEN

When there are major changes in life-style and in the kind of food we eat, it is inevitable that the shape, look and typical equipment of a kitchen will change too.

Not so very long ago, for instance, a kitchen would not have been considered well equipped without a steamer and a double boiler: the steamer for puddings, the double boiler for real custard. The pantry would have been full of kilner and jam jars; there would have been a mixing bowl, a rolling pin and a pastry board (marble if you were lucky). Saucepans were aluminium, often rather thin, which perhaps didn't matter too much if you were just using them for boiling vegetables. The only other standard pan was likely to have been a large, blackened frying pan. However, most housewives would have prided themselves on having an extensive set of well-greased baking tins in all shapes and sizes to suit the differing needs of Yorkshire puddings, jam tarts, pies and cakes. There might even have been a griddle or 'bakestone'. There would probably have been a potato peeler, a serrated bread knife and a carving knife and fork, but you would have been lucky to find much else in the way of cutting equipment. The only expensive electrical gadget there was likely to have been was a Kenwood mixer.

I have just a few of these things in my kitchen, but, steamer apart, I hardly ever use them. My baking tins are rusty from lack of use, the wedding-present carving knife and fork are tucked away in their tissue paper, and I use the rolling pin so infrequently that I always have to hunt for it on the rare occasions that I do want it. On the other hand, I do have a large collection of sharp knives, two stout chopping boards and a set of non-stick pans. Over the years I have gradually invested in various pieces of electrical equipment – but, significantly, not a food mixer.

If you are a busy person and have also decided that you want to eat healthily, then there are some pieces of cooking equipment which will make life a lot easier. This is a personal selection that I find useful because it saves time and is in tune with healthier cooking. It is not intended to be a complete *batterie de cuisine*.

CUTTING AND CHOPPING

Knives

All cookery books nag about the importance of good knives, and they are right. I once had to peel and fine-chop a pound of onions with an old table knife in a friend's kitchen: it took me about 35 laborious minutes and was the cause of considerable temporary stress in our relationship.

At its most basic, healthier cooking means that you will want to remove fat easily and quickly from meat, chop vegetables swiftly and accurately and fine-chop herbs in moments. You will also want to slice soft fruit and vegetables without squashing them. If you have bread on the table at every meal, a good bread knife is essential. Nothing is more discouraging to the enjoyment of bread than a hacked-at disintegrating loaf. My basic knife kit, collected over several years, includes:

2″ paring knife for fruit and root vegetables
4″ cook's knife for dicing and slicing
6″ broad-bladed knife for fine-chopping herbs and jointing meat
8″ stiff boning knife
9″ cook's knife for chopping meat
9″ palette knife with serrated edge for flipping over omelettes, cutting bread and cutting or lifting delicate food
6″ tomato knife for delicate fruit
Cleaver: very much an optional extra, but useful for jointing chicken and heavy chopping (e.g., of a chicken carcass)

Choosing knives is not easy. A famous name is not always a guarantee of perfection – one well-known brand, for instance, is produced by no fewer than 16 different companies, all selling under the same logo. As a result, although some of their knives are excellent, some are rather poor. Some manufacturers produce strong, well-balanced knives with dull edges: 'beautiful knife – shame they forgot to sharpen it' was the tart comment of one competitor. Picking and choosing among the various ranges seems the wisest course. My own knives are a mixture of the Kitchen Devil professional range and the Swiss make Victorinox. The cleaver came from a Chinese supermarket in Soho.

Here are a few points about buying and caring for knives:

● Wherever possible, choose knives with moulded nylon handles which can go into the dishwasher. Even if you don't have a dishwasher now, you may acquire one in the future.

● Choose stainless not carbon steel, which rusts and needs too much attention.

● Don't go for looks alone. Pick the knife up and judge the comfort of the handle. It should bulge satisfyingly into your hand (without finger indentations) and feel heavy. The blade should be firm at the top, flexible at the point. The 'tang' – the metal prong that fits into the handle – should run the whole length of the handle.

● Buy a sharpening steel, 'knife tuner' or knife sharpener and use it little and often on all your knives (except serrated ones).

● Store knives on a magnetic rack. That way they are safer to handle and will not be blunted or damaged as they may when banging against each other in drawers.

It is often said that a blunt knife is more dangerous than a sharp one. I always find this puzzling. A blunt knife is certainly time-wasting and inefficient, but at least it is unlikely to cut you badly. On the contrary, deep cuts are more common than you might think amongst even experienced users of sharp blades. Surely the reality is that sharp knives are much easier to use, but they must be employed with skill and caution.

Chopping board

A good knife deserves to be used on a good chopping board – that is to say one that provides a firm clean surface with a bit of spring. Chopping on laminates will soon ruin both the laminate and the knife. Choose the largest, heaviest wooden board you can find. Ideally, look for one made from a single piece of hardwood. Softwood dents and splits too easily, and 'joins' soon become cracks and then crevasses which harbour thriving colonies of bacteria. A board with recessed handles is easier to carry to the sink for scrubbing.

Scissors

These are useful for snipping chives and other herbs, trimming fat from bacon, cutting foil and cling-film.

GRATING, GRINDING AND SCRAPING

Grater

The traditional four-square grater is hard to beat. The thick slats will produce wafer-thin potato scallops (see page 199 for a low-fat way of cooking them). Potato toppings of this kind are a useful alternative to the pastry of conventional savoury pies. The finer surfaces of the grater are useful for grating onions, orange and lemon peel and nutmeg, and by far the best way of coping with fresh ginger – the hairier fibres are conveniently trapped, leaving only the juicy pulp.

Lemon zester

A lemon zester probably falls into the category of 'gadget', but I use mine (also made by Victorinox) frequently. Orange and lemon zest is a frequent ingredient in both sweet and savoury 'healthy' recipes because it adds zing and removes the need for salt to some extent. The small, sharp, raised circles in a zester drawn swiftly across an orange or lemon produce thin, thread-like strips of zest in no time at all, and without any risk to your fingernails.

Vegetable brush

A cheap bristle or plastic vegetable brush is the best tool for preparing root vegetables. A nylon pan-scrubber also does the job well, but does not last as long.

Mincer

Some kind of mincing equipment is useful in the healthy cook's kitchen. It is easier to control the fat content of mince if you make it yourself. However, hand mincers are awkward, slow and fiddly to use, very hard to keep clean and rust-free. They have really been superseded by electrical equipment (see pages 50–51) which will do the job much better in a fraction of the time.

Pestle and mortar

Small-scale pounding of spices, herbs and flavourings can be done with a pestle and mortar, or on a chopping-board with a knife. However, a large porcelain pestle and mortar (the only kind worth having) is expensive and, I think, a bit of a luxury. Garlic can be squashed under a flexible knife, whole spices bashed between paper with a heavy tin, and so on.

Pepper mill

The spicy fragrance of freshly ground black pepper is already well appreciated, but other spices can be given the same treatment and added at table to replace salt – especially whole coriander seeds. Choose tall pepper mills (they need re-filling less often) with an easy twisting action. The type with a rigid central spike is easier to fill than the sort where it can wobble about freely.

POTS AND PANS

I wonder how many people have, like me, set out on a quest for The Perfect Pan. This perfect pan should go equally well into freezer, or microwave, on top of or inside the oven, be equally suitable for gas or electricity, and cook evenly. It should be permanently non-stick and non-scratch, easy to clean inside and out, light to lift, but rigid enough never to buckle under heat, and should have a tight-fitting lid and handles that stay cool during cooking. It should be cheap to buy and should last a lifetime.

Needless to say, this pan does not exist, nor will it ever exist, though we should do all we can to encourage the manufacturers to keep trying. What we have instead is a situation where particular pans perform well and badly in different situations. Personal preference is important, and the type of cooker you own also has to play a large part in your choice. A friend of mine has a complete set of rather unglamorous heavy-gauge Tower aluminium pans which she bought as a newly-wed 20 years ago. They are still in perfect condition and in use every day on her electric cooker. Her teenage son, with all the confidence of one year's Home Economics behind him, pronounces these pans 'dullsville', but his mother retorts with perfect truth that they do the job, that she's the one using them and she likes them. Another friend, who cooks professionally, swears by her set of stainless steel pans, even though she admits they sometimes burn food too easily. Most chefs prefer copper, though perhaps they do not usually have to pay for the re-tinning.

While a matching set of pans may look smart, in reality a choice of one from one range and one from another may be more useful. My own suggestions would be for this mixture:

Milk pan and basic small saucepan from any range with heavy bottoms, tight-fitting lids and heat-proof handles. Cooking vegetables in minimal water is impossible without pans of this sort: the steam escapes and the food may burn. Stainless steel with a copper base is easy to clean and cooks evenly.

Very large (6 pt) non-stick saucepan for the minimal 'frying' method described on page 63; also for cooking pasta and large quantities of leafy vegetables.

Non-stick frying/sauté pan with lid. A true frying pan does not have a lid, and has sloping sides so that steam escapes. I find a lidded sauté pan with straight sides much more useful, as it is suitable for top-of-the-stove braising as well as 'frying'. A non-stick pan is essential to allow minimal use of fat. Unfortunately, non-stick coatings often have a relatively short life. They are sprayed on to the pan rather than being part of its basic structure and eventually peel off or become pitted in use, especially if they are abused by continual exposure to high temperatures. They also dislike sudden changes of temperature – for instance, being plunged when hot into cold water – and being thwacked with metal tools. A non-stick pan will last much longer with some tender loving care, but it is still unlikely to last as long as a stainless steel or aluminium pan. Personally I am prepared to renew my non-stick pan reasonably frequently for the excellent results it gives me in its youth and middle age.

Choose a non-stick pan with a heavy, scrolled base which will give it stability and good heat-conducting properties. The lid should fit tightly. A glass lid is a useful bonus – you can inspect food without letting valuable steam escape.

If you prefer a traditional frying pan without a lid (i.e., one with sloping sides) one of the best has a dimpled non-stick base and comes in two sizes, the larger of which can take four chicken joints comfortably. The dimpling on the base means that food is even less likely to sit in a lot of fat.

A non-stick pan will need non-stick tools. I find a long rubber or nylon spatula is an excellent basic tool, also useful for turning pancakes and fritters.

Wok

One of my colleagues once remarked that 'most people' were now given a 'wok set' as a wedding present, but that most of these woks stayed under the marital bed in their presentation boxes, because no one was sure how to use them. Woks, he said, had joined the ranks of the fondue set and the *bagna caôda* as a funny fad, ready, by implication, to be passed on to the jumble sales of the 1990s.

Funny fad or not, every healthy kitchen should include a wok. It is quite simply the quickest way of producing a large and satisfying meal with minimal fat and maximum preservation of nutrients. No Western pan is really a satisfactory substitute. If you live in London or another city with a large Chinese community, there will be Chinese supermarkets where you should find a good choice of woks, and you can stock up on Chinese ingredients at the same time. If you don't already have a wok under the bed, this is what to look for when you choose one:

● Thin carbon steel is better than non-stick or stainless steel, as it can be heated quickly to the correct temperature.

● The type with one wooden handle is safer than the sort with two D-shaped metal handles.

● For electric cookers you must have a flat-bottomed wok.

● A stand is essential for gas cookers, and a steaming platform and a lid are useful.

● Buy a long-handled metal spatula at the same time. This is an implement shaped a bit like a cross between a fish slice and a small shovel. It is the best implement for stir-frying, though I find a long rubber/nylon spatula is also useful.

The young Chinese woman who sold me mine gave me this pithy and useful piece of advice: 'Black wok is best.' You should season the wok according to the manufacturer's instructions. Don't attempt to scrub a wok 'clean'. Wash it briefly in water only. Wipe it dry with kitchen paper and oil it to prevent rust.

Steamer

A large old-fashioned steamer is best for steaming fish and vegetables. You can improvise (see page 58), but in the end this is messy and unsatisfactory, not least because the lack of a well-fitting lid allows steam to escape and makes timing difficult. For small quantities of vegetables a cheap expanding metal basket is all right, but if you want to steam several vegetables at once you will need the real thing. The Meyer 'Dutch Oven' is a good investment if you can afford it. The large non-stick pan can be used on its own for pasta, stews or soups, and you can buy a stainless steal steamer which fits neatly into the top with a glass lid. It is big enough to take four trout comfortably.

Auction sales and junk shops are good places to pick up second-hand steamers very cheaply, but make sure the lids fit and that the bottoms are not buckled.

Pressure cooker

Opinions vary wildly about pressure cookers. Some people think they are hissing monsters likely to throw messy soup spitefully all over the kitchen, while others find them an indispensable ally. I fall into this latter camp. I make very nearly daily use of a pressure cooker which belonged originally to my mother. It is probably 30 years old and still going strong. Pressure cooking is the simplest way of avoiding stock cubes by producing home-made stock in a very short time.

It is also important to include more pulses in our diet, and pressure cookers mean that this is possible even for people with limited time. Without a pressure cooker, most pulses have to be soaked overnight and then boiled, often for several hours. With a pressure cooker, some pulses can be cooked from scratch in about half an hour, lentils in only ten minutes. One of the best uses of pulses is in soups and dips, both ideal for pressure cooking. Using a pressure cooker means that any dish which would normally take one to two hours to cook can be ready in a third of that time. The entire procedure, including any initial sautéing, can be carried out in one pan, which also saves on washing up.

The best and most expensive pressure cookers are stainless steel with automatic timers. However, the simple 'low-tech' cooker works on just the same principle. Like steamers, they often turn up in junk shops and at auctions. Check that the metal lip of the lid and the top of the pan are not dented or damaged in any way. They should fit perfectly when swung together. The rubber gasket and the safety valve may be perished but are simple to replace, as they are widely stocked by ironmongers and kitchen shops.

Flame/oven-proof pans

It is useful to have several pans in different sizes and shapes which are both flame-proof and oven-proof. It saves time to start food off on top of the stove, transfer it to the oven, put it under the grill, and even take it to the table – all in the same pot.

Enamelled cast-iron casseroles and gratin dishes. These come in bright colours and innumerable shapes. The best known are made by the French company Le Creuset, whose flame-coloured pots have graced thousands of stripped pine kitchens. Enamelled cast iron stands up well to both direct and indirect heat but it does have disadvantages. It is heavy to lift; both the inside and the outside can become very soiled; for top-of-the-stove cooking the temperature has to be kept very low, otherwise food sticks. However, for casserole and rice dishes where a good seal between lid and pot is essential, these pans are excellent. Both the 3-pint (2-litre) and 4½-pint (2.5-litre) sizes are useful for meat casseroles well padded with vegetables. I also find the 1½-pint (1-litre) shallow gratin dish indispensable for any dish that starts off on top of the stove, then goes in the oven, and finally needs a last-minute flash under the grill.

Glass ceramic casseroles made by Corning (Vision and Vision in White) have some of the same advantages. Whereas enamelled cast iron is metal and cannot be used in a microwave, glass ceramic can. It can also withstand considerable changes in temperature – for instance from freezer to microwave – with no difficulty. It can be used on top of the stove or inside the oven. Like cast iron, it does not like fierce direct heat. I don't feel it performs as well in the oven as enamelled cast iron. However, it is not as heavy and can be cleaned without worry with a Brillo pad. I find the 4-pint (2.3-litre) square plain white glass lidded dish extremely useful. We eat a great deal of rice and this has become my rice cooker. I start off some onions and spices in a meagre amount of oil over direct heat, add the rice, then the stock, and finish the dish in the microwave. However, if I did not use a microwave I doubt if I would find it so valuable: my Le Creuset casseroles would do everything I needed.

Salad-spinner

A healthy diet will include a great many salads. It is important to wash them – a lettuce was once recorded as having been sprayed with pesticide 40 times. Dressing will not cling to wet food, so salads must not only be washed but dried. The simple way is in tea towels, but this method leaves soggy tea towels in its wake. You can also buy salad baskets, but these have to be swung around vigorously, thus spraying water everywhere – all right if it's the middle of summer and you have a garden, inconvenient otherwise. A salad-spinner is the best solution. It works by centrifugal force and drives the water out of an inner basket into the outer container. Most salad-spinners are fairly hideous objects but cheap and efficient, which is why I have one.

ELECTRICAL EQUIPMENT

The electrical departments of big stores are crammed with kitchen appliances, all of them with some virtues. However, there are drawbacks. These appliances tend to be large, so they are greedy on space. Anything electrical will be expensive. If it goes wrong it will need spares and servicing. How many of those infra-red grills, toasted sandwich makers, deep-fat fryers, rice cookers and the like really earn their keep in the kitchen? If you have a passion for toasted sandwiches, then obviously you will find a place for a toasted sandwich machine, but for basic, speedy, healthy cooking, I feel there are three appliances that are well worth considering: a food processor, a blender and a microwave.

Food processor

I was once lucky enough to have a personal guided tour round a great hotel kitchen. It struck me first how like an operating theatre it was with its super-shiny cleanliness and cheerfully irreverent atmosphere. But I noticed next that at each work station there was a compartmented stainless steel tray of about 30 exquisitely prepared flavourings and garnishes: five or six different varieties of hand-chopped herbs, anchovies, crushed garlic, flavoured oils, grated fresh ginger, finely chopped green and red chillies, and so on. The chefs did not, of course, prepare these things themselves: they were the product of many hours' hard work from innumerable hard-pressed juniors.

Just as it is often said that every working woman could do with a wife, so I often think that every home should have a commis chef to do all that hard preparatory graft as well as the washing-up, leaving the assembling and cooking of the dish to the creative cook. A healthier diet means that salt, fat, sugar and packet sauces are replaced by subtle use of herbs, spices and other flavourings, all of them needing more chopping, sieving, blending and pulverizing than is necessary for lard-basted roast pork, roast potatoes and gravy made from fatty meat juices.

Fortunately, help is at hand in the shape of the food processor. If you are short of time and committed to healthier eating, the food processor is not a 'gadget', it is an absolute essential and probably the single most useful item in the kitchen. Mine is never put away: it remains on the work-top, in use many times daily.

A food processor will chop, blend, emulsify, knead, slice, grate and shred, all in one goblet. It is powerful, easy to clean and takes up little space. Unlike blenders, which can only be used in short bursts, the motor of a food processor can normally be left running for several minutes at a time without harm. Its main advantages, though, are its extraordinary versatility and its speed.

Imagine making spicy meatballs – a perfectly healthy dish – in the traditional way. The meat needs to be minced very finely (butcher's mince is too coarse), so the mincer would have to be brought out to be clamped to a table (the type without clamps never seems firm enough), the grating plates screwed in (let's hope none of the little bits are missing) and the meat wound through – perhaps several times. The breadcrumbs would need to be grated. (In order to do this success-fully, the bread should be stale and firm.) The onions and parsley must be very finely chopped using a heavy blade on a chopping board. Any additional seasoning must also be either ground or pulverized. Then the mixture must be very well kneaded – possibly pounded – to make it smooth. Following the preparation, you would have accumu-lated quite a pile of washing-up which would include the mincer with all its blades and bits, the grater, several knives, the mixing bowl and the chopping board. By my reckoning all this would take not less than half an hour.

With a food processor the sequence could be as follows. The bread (any bread will do) parsley and onion can be chopped together, using the master blade. They are then transferred to a small bowl. The goblet does not need to be rinsed. The meat is pulverized using the master blade. The parsley, onion and breadcrumb mixture is returned to the goblet and the whole mixture is processed together until it is smooth – about 30 seconds. Time taken: five minutes. Washing up: goblet, blade, bowl and paring knife.

The processor will reduce garlic and ginger to a paste in seconds with a little water, will chop herbs, slice onions, julienne carrots, liquidize soups so that most don't need sieving, and knead bread. Most processors will now whisk eggs efficiently. The main dangers of a processor are the obverse side of its advantages. Its speedy action means that it is easy to over-process food; also the blades are so sharp that a safety routine is essential. Our rule is that the blade is always washed first and separately and never ever left lurking in a washing-up bowl where it might give someone (even the person who put it there) a nasty surprise.

I do use a hand grater and a blender for small single quantities of ingredients, but in my view the processor renders many other pieces of kitchenware obsolete. There may be a place in a perfectionist's kitchen for mandolines, herb choppers, meat mincers, food mixers and beaters, but I would use them so rarely that they would not really earn their space on the shelf. It is true, for instance, that the metal blade of a processor chops rather than squeezes minced meat and that the resulting texture is different, probably inferior. It is also true that a mandoline offers subtle variation of sizes in slicing – useful if, for instance, you are producing sliced potatoes to top a gratin dish.

Processors do not produce such a smooth purée as blenders. However, I am quite happy to compromise on these matters. To me, the speed and simplicity of food processing more than makes up for its deficiencies. Also, the manufacturers are constantly refining their machines: if, for example, you want the traditional texture of minced meat, you can now buy a mincing attachment.

Most processors are sturdy and reliable. In eight years of heavy daily use my Magimix has needed no attention except a new safety switch and replacement blades. I have added a few extra accessories – one of the most useful is a second goblet which can save time in assembling a complicated dish.

Thanks to the violence of the competition for this market, the real price of food processors has come down. It is still, however, an expensive item and it is important to choose the one that will suit you. The best processors have these features:

● A large, sharp master blade. In some processors the blade is short and stubby compared with the size of the goblet and will not process evenly. The blade should sit low down in the goblet, making it possible to process small amounts of food.

● A good range of attachments to suit your own needs: for instance, a dough kit with an extended lid for breadmaking (the basic processor will produce perfectly good dough but in smaller batches), a juicer for those who enjoy real fresh fruit juice, a whisking kit for people who make regular use of beaten egg whites.

● A large goblet with a handle for easy lifting.

● 'Direct drive' – that is, the goblet should sit directly over the motor. Processors with the motor at one side and the goblet at the other are often cheaper, but they are less powerful and the belt between goblet and motor is prone to snapping.

● Safety: it should be impossible to work the machine unless the lid is in place. The lid should fit securely – the vibration from the motor can loosen the lid in a poorly designed processor.

● An automatic cut-out to prevent over-heating.

● Easily available spares and servicing.

Many people making an initial processor purchase blench at the price and compromise by buying the smallest size. I did this myself and now regret it. The next size up or even the one after that would have cost only a few extra pounds and would in fact have suited me better. A bigger goblet is usually better (unless you are just cooking for yourself). It will handle large quantities more easily, while still coping perfectly well with small ones.

Blender / liquidizer

A blender is really a more primitive and limited form of food processor. It will produce breadcrumbs and grated cheese as well as reducing soups to a purée. Its only real advantage over a food processor is that the purées it produces are considerably smoother. However, many blenders have motors that burn themselves out rather readily; the food tends to cling to the bottom of the goblet, remaining stubbornly unblended at the top; and their capacity is often small. They are also fiddly to empty and clean.

I do find a small, cheap hand blender useful for producing small quantities of emulsified sauces or blended soups. This is shaped a bit like a torch and can be used either in its own beaker or, with care, directly into a pan. The slightly larger version has an egg-whisk attachment.

If you are looking for a traditional blender, it is probably best to buy at the top of the market and to go for a large goblet and a powerful motor. Pay special attention to the lid: it should fit very securely. There have been several accidents in which people have been badly scalded when the hot contents of a blender have spurted out accidentally through an ill-fitting lid.

Microwave

The microwave market is now worth many millions of pounds a year: it is the biggest success story in electrical retailing since the boom in freezers. The manufacturers think that by the mid-1990s 80 per cent of homes could possess a microwave.

If you read the advertising material produced by the industry, you could be forgiven for thinking that microwave ovens will do everything except boil an egg. The reality of how most people use them may be rather different. It is possible that the meal most often 'cooked' in a microwave is a ready-prepared frozen dinner from Bejam or Tesco. I know one microwave cookery teacher who swears that most microwave ovens are bought by people who actually hate cooking. Nevertheless a microwave oven must have attractions for any cook short of time. It will thaw out frozen food fast and cook it quickly. It is safe, because dishes do not get so hot as in a conventional oven. It can save on washing-up time – a china soup tureen can, for instance, go straight from the microwave to the table. There are health advantages too. Cooking times for fish, fruit and vegetables are short, so there is high vitamin, mineral and flavour retention, especially as little or no water needs to be added. Re-heated microwaved food conserves many more of its nutrients with little loss of texture and flavour.

In my experience, however, the microwave is not the all-round useful kitchen appliance it is often claimed to be. The food does not look so good because it does not brown. Roast chicken is more like steamed chicken – perfectly pleasant, but not the same as chicken cooked in the oven. Extra oil or a food-colouring mixture will have to be applied to it to 'brown' the top. Jacket potatoes do indeed cook in ten minutes, but the skins remain soft and curiously flavourless (though this can be remedied by putting them into a very hot conventional oven for ten minutes after microwaving). Oldish root vegetables remain rock hard; beef toughens and shrinks; anything with a skin will explode unless pricked. Neither is the speed element always what it appears. Rice cooks perfectly in a microwave, but it takes exactly the same time as with any of the conventional methods. It is true that scrambled eggs do not stick to their basin in a microwave, but there is no difference in the cooking time. The only sauce that really works well in a microwave is the old-fashioned floury 'roux', which most people now think has a rather limited place in cookery. All sauces need their microwave cooking interrupted constantly for stirring, turning and checking. It is a great deal easier to control and keep contact with this type of cooking on an ordinary hob.

Nevertheless, I do possess a microwave and use it frequently, mostly for rice, vegetables and fish. I find it invaluable for quickly thawing out frozen stocks and soups, and an excellent way round the problem of serving decent food in a household where people come and go at many unpredictable times. Before the arrival of the microwave, anyone coming home late would be tempted to resort to the frying pan or sneak off to the fish and chip shop. Now they know there will be a meal that can be reheated in two minutes and which will taste very nearly as good as the original.

When choosing a microwave, pocket is the main limiting factor. A conventional cooker with a built-in microwave area gives the best of all possible worlds, but these are extremely expensive.

A simple high-output (700 watt) oven with a turntable, defrost control and timer probably gives the best value for money. A browning element is a useful extra but not essential, as food can be browned under the grill. There are many microwaves on the market with other refinements, but these all add to the price. If you are unlikely to make much use of them it seems unnecessary to spend the extra money.

You need not buy whole new sets of 'microwave ware'. A browning dish with a lid might be useful, and so might a divided vegetable dish, but for the rest, existing glass, rigid plastic and pottery dishes will probably be just as good.

TECHNIQUES FOR HEALTHIER COOKING

An elderly great-aunt of mine lived in a large old house in Bristol. I used to love visiting there as a child because it was such a romantic contrast to our own suburban semi. There was a huge ginger cat which scrambled up your back, six storeys of well-polished Victorian furniture, a stuffed owl and a fish in glass cases, gas lighting, and, best of all, a stone-flagged kitchen with a scrubbed deal table and a pine dresser full of blue china. I was allowed to help prepare Sunday lunch: my job was to tidy up the sprouts. I had to cut crosses in the stalks and then put them to soak in several pints of salted water. I remember the pan being too heavy for me to lift. At 10.30 a.m. it would be transferred to the Aga with some 'bicarb' and the sprouts would be 'put on' to be ready in time for lunch at 12.30. No doubt all over Britain hundreds of thousands of other such pans were simultaneously boiling away the nutrients in vegetables because that was then the accepted method of cooking them.

Healthier eating means significant change, not just in ingredients but in the ways they are cooked. Basically, the move is away from prolonged boiling in water or immersion in fat and towards swifter, more intense exposure to heat. There has been an accompanying change in the texture that is now considered acceptable. Thirty years ago sprouts were supposed to arrive at the table dark olive in colour and very, very soft: that showed they were cooked. My great-aunt, if she were alive today, would probably be scandalized by the 'underdone' sprouts I serve, and stir-fried broccoli would, I'm sure, strike her as ridiculous.

Stir-frying apart, most 'healthy' cooking techniques are simple common-sense adaptations of the traditional methods, to bring them into line with current nutritional thinking.

BOILING

Choose the freshest, youngest vegetables wherever possible: they are moister and more pliable and therefore need only brief cooking.

Prolonged storage toughens the fibres of vegetables and means they need longer cooking time.

Always boil vegetables in a pan with a tight-fitting lid. That way the vegetables will cook partly in steam, partly in water and will need less water. Most vegetables can be cooked successfully in about half an inch of water. Vegetables begin to lose vitamins as soon as they are cut, so prepare them while the water is coming to the boil. Never soak them in water ahead of time and never start them cooking from cold – even root vegetables should always be plunged into boiling water. Bring the water back to the boil after the vegetables have gone in, cover the pan tightly and reduce the temperature immediately so that the pan lid stops rattling. In a well-designed pan, water will form a seal round the lid, preventing any more steam escaping.

Keep the cooking times as brief as possible. Sliced courgettes will be ready in four minutes, carrots in five or six, sprouts in seven or eight. Test for 'doneness' with a skewer. Add salt, if you wish, at the end of cooking time. Salt draws moisture and vitamins out of the vegetables, so it is best added last, if at all. Never add bicarbonate of soda to green vegetables: it may preserve their green colour, but it has a destructive effect on their vitamins.

Make a habit of saving the vegetable water, which will be well-flavoured and contains useful nutrients, to use as stock for sauces and soups. You can also freeze it for later use. Water from green vegetables becomes sour quickly, so needs to be used or frozen promptly.

POACHING

This technique is useful for delicate food that might break up in fierce heat – poached eggs are an obvious example. It is a good way of cooking fish and is also used in some cuisines for dumplings.

Poached fish is usually lowered gently into a lightly flavoured stock and then simmered, tightly covered, well below boiling point – the liquid should barely tremble. With some fish, salmon for instance, the heat can be turned off after reaching boiling point and the fish left to cook and cool down slowly over a period of several hours.

STEAMING

Steaming is a useful alternative to boiling for vegetables, but it is also an excellent way to cook meat and fish. Since the food does not come into direct contact with boiling water it is more likely to conserve its natural flavour. Steamed vegetables have an intense flavour which reduces the need to add salt. They take a little longer to cook than boiled vegetables, and the mineral and vitamin loss is about the same as with brief boiling, as there is some leaching into the water.

Proper steaming means that steam from boiling water is forced through holes in a steaming platform to circulate around the food. A tight-fitting lid ensures that the steam cannot escape but keeps condensing back into the pan. A large steamer gives better results than a small one because the food can be laid on the steaming platform in a single layer and will cook evenly and quickly. Bring the water to the boil before putting the unsalted food in. Reduce the heat to a simmer so that the pan lid does not rattle.

Some meat and fish dishes need to be cooked on a heat-proof plate inside the steamer, as their juices are collected for a sauce. Steaming takes a little longer with this kind of dish, as the steam cannot circulate underneath the food.

As with boiling, the juices from vegetable steaming (or fish and meat cooked without a plate) should be collected and saved for stock.

It is worth investing in a proper traditional steamer if you think you might steam a lot of food. However, there are cheaper alternatives, some more satisfactory than others. A Japanese expandable steaming basket costs only a few pounds. The ingenious overlapping metal plates will expand or contract to fit most pans. Some of these steamers have a large metal prong in the middle (for lifting), which makes them unsuitable for most fish. However, in some types the prong is removable. If you possess a really large lidded pan, a metal (not plastic!) colander may sit inside it and will work for vegetable cooking. Putting a plate inside the colander will adapt this method for fish, but it is not tremendously stable or safe. Some woks come equipped with steaming platforms and lids. Another Chinese invention is a system of rush baskets which sit one on top of the other.

PRESSURE COOKING

Pressure cooking is really just another method of steaming. The weight on the lid keeps the steam at an intense pressure, which means that the food cooks in about a third of the time it would take by conventional means. Pressure cooker design has improved recently, making those terrifying gusts of steam impossible and allowing pre-set cooking times.

In theory, pressure cooking ought to be a good way of cooking vegetables: as with steaming, they can be kept away from direct contact with the water. In practice, however, it is difficult to time the cooking with any precision. You can't easily inspect the food while it is cooking and a minute too long at such high temperatures can give disappointing results. Pressure cookers do come into their own, however, for pulses and soups and some casseroles. This can be especially important where time for cooking is limited and where a softer texture is appropriate anyway.

It is important to observe the manufacturer's safety instructions. The most vital point is never to fill the pan to more than two thirds of its capacity.

MICROWAVE

Microwave cooking is a large subject in its own right and it is difficult to do it justice here. It is most successful as a substitute for steaming and boiling, least successful as an alternative to roasting and baking. The same rules of basic vegetable preparation apply as with boiling: last-minute cutting, no soaking, pieces cut evenly sized, no salt. Most leafy or soft vegetables only need rinsing and can be cooked, covered, without any more water, so that vitamin and mineral retention is high. Root vegetables need a little more water – indeed if they are very elderly they will never become tender in a microwave.

Food reheats much more satisfactorily in a microwave than with any other technique. There is less loss of flavour and moisture and more of the nutrients are retained. Cover plated food with a glass lid or with another plate, and heat on full power for about two minutes: the exact time depends on the density and temperature of the food. Chicken and turkey can be microwaved much more satisfactorily than other meats by using a roasting bag on a plastic rack, but the results are more like casseroling than baking and the end product is often anaemic-looking. Steer clear of the 'browning glazes' sold to remedy this problem, as most of them are high in monosodium glutamate.

Use a microwave to dry summer herbs by microwaving on full power for about two minutes with the herbs scattered, whole, on kitchen paper. Store them, crumbled, in dark jars, in the usual way. These herbs will have a better flavour, texture and colour than herbs air-dried in the traditional slow way.

If you are still eating bacon occasionally, a microwave produces a good result. Cut off the fat and put the bacon on a piece of kitchen paper. Cover it with another piece. Microwave on full power for four minutes.

Fish and the microwave make perfect partners. In effect the covered fish steams in its own juices with very little loss of flavour. The fish is ready just as it begins to change colour – remember you must allow for standing time, and over-cooking is an ever-present danger with microwaves.

ROASTING

The occasional roast joint can still have its place in a healthy diet, but there should ideally be a few adjustments to the traditional way of roasting, in which typically the meat sat in a pan surrounded by potatoes, both of them basted lavishly with lard. Food cooked this way retains a lot of its own fat as well as the additional fat used for basting. Here is an alternative way to roast, which gives equally good results and is a great deal less fatty.

Red meat

Cut off all the visible fat from the meat. Season it, not with salt, but by inserting slivers of garlic or dusting a few chopped herbs over the skin. Sit the meat on a rack – either a special V-shaped roasting rack or the one from the grill pan – so that the fat collects under and not in the meat. Don't add any extra fat. Cover the top loosely with foil for the first three quarters of the cooking time. This ensures that the joint remains moist, as more steam is retained. Remove the foil for the last quarter so that the top can brown.

Poultry

Follow the same technique as for red meat, but prick the skin all over first. Discard the skin before carving.

Roast potatoes

Par-boil the potatoes for five minutes. Drain them and let them dry off a little. Now paint them sparingly with a little polyunsaturated oil and set them at the top of a hot oven for about 45 minutes.

Gravy

Let the drip tray from the roast cool down for about five minutes (keep the meat in the oven) so that the fat separates off easily on the top. Pour all the fat away. Beat in some flour creamed in water, add stock and thicken in the usual way. Alternatively, make a dark, thin sauce by caramelizing some onions in a very little fat with half a teaspoon of sugar, then adding chicken stock and puréed vegetables.

CASSEROLING

A casserole is a slow, gentle method of cooking, but a traditional red-meat casserole is probably out of the question for a busy cook on weekdays – though some chicken and fish dishes can be made with this method. Perhaps at weekends there will be more leisure time to consider them.

Casseroles are a good way to cook healthier food, as long as you observe a few simple rules. Trim any fat from the meat first, and only use minimal fat, if any, in the initial searing of meat: keeping the heat low will prevent burning. Use good home-made stock (or water or wine) rather than cubes, and keep any added moisture (stock or water) to a minimum – most food exudes a lot of its own during slow cooking. Seal the lid tightly to encourage steam. Casseroles with meat normally produce a lot of fat. Let the dish cool down for a few minutes, then spoon it off from the top. Alternatively, if you are cooking in advance, refrigerate the dish. The fat solidifies completely and will be easy to remove. Refrigerated casseroles must be very thoroughly reheated.

Traditional meat casseroles are healthier – and cheaper – 'stretched' with other ingredients. This reduces fat content and bumps up the mineral, vitamin and fibre levels. Many standard red-meat casseroles can have their meat content halved if you add pulses such as kidney beans or lentils, and vegetables such as courgettes, tomatoes, potatoes and carrots. Season with herbs and spices rather than salt. Another advantage of this method is that a casserole which includes root vegetables will probably not need thickening with flour – a technique which can sometimes give a rather gummy texture and flavour.

EN PAPILLOTE

This means cooking 'in an envelope', and is really a combination of oven-cooking and steaming in which the food is enclosed in an envelope of foil. It is an excellent way of cooking combinations of fish and vegetables, for instance, so that they retain much of their flavour and nutrients. It can also be used for fruit compotes and for vegetable combinations. It is not so successful for denser food, which is usually better casseroled.

Cut a double oval of foil, not too small, as some air space is needed for steam to circulate. Place the food in the middle. Crimp the edges tightly, twisting the two ends so that you leave yourself two 'handles': this helps you lift the food on to the baking tray without spillages. The food is usually cooked at the top of a hot oven.

A curious variation of cooking *en papillote* was the Victorian custom of cooking trout in newspaper. This unlikely-sounding technique results in an excellent if plainly cooked fish. Soak three layers of newspaper in water, parcel the fish up and put it in the oven. It will be done when the newspaper is dry all through.

FRYING

Devotees of the real purist school of healthy eating advocate throwing away your frying pan completely. I find this advice quite unacceptable. In fact I use my frying pan most days – but not in the traditional ways. When you are short of kitchen time, the frying pan is an ally, not an enemy, of healthier cooking.

Healthier basic frying

First it must be the right kind of pan. Mine is a large, heavy non-stick pan with a tight-fitting lid. I keep a pot of sunflower oil by my cooker with a bristle pastry brush at its side. When I am ready to cook, I dip the brush in once and paint the pan with oil, then heat it gently.

If I am cooking chicken I remove the skin, then slide in the meat and brown both sides. Impatience does not pay – it takes perhaps three or four minutes to brown each side. Now the lid may come into its own, depending on the recipe. For instance, if you reduce the heat and cover the pan, it will cook very quickly in its own steam, while still having a pleasantly browned crust. Don't crowd the food in the pan, otherwise it will steam from the start and will never look or taste right.

This same technique can be adapted very successfully for vegetables like onions which are normally browned in a great deal of oil. Slice the onions in the usual way. Choose a large, deep saucepan, preferably non-stick (although it works almost as well with other pans). Brush it with polyunsaturated oil – just one dip in the pot is enough. This time have the initial temperature a little higher (but well short of smoking point). Put in the onions and turn them vigorously and continuously with a wooden spoon or fork for about four minutes, when they will be well browned. The temperature can be reduced for the latter part of the cooking. A saucepan is better than a frying pan for this technique, as less steam is lost and the onions cook partly through contact with the hot oil, partly in their own moisture given off as steam.

Stir-frying

Stir-frying proper is slightly different. It is possible to improvise with a large frying pan, but using a Chinese wok (or Indian *karhai*) is really the only way to do it properly, and much safer and tidier. Stir-frying in any other kind of pan tends to mean that much of the food flies about uncontrollably, often ending up on the floor. The round bottom and steep sides of a wok mean that a lot of food can be stir-fried safely and quickly in absolutely minimal oil.

Stir-frying is the busy cook's friend. In the time it takes the rice to cook you can prepare and make perhaps two pleasant meat or vegetable dishes one after the other using the same pan. The secrets of success are:

● The wok must be well seasoned by an initial heating with oil. It should never be washed in detergent after that. Wash it in hot water, wipe it dry and oil it between uses.

● Food must be cut up small, with all the pieces exactly the same size, otherwise some will be under-cooked and some over-cooked.

● All the ingredients should be prepared in advance, including any sauce.

To stir-fry, heat a teaspoonful of oil in the wok under a high heat until it is on the verge of smoking. The oil should be safflower, sunflower or corn. Olive oil is not suitable as it smokes at too low a temperature. First add the ingredients that will take longest to cook, then the others in descending order. Keep lifting and turning the food so that it keeps continuous contact with the hot sides of the pan. In Chinese cooking, a well-seasoned sauce made from stock or wine and thickened with cornflour is often added at the last moment. The actual cooking time may be as little as two minutes for vegetable dishes, slightly longer for dishes containing meat.

'Dry' frying

Some food will cook over a low heat in a non-stick pan without any fat at all. This is a good technique for mince, as the fat will run out and can then be drained off. By and large, though, only fairly fatty foods can be cooked this way, and this is the kind of food to avoid where possible.

Deep frying

I avoid deep frying altogether, but it is true that done with care it can be less unhealthy than you might think if you observe the following guidelines:

● Cook the food in a polyunsaturated oil such as sunflower or corn oil. These particular oils have high smoking temperature (200° C, 400° F).

● Heat the oil to just below smoking point in a pan less than half full. Test the temperature by dropping in a piece of bread. It should brown in not more than 30 seconds, not less than 20 seconds.

- The food should be dry, or coated in a light batter to protect it.

- Cook in small batches, drying each batch on kitchen paper.

- Never re-use the oil more than once. Even a polyunsaturated oil will change its chemical nature on frequent re-heating to very high temperatures.

- If you are cooking chips, cut them thick and straight. They absorb less fat that way.

- Fat can quickly catch fire if it becomes too hot and chip pans are one of the most common causes of domestic fires. Always stay within reach of a frying pan. If the worst happens and it does catch fire, DON'T TRY TO LIFT IT TO SAFETY. Quickly soak and wring out a tea towel and throw it over the pan. It is better to have a ruined, burnt tea towel than ruined, burnt hands and face.

GRILLING

This must be one of the simplest and quickest healthy cooking techniques of all, enabling fat to run out of and away from food.

Grilling is often advocated as the 'standard' method of healthier cooking. However, like all other cooking techniques, it has its particular place and is not a cure-all. It does not work well for cheap, tough cuts of meat and it can dry out some kinds of white fish (unless a lot of fat is added, which defeats the object). It is often difficult with thick or dense food to achieve an end product which is cooked all through without also being burnt on the outside. And some grilled food can be unpalatably dry.

Better grilling

Trim the fat from meat. Protect delicate parts of fish with small pieces of foil for the first part of the cooking – a frizzled trout tail is an unappetizing sight. Food should be at room temperature. If it is chilled it will steam rather than grill.

The grill must be pre-heated – this gives you more control over the cooking. Do use the rack. If you grill meat on foil or on a plate, the advantage of grilling is lost because the fat can't escape. The first part of the cooking is usually best done at medium distance away from a moderate heat. Move the food nearer at the very end if you want a more browned result.

Marinating food, even for a few minutes, before grilling increases its moisture level, tenderizes it, and will provide you with a basting liquid during grilling. Steer clear of very oily marinades (though a little olive or safflower oil is fine). Try mixtures of plain yoghurt, lemon juice, herbs, wine and ginger. Alternatively, brush a mean amount of oil over the food before grilling. This will give a pleasantly browned result without substantially increasing the fat level: a teaspoon is quite enough to coat four fish. Spiced oils are a useful alternative to plain cooking oils (see recipe on page 228).

Much plainly grilled food is more palatable if it is accompanied by a sauce – often a cold sauce. On page 224 there are some easy recipes for simple sauces to accompany grilled fish.

THE HEALTHY LARDER

Fifteen or so years ago I acquired an enormous second-hand chest freezer. I remember proudly rushing out to Bejam and spending a large sum of money on stocking it. I followed the advice in all the books on freezing and made a list of contents as soon as I got home. I recently discovered this list at the back of a cupboard (it was the only one I ever made – so much for good intentions). Listed there were bags of pork chops, lamb chops, chicken quarters, steaks, joints of New Zealand lamb, liver for the cats, ice-cream, whipping cream, butter, lard, frozen fancy cakes, and some 'luxury' ready-prepared meals. There were a few bags of cauliflower, peas and courgettes, but no other vegetables, no fruit, no fish at all, and one loaf of white bread.

Today the chest freezer has gone, together with the inconvenience of diving into the inevitable muddle at the bottom. Today's list, if I made one, would include eight wholemeal loaves; two packs of wholemeal baps; several different types of fish; fish fingers for the children; pizza bases and pizzas; large bags of vegetables, mostly peas, spinach, broad beans and sweet corn; cooked kidney beans; small packs of herbs; home-made tomato sauce, and home-made stocks of several different types. The difference could hardly be more startling.

People hoping to convince us of the need to switch to a healthier diet often underplay the amount of change that is involved. 'Just give up a little bit more of this and eat a little bit more of that,' they wheedle. I believe this approach is misleading. Depending, of course, on what you are already eating, the degree of change can be profound and will be reflected in what you buy. Eating healthily undoubtedly means a pattern of shopping different from that of the recent past: for instance, stopping as a matter of course at the herb and spice rack to replenish supplies; choosing a supermarket that sells fromage blanc, thickened yoghurt and decent olive oil; spending a far greater percentage of the weekly food bill on fruit and vegetables; patronizing specialist ethnic grocers for food like fresh ginger, fresh coriander or ricotta cheese that might be more difficult to track down in supermarkets.

Healthier eating should not involve more expense. Highly

processed foods are not cheap: a ready-prepared potato salad, for instance, costs roughly three times its home-made equivalent. Tinned pineapple in heavy syrup may look cheap and a large fresh pineapple expensive, but the fresh pineapple will probably make three meals for a smaller outlay than the cost of three tins. The idea of healthy eating is to replace the expensive, fatty, sugary and salty convenience foods by fruit and vegetables, not to add more fruit and vegetables to an 'unhealthy' diet. If you eat a lot of pulses and stick to strictly seasonal fruit and vegetables your food bill could actually be smaller.

BREAD AND FLOUR

Bread is not fattening. Wholemeal bread is an important source of dietary fibre and minerals. Decent bread should, ideally, be on the table at every meal. The best choice is wholemeal, from a baker who still makes his loaves in the traditional way. 'Wholemeal' (or 'whole-wheat') means that the whole grain has been used to make the flour. This should have the best flavour and all the nutrients of the original grain. It often takes a while to find a palatable loaf. Some 'hand-made' bread is horribly dense and heavy; supermarket wholemeal is still preferable to supermarket white sliced, but may be equally full of air and moisture. The ideal theoretical solution is to make your own, but few busy cooks have time for this. Bread freezes well. Once you find a source of good bread, buy it in bulk and freeze it.

Some people find wholemeal bread too heavy. 'Brown' (which used to be called 'wheatmeal') is the next best choice, as it is made from flour which is '85-per-cent extraction' – that is, it contains 85 per cent of the original grain, so it still retains a high percentage of the nutrients. 'Granary' bread is usually made from brown (wheatmeal) flour with some malted grains added.

Purists advocate using wholemeal flour in every case instead of white. My own feeling is that while wholemeal flour makes excellent cakes, biscuits and pancakes, I have yet to find a way of cooking wholemeal pastry satisfactorily: the results are always too soggy or too brittle and the colour is off-putting. I also feel that wholemeal flour is sometimes difficult to use successfully in sauces. If you are eating plenty of fibre in other ways, the use of white flour in such cases is not going to matter too much.

CHEESE

Most hard cheeses are high in both saturated fat and salt, so they should be used sparingly. However, the strong flavour of mature cheese means that little is actually needed to add dash and flavour to a dish. Half an ounce of grated Parmesan sprinkled on pasta adds a very small amount of fat in return for a big bonus on flavour and texture.

Some softer cheeses like Brie, Camembert, Mozarella, Gouda and Edam are lower in saturated fat. Edam, Gouda and Mozarella melt well, so they are useful for toppings. Beware that the milder flavour does not lead you into using larger quantities: traditional recipes often quote far too much. An ounce or two of grated Edam is quite enough to top a potato gratin, for instance.

Low-fat soft cheeses

Ricotta. An Italian soft cheese available from delicatessens, but, mysteriously, not from supermarkets yet. This is tragic as it is a wonderful cheese – unsalted, moist and smooth. It can be used in sauces and stuffings for pasta, or in puddings. It makes an excellent light lunch eaten in a slice with some cherry tomatoes and a wholemeal roll.

Cottage cheese. The lumpy texture and added salt make this a less useful ingredient than it might be. However, cottage cheese can be mixed to a paste with stronger cheeses to stuff baked potatoes and pancakes, used in cheesecakes or eaten on its own with salad.

Quark. This curiously named German cheese, now widely available in supermarkets, is sold in tubs and looks exactly like a cream cheese, but has only a fraction of the fat. It has a dense texture, a slightly sour flavour and leaves a 'dry' after-taste on the palate. Use it wherever you would use cream cheese – in cheesecakes, to stuff canapés, make sweet puddings, and so on. However, I do not find it a good substitute for cream on raw fruit – it is too sour and too thick. Quark can be used very successfully for thickening sauces instead of cream or egg yolks: it will not separate when boiled.

Shape. A bland low-fat 'cream' cheese manufactured by St Ivel. It is about 9 per cent fat. It has a soft, spreading texture and is a good substitute for cream cheese. It is also an excellent thickener for sauces, especially pasta sauces, as it can be boiled without separating.

Fromage blanc/fromage frais. I have included this useful commodity here, only because its name means 'white cheese' or 'fresh cheese'. However, it is much more like cream or yoghurt in both texture and flavour. The texture is like thick yoghurt, but the flavour is distinctly less sour. Fromage blanc is a fermented milk product, so it will always have a slightly tart flavour, but it is delicious with soft fruit or hot puddings. It makes a pleasant stuffing with cooked dried fruit for pancakes and can also be used, with very great care, to thicken sauces. Whisk a spoonful at a time into a liquid that is hot but not boiling. I now automatically put a tub of fromage blanc into my shopping trolley every week – fortunately Sainsbury's now sell their own label, and other supermarkets and chains are following suit. Look for the label that tells you what percentage of fat it has: some of the French imported brands have a high percentage and are therefore not low-fat. The carton will say 'x% matière grasse'. Look for a brand that offers under 3 per cent fat.

Low-fat hard cheeses

Some manufacturers are now responding to the 'health lobby' by producing low-fat Cheddars and so on. Though we must be pleased that these products are available, they do, unfortunately, leave quite a lot to be desired from the cook's point of view. The texture is crumbly, the taste slightly sour, and the cheese does not melt or brown appealingly: it remains a moist deep-yellow mass.

FATS AND OILS

One of the main aims in a prudent diet is not only to cut down on total fat intake in general but to reduce the quantity of saturated fat in particular.

Fats

Butter undoubtedly tastes far better and is far more useful in cooking than any of its rivals. Unfortunately, however, it is also a saturated fat and should be used very sparingly. Unsalted butter is widely available.

Polyunsaturated margarines are a healthier choice, even if less appealing in taste and texture. Look for tubs that say 'High in polyunsaturates'. Other margarines may be just as full of saturated fat as butter. Polyunsaturated margarines can be used for baking and, with care, for frying. It is difficult to find polyunsaturated margarines that are unsalted. They also, it must be said, contain additives and artificial colourings, unlike butter.

Low-fat spreads are margarines whipped up with water. For this reason they have fewer calories. (Butter and margarine have equal numbers of calories.) Some have a high butter content: look for the brands which are high in polyunsaturates. Low-fat spreads cannot be used for frying or, unless the recipe specifically says so, for baking – they contain too much water and break up under heat.

Cooking fats. Lard is an animal fat and highly saturated, and so are most hard margarines. Use polyunsaturated margarine or polyunsaturated oils instead.

Oils

Like margarines, some oils also contain saturated fat. The ones to avoid are palm and coconut oil.

The best all-round choices on health grounds are the polyunsaturated oils: corn (maize), safflower, sunflower, soya and groundnut (peanut). Safflower and sunflower make the best choices of these four where salad dressings are concerned. Corn is a heavy-tasting oil better kept for frying.

Olive oil is monounsaturated, so is neutral in its effect on blood cholesterol level. It has easily the best flavour of all oils for salad dressings, and can be used successfully for initial sautéing as long as the temperature is not raised too high. Look for cold-pressed 'extra virgin' olive oil, which will have the best flavour.

Don't re-use oil more than once – the heat will alter the flavour and may also change it from a polyunsaturated fat to a saturated one.

FISH

My favourite fishmonger, like many in his trade, is a fish fanatic. He often tells me with pride that he eats fish twice a day, every day, even on Sunday without ever feeling bored, because the tastes and textures of fish vary so much. Some people might feel, 'Well he would say that, wouldn't he?' Others might think, wryly, that they should be so lucky . . .

Unfortunately, there's no getting away from the fact that almost until yesterday, the wet fish shop was in decline. Thanks to EEC policy and the 'Cod War' with Iceland, fish has become much more expensive. The habit of fish-buying was lost by a whole generation which regarded boil-in-the-bag cod in parsley sauce as an exciting and risky dish.

Now, however, there are signs that the fish trade is looking up again. Fish has had a series all to itself on television; the Sea Fish Industry Authority has launched several effective campaigns including TV commercials to promote fish. Fish is now on sale in supermarkets; it is noticeably featured in many more ready-made dishes and magazine articles than was the case a year ago. New fish shops seem to be opening everywhere.

Fish is low in saturated fat so it can be eaten in unlimited quantity. Oily fish is high in polyunsaturated fat and is thought therefore to have beneficial effects on arteries. All fish is high in protein, minerals and vitamins. It should feature prominently in any prudent diet.

Buying fresh fish

Look out for:

- Bright eyes
- Bright red gills, bright-looking skin
- Fresh smell
- Firm, stiff flesh

Beware of:

- Dull, sunken eyes and pale gills

72

- Fishy smell
- Flabby, yellowing flesh
- Oily fish, whose blue and green lights are fading
- Shellfish should be bought live wherever possible.

Don't patronize a dirty fish shop with broken tiles, sullen service, flies everywhere and a fishy smell. A fish shop, like fish, should smell of the sea. The fishmonger should always offer to scale, clean, behead and fillet fish for you: most are only too willing to help. Many will suggest favourite recipes for unfamiliar fish. And almost all decent fishmongers will be able to obtain fish for you if you want to order an unusual variety.

Fresh supermarket fish is often excellent, though a little more expensive and available only in a limited range. Personal service is not always on offer, but the fish have usually been cleaned as a matter of routine.

Frozen fish is good value, as the fish are likely to have been frozen speedily after catching. The flavour is usually good, though the texture is a little softer than that of fresh fish and the range of choice limited. Avoid the ready-breaded type: the stiff, dyed-orange coating is unpleasant and it is so easy to make a superior version of your own (for one recipe see page 188). Thaw frozen fish before cooking it. Put it on a plate lined with kitchen paper and let it thaw gradually in the refrigerator or quickly in a microwave.

Tinned fish is a useful back-up for busy cooks, in spite of its salt and oil content. It can make a quick sauce for pasta and pizza or a pleasant ingredient in salads and soups. Especially useful: clams, mussels, oysters, sardines, tuna, salmon and anchovies.

Smoked fish (e.g., kippers, mackerel, bloaters, salmon) is salty, so use it sparingly.

Preparing fish

While most fishmongers are obliging, there is the occasional rogue who is not. You may also have the rare treat of being presented with a freshly caught fish which needs cleaning. Fortunately, most fish are designed in the same way, so dealing with them is easy.

● *Scale* the fish by pulling a blunt knife from tail to head. Do this over a sink and be prepared later to remove scales from a wide area around, including your hair.

● *Gut* the fish by slitting the belly neatly and pulling out the innards. Remove all traces of blood, as this can be bitter.

● *The head* can be left on or removed, as you please. If you leave the head on remove the gills, as they will taste bitter.

● *Fillet* the fish, if necessary, by holding the cleaned fish on the work surface and cutting neatly round its head. Now slit the flesh along the backbone to the tail. Ease the flesh away from the bone with the knife. Turn the fish over and do the same on the other side.

● *Skin* the fish, if you wish, by placing the fillet skin-side down on the work surface. Slide the knife just under the skin at the tail end. Grip the tail, then work the knife under the skin, pushing the knife away from you.

Cooking fish

Fish is fast food. The only real problem it presents is the danger of over-cooking. As a very rough and ready guideline, each half-inch depth of fish takes about four minutes. Fish is cooked when it has changed colour and become opaque all the way through, and when a thin-bladed knife will readily be able to ease it from the bone. Remember that fish, like scrambled egg, goes on cooking after it has been removed from the heat.

Fish may be poached, fried, grilled, microwaved, steamed, barbecued, casseroled, roasted or eaten raw, depending on its type. The best fish to grill are the oily fish; firm fish like monk are the best for barbecueing, but most fish may be successfully steamed and fried. Fish can be used for pasta sauces, and makes a superb ingredient in rice dishes.

FRUIT AND VEGETABLES

As a newly-wed I always tried to keep a fruit bowl on the table. The bowl was filled with a pound of apples, a few pears and a couple of oranges on Fridays, and that was it. Fruit was also eaten cooked in tarts and flans, but it did not have a significant part in our diet. Similarly with vegetables: the basic plan of meals was the usual 'meat with two veg'. The meat was the important element; the vegetables were the garnish.

Today the situation has totally reversed. I buy very little meat. My shopping is dominated by fruit and vegetables. The fruit bowl is still on the dining-room table, but it is replenished daily from the refrigerator, whose whole lower area is entirely taken up with vegetables and fruit of every description. Although we are not vegetarians, many of the meals we eat are, in practice, meat-free: for instance, a red pepper or broccoli soup, then a spiced mushroom pilau followed by fresh fruit. The meat we do eat tends to be an adjunct to the vegetables, pasta or rice rather than the other way round.

Fruit and vegetables should be eaten very fresh, and raw as often as possible: this is the best way of obtaining the maximum benefit from their minerals and vitamins. Leaving them unpeeled and cooking them briefly is also important. Cooking methods are described in more detail on pages 56–9.

Frozen fruit and vegetables are also a good buy. They are packaged under strictly hygienic conditions and frozen so quickly after picking that they will often contain more minerals and vitamins than their fresh equivalents. They do not usually have sugar or salt added. Firm fruit and vegetables normally freeze better than those with soft structures. However, even frozen raspberries and strawberries can be used successfully for fruit purées and sauces.

Most people are probably reasonably familiar with the main groups of fruit and vegetables and know how to deal with them. For those who are baffled by vegetables, the best book is John Tovey's *Feast of Vegetables* (Century, 1985). The wide range of fresh salad leaves available is probably more unfamiliar, so I have taken a little space on pages 87–91 to describe some of the varieties available and how to treat them.

HERBS

Until a few years ago the use of herbs in cookery had almost died out. An interest in herbs was regarded as dubious and slightly cranky: possibly there was more popular interest in the medicinal than in the culinary properties of herbs. In just a short time this has all changed. There are now several nurseries making a good living out of selling nothing *but* herbs, and most stock at least ten varieties. In my local market it used to be only the Greek shop that sold herbs. Now the three plant stalls sell them too and you have to be there early on Saturday if you want to buy. The general improvement in standards of cooking has helped this revival; so, too, has greater knowledge of ethnic cuisines which make extensive use of herbs. *Nouvelle cuisine* emphasized the complementary nature of herbs, but this was never a grass-roots cookery fashion. The real revival in the fortunes of herbs has certainly been helped enormously by the widespread interest in healthier food, because herbs make food more interesting without needing to resort to butter, salt and lard.

The main uses of herbs

Garnishing. A garnish should be both edible and complementary in flavour and colour to the food. Parsley is the traditional herb to use, either finely chopped or in sprigs. However, most herbs may be used for garnishing in exactly the same way. The quantities will vary according to the dish, its taste, and the pungency of the herb.

Flavouring. Some herbs seem to have a natural affinity with certain foods: fennel and dill with fish, basil with tomatoes, sage with pork, rosemary with lamb, tarragon with chicken, and so on. The flavour of a herb should never swamp the food but should enhance it. Delicate herbs are often better added at the last minute; the tougher, woodier herbs like thyme, sage and rosemary are usually incorporated at the start of cooking.

There are no hard-and-fast rules about using herbs. For many dishes the best results do seem to come from using only one or at the most two herbs, but this rule, like most, is made to be broken. Mixed herbs make excellent coatings combined with breadcrumbs in shallow-fried dishes, and they are equally good in meatballs or casseroles.

● **In their own right.** Many herbs are rich sources of minerals and vitamins and make excellent salads. A beautiful summer salad can be made from a frilly lettuce, a few sorrel leaves, and a generous handful of other mixed fresh herbs lightly chopped or torn.

Growing herbs

Fresh herbs are expensive to buy. Even a bunch of good old parsley often costs as much as a pound of apples. Summer herbs can cost even more: those beautifully presented sprigs of tarragon or basil are outrageously expensive. It makes sense to grow your own if you possibly can. Some perennial herbs such as rosemary and bay are easily grown shrubs and, once established, will carry on happily, needing little further attention. Many of these herbs are also evergreen, so will continue to be a source of fresh leaves even in the winter. Perennial deciduous herbs such as sorrel, chives and mint are sturdy, and their rampant growth may even need to be kept strictly under control. Parsley is a biennial. It likes rich, moist soil and some shade from strong sunlight. The seeds take a long time to germinate, but once the plants are growing well they are quite robust. It is really only the delicate summer herbs such as basil, coriander and tarragon that are at all difficult to grow. They need a light, well-drained soil and plenty of sun. A sunny window-sill is perfect. A friend of mine who is a talented cook lives in a small flat. In summer her tiny balcony is crammed with Gro-Bags containing, not the usual elegant geraniums and pansies, or sensible tomatoes, but dozens of thriving basil and tarragon plants. Two terracotta pots house respectively a large rosemary bush and a bay tree.

There is another good reason to grow your own herbs: the taste is far superior to that of preserved herbs, even though the quality of dried and frozen herbs is improving all the time.

Storing fresh herbs

If you do have to buy fresh herbs, they can be stored successfully for up to two weeks. Put them in a large jam jar full of water. Cover the whole thing with a plastic bag and store in the refrigerator. Inspect them occasionally and remove any yellowing or slimy leaves.

Preserving herbs

Air-drying over several weeks is the traditional method, but this gives poor results. The herbs become dusty and lose flavour. There are three modern alternatives.

● Spread the herbs in a single layer on a tray. Put them in an airing cupboard or the plate-warming drawer of the oven for about 24 hours until they are dry and brittle. Store in airtight bottles away from light.

● Microwave the herbs on kitchen paper. The time taken will depend on quantity – about three minutes at full power should be enough for a handful of fresh herbs. The herbs are ready when they crumble easily. Let them cool, then store in bottles as described above.

● Chop or tear the herbs. Spread them on trays and fast-freeze them for about six hours, or until they are stiff. Store them in small plastic bags or yoghurt containers.

It is really worth going to this trouble only with summer herbs like basil, tarragon, chervil and sorrel.

Bought dried herbs

Although the real fresh herb is incomparably better in taste and texture than its dried counterpart, there are many situations in which dried herbs make perfectly good sense. Not everyone has a garden, or the time and patience to grow their own herbs. Commercially dried herbs are not expensive and the range of choice is enormous.

● Look for reasonably bright colours – anything too faded may have been sitting on the supermarket shelf for too long.

● Independent food shops often sell an enormous range of loose herbs much more cheaply than the supermarkets. The quality may be more variable, but you are not paying extra for packaging in smart little bottles.

● Basic herbs (e.g., mixed herbs, parsley, thyme and sage) are often also available much more cheaply in refill drums.

● Store herbs away from direct sunlight if possible.

● Give your herbs a sniff every time you use them. Be ruthless about throwing away anything older than six months, as it is unlikely to have much flavour.

Fifteen useful herbs

There are many dozens of culinary herbs, but this is my own top fifteen:

Basil. This wonderful fragrant annual herb is one of the delights of eating in Italy, where it is used to flavour tomato salads, to make *pesto* with pine-nuts as a sauce for pasta, and in many other ways. It does not dry well and is rarely on sale fresh except at vastly inflated prices in modish London greengrocers' shops. Growing it yourself is really the only way to ensure a steady supply. I find that slugs and snails have very good taste where herbs are concerned and can instantly detect a new young basil plant, so protect the plants from their unwelcome attentions if you can.

There are many varieties. *Common or sweet basil* has the juiciest leaves and is the best all-round choice. *Bush basil* has a milder flavour, but is slightly easier to grow.

Bay. A perennial evergreen often grown as a decorative tub plant. It dries well. A useful herb for rice dishes, fish, and meat casseroles. Essential for marinades, useful for Indian food.

Chervil. A tall, frondy annual or biennial that is easy to grow. It has a faintly aniseed flavour and is a useful garnish for fish and vegetables.

Chives. Food shops usually sell chives as complete potted plants, as they wilt so quickly after cutting. Take them home, split them up carefully into smaller clumps and you will soon have many thriving bushy chive plants. Snip them up with scissors for last-minute sprinkling on soups or fish: their mild, oniony flavour is lost in prolonged cooking. The pretty purple flowers are also edible and look good in salads. Chives freeze well but do not dry successfully.

Coriander. This herb provides both interesting seeds and fragrant leaves. It is probably the most widely used herb in the world, but is usually only available here from specialist greengrocers. It looks very like flat-leaved parsley, but the flavour is completely different: sharp, almost lemony. It is a superb herb, useful for garnishing, in casseroles, soups and on fish. Unlike parsley it is always sold with its roots still attached. It freezes well, so if your supplies are uncertain, it may be worth buying and freezing in bulk.

Dill. Both leaves and seeds of this tall hardy annual are useful. Classically, dill partners fish, but it also goes well with scrambled eggs, cucumber, and even tomato salads.

Fennel. Fennel comes from the same botanical family as dill, and the leaves are similarly feathery in appearance. However, unlike dill, fennel has a strongly aniseed flavour and is a perennial. It can be used with fish, but is also pleasant on new potatoes and in pickles.

Lovage. This handsome tall perennial looks and tastes like celery. Use the chopped leaves sparingly in salads, soups and casseroles.

Marjoram. Marjoram is a close relative of the much stronger-tasting oregano, which grows wild all over the Mediterranean. The flavour is a little like thyme, but sweeter. Add marjoram raw to salads, or to braised vegetable dishes and tomato sauces. It should only be added at the last stages in cooked dishes. It dries well: look for 'oregano' in the commercially available ranges.

Mint. Apple mint is probably the most useful of the many different varieties. Use it for summer drinks and chopped in salads; add a sprig to new potatoes or young carrots. It has a natural affinity with orange zest in stuffings, and for meat dishes, especially pork.

Parsley. There are two common varieties of this useful herb. Curly parsley is probably more attractive for garnishing, but flat-leaved parsley has the better flavour. Parsley is a mild herb, so can usually be added generously to a wide range of savoury dishes.

Rosemary. This evergreen shrub is useful for both pork and lamb dishes. Strip the spikes from the woody stems and chop them well unless they are destined for long, slow cooking. A little rosemary goes a long way.

Sage. Sage is a handsome garden plant in its own right: the purple flowers and grey leaves are often prized by gardeners oblivious to their culinary charms. Sage can be overpowering: use it sparingly raw (chopped finely, as the leaves are tough) in salads, or more generously for meat balls, grilled fish or pork.

Tarragon. There are two varieties, but only one of them, French tarragon, has the proper flavour. Russian tarragon (also known with a little unfairness as 'false tarragon') has much less taste. Tarragon is a delicate perennial with a superb flavour. Use a sprig inside roast chicken, chop it raw in salads, infuse a few sprigs in vinegar, add a tarragon garnish to vegetables and fish. Tarragon dries well and reconstitutes itself quickly in sauces.

Thyme. There are many different varieties of this half-hardy evergreen creeping herb. It has a strong flavour, so needs to be used sparingly. It is an excellent herb for use with poultry, and can often liven up an otherwise bland pulse dish or soup. Thyme is best used at the start of cooking.

MEAT AND POULTRY

Meat is a good source of protein, vitamins and minerals, but it is also a source of saturated fat. It is important to avoid the 'made-up' meats as far as possible. These include sausages, pork pies, luncheon meats and salamis, which all normally contain high percentages of fat. The amount of fat in other meat varies according to the cut. But, on average, these are the percentages of fat in the different types of meat:

BEEF	Roast, with fat	29%
	Rump, with fat	12%
	lean only	6%
LAMB	Chops, with fat	29%
	lean only	12%
	Leg, roast with fat	18%
	lean only	8%
PORK	Chops, with fat	24%
	lean only	11%
CHICKEN	with skin	14%
	without skin	5%
TURKEY	with skin	6%
	without skin	3%
RABBIT		4%

This list shows how widely varied the fat content can be in red meat: a lean grilled rump steak with all the fat removed will have as little fat as chicken with the skin removed. Chicken with the skin left on is more fatty than a lean grilled lamb chop with the fat removed. Unfortunately, the leanest cuts of red meat are also the most expensive. However, healthier ways of cooking meat also make a small amount of meat go a long way. For instance, a stir-fried beef dish may need only one small sirloin steak to feed four people.

Some ways of reducing the fat content of meat in cooking are discussed on pages 60–66. In general, however, the best way of using meat in a prudent diet is to incorporate it in 'stretched' dishes with pasta, pulses and rice: Spaghetti Bolognese, Chilli con Carne and Chicken Risotto are all good examples of healthy, filling and tasty dishes in which the meat goes a long way. For traditional 'meat and vegetable' dishes, chicken and turkey are better choices than red meat.

MILK

Changing to a low-fat milk is an easy way to reduce the amount of saturated fat in the diet. Most milkmen will now deliver fresh skimmed milk and it is widely available in supermarkets too.

The milks with the highest fat content are: gold top, Jersey or Channel Island, green top, silver top and homogenized.

Low-fat milks

Semi-skimmed milk has a striped red and white top and has only 2 per cent fat. This milk is a good compromise for people making the change from higher-fat milks.

Fresh skimmed milk has a blue top and a thin, slightly blue appearance. Some people find it 'watery' at first, but it is the best choice on health grounds as it has almost all the fat removed. It is also available in Ultra-Heat-Treated form (UHT), which means that it has been sterilized at high temperatures and will keep unopened for several months.

Powdered skimmed milk is an acceptable substitute for fresh milk in cooking, but harder to use successfully in tea and coffee.

Powdered coffee whiteners usually contain a lot of saturated fat as well as additives, so are better avoided.

Skimmed milk is certainly the best choice on health grounds. Although semi-skimmed appears to have so little fat, the figure of 2 per cent is quite deceptive. It is calculated on the weight of the milk. Milk is mostly water. When this factor is allowed for and the fat calculation is done on the percentage of the energy (calories) the milk contains, the fat percentage in semi-skimmed milk jumps to 36 per cent.

NUTS

Nuts are good sources of fibre, minerals, vitamins and protein. The fat they contain is mostly polyunsaturated. They are high in calories, but it is difficult to consume 'too many' as they are so filling. It is best to avoid salted peanuts because of the salt. Some uses of nuts in a healthier diet include:

- Dried fruit and nut mixtures as snacks and for packed lunches.

- Cashews, pine-nuts and hazel-nuts in breakfast muesli.

- Pine-nuts, cashews and almonds go well in savoury rice dishes.

- Vegetarian nut roasts and rissoles.

- Toasted nuts make an excellent garnish for sweet and savoury dishes.

PASTA

It is interesting how certain ideas about food take root in popular consciousness and are then extraordinarily hard to shift. In the 1960s and early 1970s pasta was denigrated as 'starchy' food and was on the forbidden list for anyone trying to lose weight, along with potatoes and bread. This idea lingers on even now. One still overweight celebrity, recently interviewed about his substantial weight loss, mourned the fact that he must avoid spaghetti. This legacy from the 'high protein' diet will no doubt eventually fade away as people realize that 'starchy' food is perfectly healthy as long as it is not the sweet, sugary kind. Pasta is a starchy food, an 'unrefined carbohydrate', and therefore an excellent food in a healthy diet. It also cooks quickly – fresh pasta in three minutes, dried in never more than twenty. Of course it will be 'unhealthy' if served with fatty, salty sauces, but pasta lends itself beautifully to sauces that are anything but unhealthy: simple sauces quickly made from vegetables or seafood, for instance, or traditional meaty sauces adapted to modern thinking. I give several in this book.

Traditionally, pasta is served as a first course in small enough quantities to leave an appetite for what is to follow. However, pasta is the perfect healthy food for people looking for a quick, no-fuss supper, and the quantities I give in this book are for main-course eating.

There are hundreds of different pasta shapes, and several colours and flavourings. The main points to look out for when buying and cooking pasta are:

● The small roundish shapes are best for soups.

● Chunky tubes like penne are usually best complemented by hearty, tomato-based sauces.

● Thin ribbon and thin tubular shapes like tagliatelle and spaghetti are the most useful kinds of pasta for all purposes, as they will take both delicate and strongly flavoured sauces.

● Flat sheets such as lasagne are best for stuffing and for dense sauces baked in the oven. 'Pre-cooked' lasagne generally has a very inferior flavour and saves little time anyway.

● Wholemeal pasta is available in a limited range and has a much more chewy texture and a more intrusive flavour than white. It takes a few minutes longer to cook. By and large, wholemeal pasta needs a strongly flavoured sauce with plenty of texture: it is excellent, for instance, for Spaghetti Bolognese (page 165) or for Spaghetti with Anchovies and Olives (page 159), which has a spicy, pungent sauce made from anchovies, chillies and olives. It is absolutely hopeless with a mild sauce such as Spinach and Ricotta (page 167).

● Fresh pasta is delightful, but it is more expensive and does vary greatly in quality. If it has been left for too long on an open shop counter it may have dried out and lost its fresh flavour.

- *Quantities*: Roughly 4 oz (100 g) dried pasta per person is about right for a main course, 2 oz (50 g) for a first course. Fresh pasta weighs more because of its higher moisture content. Allow 5–6 oz (120–150 g) per person.

- *Cooking time*: Varies according to the shape, age and density of the pasta. Keep tasting until the pasta is soft but still has a little bite left in it. There is no need to add salt to the water, or to drown the pasta: 5 pints to one pound of pasta is about right. Add the pasta all at once and when the water is boiling. Stir a few times to stop it sticking together.

- *Serving*: It is possible to have fierce arguments about the best way to serve pasta and for everyone to be right. A communal serving bowl is not usually a good idea, especially for spaghetti, which tends to slither uncontrollably into the gap between the serving dish and the diner's plate. I find the best solution is this: drain the pasta, then return it to its pan. Add about half the sauce and toss it thoroughly into the pasta. Put the tossed pasta on to individual plates, then add a little sauce on top. The plates should be deep to make eating easy – large soup dishes are ideal – and they must be well warmed, as pasta loses its heat so easily.

- *Re-heating*: pasta re-heats well in a microwave.

PULSES

Pulses are the dried seeds of podded vegetables. They are the perfect healthy food: full of fibre, high in vitamins and minerals, filling, low in fat and also cheap. They are excellent in salads, for dips, to 'stretch' meat dishes and to make soups. Most need pre-soaking and lengthy cooking, so they are not ideal for time-conscious cooks. Split (orange) lentils cook in about 20 minutes, but although still a nutritious food they do not quite have the flavour or texture of the whole green or brown lentils which take about double the time. Mung beans do not need soaking and can be cooked in 30 minutes.

Soaking and cooking times for other pulses

Soak 8 hours, boil 45 minutes	Aduki beans, kidney beans
Soak 8 hours, boil 1 hour	Butter beans, haricot beans, black beans
Soak 8 hours, boil 1½ to 2 hours	Chick peas

Pressure cooking can reduce cooking time considerably. The beans do not need to be soaked first. Divide the cooking times above by a third. With conventional cooking, the toxin in beans must be destroyed first by 10 minutes of hard boiling. This is not necessary with a pressure cooker, as the water temperature is so high throughout the cooking time.

Tinned pulses are widely available, but normally have salt and sugar added. Rinsing the beans well under cold running water gets rid of some of this. Don't add any more salt to dishes in which you are using tinned beans. On the whole, I feel that the convenience factor of tinned pulses outweighs the disadvantages. And perhaps the manufacturers will respond soon to pleas to produce salt-free beans.

RICE

Like pasta, rice is important in a healthy diet. It makes a small amount of meat or fish go a long way and is a complex carbohydrate, so it is a food that should be a staple of healthier eating. Its other virtue is that it cooks very quickly.

There are many ways of cooking rice successfully. The one I prefer is this:

Put the rice in a large strainer and let cold running water play through it vigorously while turning it gently with your fingers. Continue until the water runs clear. This means that all the excess starch has been washed away.

Put the rice in a heavy pan with a tight-fitting lid. Add the same volume of water or stock plus one third. Bring to the boil, reduce the heat to the barest simmer, cover tightly and cook, undisturbed, for 20 minutes, when all the water should have been absorbed.

For flavoured rice, wash the rice as before. Heat a little oil in the bottom of the pan and sauté onions or spices before adding the rice.

An alternative method is to cook the rice in the oven. This is totally foolproof but does take longer. Pre-heat the oven to Gas Mark 3, 325° F, 170° C. Wash the rice as before. Put it in an oven-proof dish with a tight-fitting lid. Add the same volume of boiling stock or water plus one third. Cook, undisturbed, for 25 minutes.

There are innumerable varieties of rice. The best all-purpose long-grain is *patna* which is cheap, available everywhere and has a good flavour. *Basmati* has an even better flavour, but is more expensive. *Easy-cook rice* has already been partially cooked and gives a rounder, heavier grain with substantially less flavour.

For risottos and stuffed vegetables the absorbent Italian round-grain *arborio* is the best choice. The cooking method is different from that used for long-grain rice. It is simmered and constantly stirred in an open pan with fresh stock or water added from time to time. *Pudding rice* is an alternative round-grain rice, but does not have the same flavour as arborio.

Brown rice may be long or short grain. Nutritionally it is superior to white rice, as it retains far more fibre, vitamins and minerals. Rinse it very briefly in cold water. Cook it in a tightly lidded heavy pan with double the volume of water for 40 minutes. Brown rice rarely sticks, even when overcooked.

All the rice recipes in this book are for white rice, because it cooks much more quickly. But if you have more time, brown rice can of course be substituted.

SALAD LEAVES

Salad leaves are important to health-conscious cooks who also have limited time. They add colour, flavour, texture and nutritious ingredients to a meal, and best of all, they don't need peeling or scraping. Since the choice is now so wide, I have listed some of the main types here, with notes on how to prepare them. There are many people who still talk disparagingly of salad leaves as 'rabbit food'. When a salad consists only of a few limp green cabbage-lettuce leaves, perhaps this judgement is correct. At my children's school the lunch menu, typical of so much institutional catering, offers as 'salad' either a few pieces of green lettuce without dressing (though of course 'salad cream' is available) or commercially produced coleslaw. And yet only a few hundred yards away an excellent street market sells, at a rough estimate, at least 30 different ingredients for leafy salads.

One of the most pleasant results of the trend towards healthier eating is that suddenly such a wide variety of fruit and vegetables are being made available. Sometimes this happens with surprising speed. On the day I read in a magazine that purslane was never offered for sale in Britain (readers were encouraged to grow it), I saw it neatly packaged in a suburban supermarket with clear instructions on how to use it. Some Sainsbury branches sell nasturtium leaves; most Marks and Spencer food stores offer Batavian endive or other frilly endives. In general, however, it is still the case that the more unusual salad leaves need to be either hunted in street markets and specialist shops or home grown.

Storage

Most salad leaves need careful handling to avoid bruising. Remove any wilted leaves, then store them wrapped in a plastic bag at the bottom of the refrigerator. Most loosely packed green leaves will keep for up to four days this way. The dense, heavy lettuces or cabbages should be tightly wrapped in cling film and refrigerated. They will keep well for up to a week.

Preparation

Never soak salad leaves; their water-soluble vitamins will be lost. Wash them briefly in cold running water, shake off any excess, then dry in a salad spinner or tea towel. Lettuce with stiff, coarse leaves can be chopped, but soft leaves should be either left intact or gently torn. Prepare lettuce at the last minute and make sure the leaves are absolutely dry before adding dressing, otherwise it will not be absorbed. Bitter leaves need a strongly flavoured dressing; delicate lettuces are best complemented by a light dressing.

Lettuces

Cabbage head. The 'crisp head' versions have stout, crisp leaves. *Iceberg* is a heavy, pale lettuce that keeps exceptionally well and will provide several meals. It is not a lettuce with a powerful flavour, but has a pleasant, crunchy texture. *Webb's Wonderful* has a better flavour than Iceberg and an equally good texture.

Cos lettuces. These have long, crisp-textured, well-flavoured leaves. They keep well and can be torn or chopped for salads. *Little Gem* is a variety of cos with wavy leaves, tight hearts and an excellent sweet flavour. Available now in many supermarkets.

Loose-leaf lettuces ('Salad Bowl'). These attractive-looking lettuces have the agreeable habit of growing again if cut. Some, like the Italian *Lollo*, have crisp, curly leaves; others, like *Oakleaf*, have soft, floppy leaves shaped just like oak-leaves. Oak leaf bruises easily but has a delicate, sweet flavour. Some loose-leaf lettuces have a reddish tinge, which makes them especially valuable for colour contrast in a salad.

Cabbages

Cabbages make excellent salads, though most people find the very dark-leaved types too tough and bitter to eat raw.

Dutch cabbage is the type finely shredded for coleslaw and other similar salads. Cut out the main stalk.

Red cabbage is tough unless very finely shredded, but also makes a pretty coleslaw.

Chinese leaves. An elongated pale green cabbage with tender leaves. It can be chopped for salads or cooked. It is especially good stir-fried.

Pak-choi. A small succulent leafy oriental cabbage with bright green leaves and thick white stalks. Use it like Chinese leaves.

Spinach/Swiss chard

These dark green vegetables are excellent value nutritionally as they are good sources of folic acid, vitamin C and iron. For salad use the young tender leaves are best. Roll them into a cigar shape and chop them finely.

Chicories

All chicories share a slightly bitter flavour, so should be used in raw salads with discretion. However, they do come in a splendid range of colours and textures.

Raddicchio (red lettuce) is a small, tightly hearted chicory from Italy. It is expensive, but a little goes a long way and provides an excellent colour contrast in a mixed leaf salad.

Belgian chicory is a blanched shoot with creamy, spear-like leaves. It has a juicy texture and makes an excellent partner to salads containing fruit, especially oranges and grapefruit. Leave it wrapped in cling film in the refrigerator. Always store this chicory in the dark: exposure to light increases its bitterness. To prepare it, cut off the root end. Chicory can either be sliced into rings or the leaves can be separated and kept whole. Wash, dry and add dressing immediately to prevent browning. Whole chicory leaves are a useful garnish to soft grain or bean salads and can be used as edible food scoops.

Endive (Bavarian endive, frizzy endive, frisée). Endive actually belongs to the chicory family. It is a useful, crunchy, winter or summer salad with striking good looks: a huge, sprawling, shaggy head of green saw-toothed leaves, with the sweeter bright yellow leaves in the centre. A whole endive can be expensive, but supermarkets are now beginning to sell smaller packaged portions. The taste is pleasantly bitter. A useful addition to other leaves – overpowering on its own.

Storage. Wrap in a damp cloth or newspaper and refrigerate. It will keep for up to five days.

Preparation. Remove any coarse or damaged outer leaves. Snip the endive into individual spears. Wash them, then spin or pat dry. Endive needs a strongly flavoured dressing – anything too delicate will be lost on it.

Miscellaneous

Sorrel. Sorrel can often be found growing wild, but it is a perennial which is also easy to cultivate. It has a strong, sharp, almost lemony taste, so is usually used as a herb – with discretion. It can also be used for soups and sauces, where it cooks down like spinach.

Corn salad/lamb's lettuce. Like sorrel, this plant often grows wild. The soft, floppy leaves have a mild flavour but need to be eaten very fresh, as they quickly become limp after cutting.

Cress. Watercress has a pungent, peppery taste and is full of goodness. It is related botanically to nasturtium and has a rather similar flavour. Store it in a loose plastic bag in the refrigerator.

Dandelion. This prolific weed is often served as a delicacy in France with bacon and a bacon-fat dressing – not tremendously healthy. Dandelion has a strong taste and is probably better thought of as a salad herb: useful in small quantities as a garnish. Gather only young leaves from plants that have not yet flowered. Don't pick them from the verges of busy roads: the danger of pollution is too great.

SALT

Salt is an acquired taste, therefore it can be unacquired. 'Rock salt', 'mineral salt', 'salt crystals' and 'sodium' are all usually sodium chloride – common salt. I discuss some strategies for cutting down on salt on pages 31–2. Some useful salt substitutes are:

Low-salt products. These are generally mixtures of potassium with sodium. They are expensive compared with sodium chloride, but a little goes a long way. Some brands have a much higher sodium content than others – it can be as much as 40 per cent – so look on the label. The taste is very similar to salt, with perhaps a slightly more tart aftertaste. It is harder to detect the difference in cooked food. People with diabetes or kidney conditions should discuss these salt substitutes with their doctors, as too much potassium can cause problems in such cases.

Lemon juice. The strong flavour is nothing like salt, of course, but it seems to satisfy the need for seasoning.

Other herbs and spices also have an important part to play (see pages 76–81, 93–6).

STOCK

Good stock is an essential foundation for healthier cooking. It will flavour rice and add distinction to casseroles, pasta sauces and soups. A good stock gets round the need to add masses of salt because it provides both flavour and that favourite of the food industry, 'mouth feel'.

Unfortunately, for time-saving cooks, a stock cube is not the answer. Stock cubes taste of . . . well, stock cubes. Almost all of them have the overwhelming sour chemical saltiness which indicates a lot of monosodium glutamate. The colours are usually azo dyes, the flavours may also come from the laboratory.

The only way to achieve good stock is to make it yourself in bulk and then freeze it in smaller containers. I give several stock recipes on pages 225–8, but the basic rules are actually very simple:

● Never, ever, throw away a carcass or trimmings if you can use them for stock.

● Cover the meat or vegetable trimmings with water and simmer for several hours.

● Pressure cookers will produce good concentrated stock in anything from ten minutes to an hour, depending on ingredients.

● Add carrots, onions, onion skins, bay-leaves, spices or herbs to suit your taste.

● Dark stock is produced by dry-roasting meat or bones for about 45 minutes, 'deglazing' the pan to scrape in all the dark juices, and then simmering as before.

● Meat stock can simmer for several hours. Vegetable stock takes about 45 minutes, fish stock no more than 20 minutes. (Longer cooking may result in a sour-tasting liquid.)

● Strain the stock and let it chill in the refrigerator, then remove the fat before freezing. Don't add salt.

- Frozen stock will keep for up to six months in the freezer.

SPICES AND FLAVOURINGS

Artificial flavourings for highly processed food are big business. 'Prawn cocktail flavour crisps' have never been anywhere near prawns; 'orange flavour jelly' is a synthetic substitute for real orange juice; monosodium glutamate can provide 'flavour enhancement' for anything from barbecue sauce to tinned tomato soup. Yet cooking with the real thing is within anyone's grasp. Spices which used to be available only from an Indian or Chinese grocery shop are now sold in most supermarkets; they are sold loose, by the ounce, in many independent whole food shops; and there's still the little Indian shop on the corner for anything really tricky and unusual.

Cooking with spices and flavourings is not difficult. There are a few basic hints which make it easier to achieve a good result:

- If you have both the time and a coffee grinder, buy whole spices and grind them yourself. The flavour is much better.

- Ground spices quickly lose colour and flavour, so buy them frequently in small quantities rather than in bulk. Throw out any that have been sitting around for more than six months.

- Frying spices in a little very hot oil for savoury dishes is the most effective way of releasing their 'essential oils'. The oil should not be smoking, otherwise it will burn the spices.

- Be exact in following an unfamiliar recipe or one using unfamiliar spices. Use a set of measuring spoons to give correct quantities.

- Keep a good range of store-cupboard spices so that they are always on hand. Whole spices will keep satisfactorily for a year or more.

A basic spice kit: Like herbs, spices have their own folklore and history. The best book for further study of this vast subject is Tom Stobart's *Herbs, Spices and Flavourings* (Penguin, 1977). This is my personal list of favourites – spices I always keep in stock:

'Hot', pungent spices and flavourings

Black pepper. A mildly hot spice, available everywhere as whole peppercorns. Don't buy it ready-ground, as the flavour is very inferior.

Cayenne. The hottest spice from chilli peppers, to be used with great caution.

Chillies. Fresh or dried, green or red. They vary in hotness, but treat them with respect. Discard the seeds.

Garlic. Culinary life without garlic would be dull indeed. Raw garlic is a perfect flavouring for salad dressings, and is an essential ingredient of classic dishes from the Mediterranean and from Asia. Crush it with a flexible knife against a wooden board. A swift way of using garlic for a time-conscious cook is to buy a tube of garlic purée. A half-inch squeeze is about the equivalent of one clove. Garlic purée contains salt, so don't add any more salt to the dish without tasting it first. Garlic burns easily when fried, and then becomes bitter. If this happens, discard it and start again.

Mustard. English mustard is the hottest type, though it becomes less hot after cooking. It is cheaper to buy in powdered form. French mustards are mixed with herbs, vinegar and other spices. Dijon is the best for vinaigrette. Whole made-up mustards are best kept for eating with cold meats – they are not so suitable for cooking. Loose mustard seeds are useful in Indian dishes.

Mild aromatic spices

Cardamom. An expensive spice. Always buy it whole. Crush the pods to extract the seeds. About six pods will be quite enough to flavour a rice dish.

Coriander. May be used whole or ground. A superb spice with a faintly 'orange' tang. Can be used lavishly.

Cumin. May be used straightforwardly as whole seeds, 'roasted' in a dry pan for a few minutes (when it changes flavour), or ground. The essential 'curry spice'.

Paprika. A sweet bright-red spice classically used for Hungarian goulash. Can be used generously.

Saffron. The most expensive spice in the world, made from the stigma of the saffron crocus. A few threads can be heated in a dry pan, then soaked in milk to flavour and colour rice.

Turmeric. A yellow ground spice with a slightly sour flavour. Useful for colouring rice, but needs to be used cautiously.

Salty flavours

All the oriental salty sauces are high in sodium, so should be used sparingly.

Soy sauce (shoyu). A fermented by-product of soya beans. 'Light soy sauce' is saltier than 'dark soy sauce'. **Tamari** is a milder version of soy sauce. **Miso** is a soya-derived paste.

Tart, sharp flavourings and spices

Capers. The small flower buds of a Mediterranean plant, usually pickled in brine. Rinse and soak them in cold water before use. They are especially good in fish casseroles and in tomato sauce for pasta.

Ginger. This knobbly rhizome will keep for several weeks in a refrigerator. A one-inch (2.5-cm) cube is the usual amount to give a sweetish, sharp, semi-hot flavour to food. Peel it, then grate it. This leaves the hairier fibres behind. If you are really stuck for fresh ginger, a pinch of dried ginger will give some of the flavour. However, while dried powdered ginger has the 'hot' quality of fresh, it lacks its sharpness.

Lemon/orange. A lemon-juice marinade helps to tenderize meat and will also coagulate the protein in raw fish to produce a palatable texture. Both lemon and orange zest contain highly concentrated flavours. Wash the fruit first to remove wax and dye, then peel, scrape or grate the thin zest. A lemon zester (see page 43) is the most efficient weapon for this job.

Tomato purée. Some Italian cooks regard resorting to tomato purée as the lazy substitute for hours of gentle simmering with fresh tomatoes. This may be true, but the concentrated flavour of tomato purée is a wonderful time-saver. It does contain salt, so do not add more salt to the dish without checking the seasoning first.

Sweeter aromatic spices for sweet or savoury food

Allspice. Looks like a large peppercorn. Flavour akin to both cinnamon and nutmeg.

Cinnamon. Much better bought whole as a 'stick' than ground, even though ground cinnamon keeps its flavour well.

Cloves. Used whole, they give a pleasant tang to fruit pies. Also good whole or ground for mild Indian dishes.

Mace and nutmeg. Mace is the inner casing of the nutmeg. Keep whole nutmegs and use them as necessary on a fine grater. Mace and nutmeg are good in bread puddings or in the Middle Eastern savoury dishes. They are excellent with rice and cheese.

Rosewater/orange flower water. Fragrant distilled essences diluted with water, sold in chemist's shops. Useful for fruit compotes and fruit salads.

Vanilla. A vanilla pod will last a long time and can simply be wiped down after use. Vanilla essence is sold in liquid form – but beware of 'vanilla flavouring', which is not made from the real thing.

SWEETENERS

It would be foolish to advocate banning sugar from the kitchen altogether. I have always liked the idea advocated by the science writer Colin Tudge of regarding sugar as a 'spice', to be used occasionally and with discretion where nothing else will do. A tablespoon added to two pints of home-made lemonade or elderflower cordial will make all the difference between a palatable refreshing drink and one likely to be roundly rejected as 'too sour'. The amount in each glass will be extremely small, especially when compared with commercially produced colas or squashes. Similarly, a little sugar may be added with profit to tomato sauces, fruit compotes and cooked fruit purées. Choose whichever sugar is best for the job in hand: a pinch of ordinary white sugar for savoury sauces, molasses for plain yoghurt, and so on.

Generally, however, the craving for sweetness is best satisfied by using naturally sweet food which will also give fibre, minerals and vitamins.

Dried fruit can be soaked, cooked, or puréed to make puddings, pancake fillings, fruit spreads for toast, muesli, and flavourings for yoghurt. It makes excellent chutney, to which very little extra sugar need be added. It can be pulverized in a food processor and rolled into balls to make 'sweets'. I always keep a bowl of dried fruit on the dining-room table for children and adults to help themselves. The range of dried fruit available includes apple, pear, plum, pineapple, grapes of various types, mango and peach.

Deal with the fruit by rinsing it first to get rid of the sulphur dioxide coating used to keep it supple. Then it may be either soaked overnight or simmered for 15 to 20 minutes in water, fruit juice or wine. Alternatively, five minutes' cooking, covered, in a microwave will give the same result.

Fresh uncooked fruit is naturally sweet and can form the basis of many excellent puddings. A fruit salad made from a well-balanced mixture of ripe fruit does not need added sugar. Some fruit lends itself particularly well to proving a sweet base for other flavours – in particular, mango and banana.

Carob powder comes from the pod of a tree growing all round the Mediterranean. It has a chocolate-like flavour and can be used for baking. However, 'carob bars' often have a lot of added sugar.

Fruit juice. Natural juices labelled as having 'no added sugar' are useful for children's lollies, jellies, and fruit salads.

Fruit spreads made from concentrated fruit juice are available in about five flavours. They look unappetizingly dark, but can add a touch of flavour and sweetness to puddings. They are available in health food shops and from large supermarkets.

Low-sugar jams. The choice of these jams has been greatly enhanced recently by the addition of a new range from Robertson's. The colour, texture and taste are very acceptable. Most low-sugar jams have to be refrigerated once opened.

VINEGARS

Flavoured vinegars add an extra zing to salad dressings and are easy to make. The best herbs to use are the delicate herbs of summer: dill, tarragon and basil. Pick a bunch of herbs on a dry day: to keep bacterial contamination at bay it is important for the herbs to have no moisture on them. Wash out a bottle with a plastic cap in hot soapy water and then let it dry off completely. Put in just enough herbs to occupy about one third of the space in the bottle – don't overcrowd it. Pour in white wine vinegar to the top of the bottle and cap it. Leave the vinegar in a cool dark place for about three weeks, then strain it.

YOGHURT

Yoghurt is available everywhere: even the smallest village shop now stocks it. Many yoghurts proudly proclaim that they are 'low fat'. However, many are also heavily laced with sugar, azo dyes and synthetic flavourings. It is much easier and cheaper to buy a large tub of plain yoghurt and then to mix in some fruit (or even home-made jam) yourself for the children.

The sour flavour and thin texture of low-fat yoghurt means that it is not such a good substitute for cream as fromage blanc where puddings are concerned. However, thickened yoghurt may be much more acceptable. Strain the yoghurt through two layers of kitchen paper lining a sieve to drain off the watery whey.

Yoghurt made from whole milk, like Greek sheep's or cow's milk yoghurt, is thicker than the low-fat variety. However, although it has more fat than yoghurt made from skimmed milk, it still has less than single cream.

Yoghurt is simple to make at home and is about a third the price of the bought variety. Boil a pint of skimmed milk, then let it cool to just above blood heat (113° F, 45° C). Stir in a teaspoon of ordinary plain unpasteurized yoghurt (no special 'cultures' are needed) and leave the milk in a warm place (e.g., an airing cupboard) for about six hours, preferably well wrapped in insulating layers of blanket or towels.

When cooking with yoghurt, whisk it in a tablespoon at a time and do not let it boil if you want to stop it curdling (though this separation does not affect taste, only appearance). Beating in a teaspoon of cornflour will also prevent curdling in low-fat yoghurt, while yoghurt made from whole milk is less likely to separate.

BEATING THE CLOCK

I have a friend who is a clever and talented cook, but it never pays to expect a quick meal from her. She likes you to be in the kitchen with her while she is cooking, and I have often watched while she stands, knife suspended, because she is recounting an amusing little story – for instance about the fishmonger who supplied the fish we are to eat. The fish might wait at least ten minutes to be filleted. As a guest you are not allowed to 'help' and you are also generously plied with wine, so the hours pass in a pleasant haze of good companionship, even while your stomach is rumbling.

I do not have this delightfully casual attitude to cooking. Once started, I am keen to finish as quickly as possible. Cooking healthily does not demand hours of intricate attention. In fact it can be much quicker than traditional cooking. Think, for instance, of a roast joint with roast potatoes and vegetables. This is a meal which cannot ever really be prepared in under an hour and a half. It also needs split-second timing at the end of cooking. It leaves a dirty oven and a pile of greasy washing-up. There is even more work in a steak and kidney pie: the meat to prepare and tenderize first and the pastry to make, before the pie is even put in the oven; vegetables to wash, peel and cook. By contrast, a satisfying pasta or stir-fry dish can be cooked from start to finish in about 20 minutes with only one or two pans to wash at the end.

Nevertheless, even for quick recipes there are a few hints and tips for saving time:

THE KITCHEN

It may seem like stating the obvious, but a well-planned kitchen will make the work more efficient and will therefore save time. If you find you are always having to pause while you plod to the refrigerator, then think about whether you can move the refrigerator. Put all the herbs and spices together, all the tins together, all the dried goods together. Put the knives within half an arm's reach of the main work surface.

99

Put the cooking utensils by the side of the cooker: there's no need to buy fancy racks – an old jug will do just as well.

The rubbish bin. Assuming you are right-handed, move the rubbish bin out just to the right of the main work area while you are at the trimming, peeling and chopping stage of preparation. A large swing-top bin needs to be emptied much less frequently and is easier to work with than a pedal bin. Take the lid off while you are working so that you can scrape trimmings straight into it.

Washing up. Keep a well-filled bowl of hot, soapy water ready all the time you are working and put dirty pans straight into it.

Equipment. Investing in the right equipment (see pages 40–55), especially a decent set of knives and a food processor, will make a great deal of difference.

PREPARATION

For any demonstration programme on television it is essential to have every single ingredient and tool set out in advance. The Assistant Floor Manager has one of the most important jobs on the set: he or she makes a plan of the work-top indicating every spoon, knife, J-cloth and ingredient that will be needed and exactly where it is to be placed. This is checked and double-checked before the recording. The reason for this care is to save precious seconds in the finished programme. Before working on this kind of programme I was a notoriously sloppy kitchen worker. Not only did I leave piles of hideous mess and washing up in my trail, I also frequently burned or spoiled food through having to take my attention away from the cooker while I hunted for some special knife, or weighed the flour.

Today I am a reformed character. Before I start I spend a few minutes reading the recipe, preparing all the utensils and pots I shall need and assembling the ingredients. I reckon this probably saves me as much as ten minutes in total cooking time and makes the whole process much more enjoyable because it is more efficient.

In advance

It is often worth making large quantities of frequently used mixtures and refrigerating or freezing them. It takes virtually no extra time, for instance, to make a week's rather than one meal's supply of salad dressing. Store it in a screw-top jar. Other useful mixtures or ingredients include:

> Flavoured vinegars (page 98)
> Flavoured oils (page 228)
> Muesli (page 229)
>
> To freeze
>
> Breadcrumbs
> Chopped herbs
> Stock (page 92)
> Basic tomato sauce

READY-PREPARED INGREDIENTS

When you are truly short of time for cooking, it might be the case that time is the economy rather than money. The supermarkets have catered to this need by producing ready-prepared ingredients: for instance, pre-chopped braising steak, skinned chicken breast fillets, skinned and boned chicken thighs, squid 'tubes' (cleaned, skinned and gutted), and so on. These are all useful and time-saving products, but be prepared to pay a lot extra for the privilege. For instance, a packet of two skinned and filleted chicken breasts will probably cost about a third as much again as the same breasts on a whole chicken. And with the whole chicken you will also have more meat plus the carcass and the giblets for other meals.

One splendid addition to the range of time-saving ingredients is garlic purée. This is sold in a tube the same size as a large tube of tooth-paste, and gives an authentic garlic paste without the bother of peeling and crushing fresh cloves. Other useful flavourings presented in tubes include tomato of course, onion purée and mixed herb purée.

Where tins are concerned, tinned tomatoes are always useful. If you have access to a continuous supply of sweet, well-flavoured 'real' tomatoes, and plenty of time, then of course it will be better to use them for tomato sauces, slipping off the skins in boiling water and then sieving them. Mostly, however, the fresh tomatoes in shops are grown for appearance not flavour. Tinned Italian 'plum' tomatoes are usually sold unsalted, have a good flavour and are much more useful for year-round use. I buy five or six tins at a time so that I always have the makings of a quick sauce or soup. Other tinned vegetables worth keeping in stock for their time-saving value include green, red, white and brown beans. These are always useful as the makings of cheap high-fibre dips and soups.

Pound for pound, tinned fish is an expensive substitute for the fresh product. Some tinned fish (e.g., prawns) are so inferior in taste and texture that they are not worth bothering about. However, I always have in stock a few tins of sardines, cod roe, oysters, anchovies, mussels, tuna, clams (when I can find them) and crab. Not only are they endlessly useful for snacks-on-toast, but mussels, clams, crab, tuna and even cod roe will provide the basis for a pasta or rice sauce which can be made in ten minutes.

Bottled sauces are usually heavily dosed with additives, and as a result many taste unpleasantly synthetic. I make an exception for the Italian pesto and parsley sauces (obtainable from large supermarkets and delicatessens). Both have more of the authentic flavour of basil or parsley than the dried herb; a teaspoonful is useful in a winter casserole or pasta sauce. Even opened they keep, refrigerated, for several months. I usually also have small jars of cranberry sauce and red-currant jelly in my cupboards. I use them for adding a sweet-sour touch to sauces for meat. Of the oriental ready-made sauces, I do keep soy sauce, hoisin sauce and oyster sauce, tabasco and a mild curry paste in stock, but I use them warily. Most are very salty and contain MSG as well as azo dyes.

Finally, I usually have a large drum of ready-grated Parmesan cheese in my refrigerator. It is true that the whole cheese grated as you need it has a much superior flavour and texture and also keeps better. However, you have to be near a good source of Italian cheese to buy it in a piece, and of course grating it is one more task to do before sitting down. I find that there are many occasions when I prefer to save the time.

Time-saving Recipes
for Healthy Eating

SOUP

Soup is ridiculously easy to make and is usually remarkably quick to cook. Soups can be totally healthy: only a minute amount of fat is necessary, and they are also one of the best ways of increasing the amount of vegetables and pulses in the diet.

The foundation of a good soup is home-made stock (see pages 225–8 for recipes). A stock cube heavily diluted (use it at half the recommended strength) will do in an emergency, but it never really tastes authentic.

The techniques of soup-making are simple. The recipe usually includes a root vegetable to provide a natural thickener. This is briefly sautéed in minimal oil with other vegetables, then the stock and any other flavourings are added. Some soups are made with diced vegetables which are intended to be eaten as they are. Others have to be puréed. A blender gives a smoother result than a food processor.

There are a few soups which a perfectionist would sieve on cosmetic grounds – for instance, soups containing tomatoes. However, there is really no need to do this if you are short of time, and you will also have a higher vitamin and fibre content if you do not.

Many soups, especially the ones containing pulses, are filling enough to provide a complete light meal, with wholemeal bread and fruit to follow. We often have this kind of soup on Sunday evenings when we have had guests for an elaborate Sunday lunch, or on Saturdays when shopping for food has temporarily exhausted our interest in cooking.

SWEET RED PEPPER AND TOMATO SOUP
WITH SUMMER HERBS

The brilliant red of this light soup makes a colourful and refreshing start to a summer meal. It can be served hot or chilled.

SERVES 4 GENEROUSLY

12 oz (350 g) red peppers
1 small eating apple
1 onion
2 teaspoons lemon juice
14 oz (450 g) tin tomatoes
1 pint (600 ml) strong stock
1 tablespoon soy sauce

Handful fresh herbs: ideally
  mint, tarragon and basil
  (or ½ teaspoon of each, dried)
Salt to taste

GARNISH
6 fresh basil leaves or a few sprigs
  of parsley
A little yoghurt (if served cold)

De-seed the peppers, peel and core the apple. Chop these roughly, together with the onion. Put them in a deep saucepan with the lemon juice, tomatoes and their juice, the stock and soy sauce. Bring to a simmer, cover tightly and cook for 20 minutes or until the peppers are soft. Add the fresh herbs, unchopped, and simmer for another minute. Blend to a smooth purée. If you have time, sieve the soup to remove the tomato pips, though this is not essential. Check the seasoning and add salt to taste. Serve immediately with a few torn basil leaves floating on top, or chilled with a little yoghurt.

CARROT AND CORIANDER SOUP

There is only one herb – coriander – in this soup, and one spice – cardamom. Nevertheless, the soup has an exotic taste, for what is actually little effort. This soup does not really need salt, but add it if you wish.

SERVES 4

1 lb (500 g) carrots
1 onion
1 medium potato
6 cardamom pods

2 pints (1.25 l) stock
1 bunch fresh coriander

GARNISH
A little low-fat plain yoghurt

Scrub the carrots, peel and chop the onion and potato. Let them sweat for a few minutes in a deep saucepan brushed out with oil. Meanwhile, crack the cardamom pods and extract the seeds. Add them to the pan with the stock. Simmer, covered, for 20 minutes. Wash and trim the coriander. Keep a little aside for garnish. Add it whole to the soup and simmer for about 5 minutes. Blend or process until the soup is as smooth as possible. (The soup can be cooled and stored at this stage as it reheats well.) Ladle the soup into individual bowls with a swirl of yoghurt and a sprinkling of coriander on top.

CARROT SOUP
WITH ORANGE AND TARRAGON

Carrot and orange soup is often spoilt, I feel, by the use of far too much oil to sauté the vegetables initially and adding cream at the end. Neither is necessary. Nor does the soup need much, if any, salt – it will spoil the delicate, rather sweet flavour and light texture. Fresh tarragon is wonderful for this soup, but dried is perfectly all right – it reconstitutes itself quickly in the liquid.

SERVES 4

1 lb (500 g) carrots
1 onion
1 medium potato
1 orange

6 cardamom pods
1½ pints (1 l) chicken stock
1 tablespoon fresh chopped
   tarragon, or 1 teaspoon dried

Roughly chop the carrots, onion and potato. Brush out a heavy saucepan with oil and sauté the vegetables for about 3 minutes. Meanwhile, grate the peel of the orange, then squeeze its juice. Crack the cardamom pods and extract the seeds. Add the orange juice and rind, the cardamom, and stock. Bring to a simmer, cover and cook for 25 minutes. Add the tarragon in the last 5 minutes of cooking. Blend very well: the texture should be as smooth as possible. Serve with triangles of wholemeal toast or warmed brown rolls.

CREAM OF CELERY SOUP

As a child, I had an unreasonable loathing for the sharp taste and sneaky fibrousness of raw celery. Even now, I prefer it cooked. It makes wonderful soup: this one has a light, delicate flavour and gives a good start to a meal which is to have a substantial main course.

SERVES 4

2 onions
4 fat celery stalks
1 leek (or in summer, 3 spring
    onions)
1 potato
1½ pints (1 l) chicken stock

1 teaspoon dill seeds or celery
    seeds
1 bay-leaf
5 fl oz (150 ml) skimmed milk
Salt and pepper to taste

Slice the onions and sweat them in a little oil in a heavy non-stick saucepan. Meanwhile, finely chop the celery (save the leaves, if there are any), washed leek and scrubbed potato, then add them to the pan. Sweat for a further two minutes. Now add the stock, the bay-leaf, and the dill or celery seeds. Cover tightly and simmer for 20 minutes or until the vegetables are soft. Add the milk and let the soup heat through without boiling for another minute.

Celery is very fibrous, so this soup should be sieved. Blend it first, then pass it through a metal sieve, using the side of a ladle. Add a tablespoon of the celery pulp to the soup and discard the rest. Heat the soup through gently, add salt and pepper if you wish, and serve garnished with a few of the chopped celery leaves floating on top.

FISH CHOWDER

A chowder is a thick soup substantial enough for a light lunch or supper dish. Traditionally it is made with salt pork and a mixture of fish (or meat) and diced vegetables. Milk is usually added to the liquid. This one is made with simple, familiar ingredients and uses a small amount of lean bacon instead of the salt pork. It produces a splendidly filling and tasty dish.

SERVES 4

4 medium potatoes
1 medium onion
1 leek (or, in summer, 3 spring
    onions)
1 stick celery
2 carrots
1 slice unsmoked back bacon
1 teaspoon sunflower oil

10 fl oz (300 ml) stock, preferably
    fish stock
2 tablespoons fresh chopped mixed
    herbs, or 1 dessertspoon dried
    mixed herbs
Black pepper
½ teaspoon garam masala or mild
    curry paste

6 oz (175 g) white fish fillet, e.g.,
   cod or hake
10 fl oz (300 ml) skimmed milk
2 oz (50 g) defrosted prawns
Salt to taste

GARNISH
1 tablespoon finely chopped fresh
   parsley

Peel and dice two of the potatoes. Peel the other two and keep them whole. Slice the onion, carrots, celery and leek very finely. Finely chop the lean part of the bacon, discarding the fat. Heat the oil and sweat all the vegetables for about 5 minutes with the bacon. Add the stock and the herbs, the pepper and the garam masala or curry paste, and simmer for 15 minutes. Lift out the two whole potatoes, mash them to a pulp and return them to the soup. Simmer, covered, for another 5 minutes. Meanwhile, cut the cod into one-inch (2 cm) cubes. Add it to the soup. Lower the heat so that the liquid is barely trembling and cook, covered, for one minute. Add the milk and heat it through. Do not let the soup boil. At the last moment add the prawns. Stir well to heat them through. Make sure that the cod is cooked. Check the seasoning, adding salt if necessary. Garnish with parsley and serve on well-heated deep plates with granary bread.

CULLEN SKINK

A simple fishy soup from Scotland, best made with Finnan haddock.

SERVES 4

1 lb (500 g) potatoes
1 large onion
1 Finnan haddock
1 bay-leaf
1 pint (600 ml) skimmed milk

¼ nutmeg
Freshly ground black pepper
2 tablespoons finely chopped fresh
   parsley

Peel, chop and then simmer the potatoes in a large saucepan until they are tender. Meanwhile, chop the onion finely and sauté it with a hint of oil for about 4 minutes in a deep, lidded frying pan. Now add the fish, the bay-leaf and the milk. Grate on the nutmeg and add some freshly ground black pepper. Bring to a bare simmer, cover and cook for about 6 minutes. Lift out the fish, flake it and discard the skin and bones. Drain the cooked potatoes, mash them well and return them to their pan. Add the flaked fish and the strained milky liquor. Now add enough water to produce a pleasant texture to the soup: it should not be too thin. Stir in half the parsley and simmer for a minute. Ladle into deep soup dishes with the remaining parsley sprinkled on top. Serve with warm rolls.

PRAWN AND CRAB BISQUE

I have often enjoyed reading the sort of recipe for fish soup where it is assumed that one has a whole leisurely day to prepare it. The list of ingredients will include six or seven different varieties of rare fish, and there are usually many stages of intricate preparation before one can sit down to enjoy the resulting rather grand soup.

This is not a grand soup, but it does have a rich, true shellfish flavour and an attractive deep-pink colour, and it is always popular with guests. Even the most ordinary of fish shops or stalls will sell whole pink prawns at a very reasonable price and the fishmonger will usually have the odd plaice or cod head that he can throw in for a few pence or for nothing. There is very little fiddly preparation in this soup and the end result is superb. Shellfish are naturally quite salty and are often boiled in sea-water, so there is no need to add any extra salt.

SERVES 4

2 small crabs
12 oz (350 g) whole pink prawns
1 onion
1 potato
2 small fish heads (e.g., plaice, trout) or 1 large cod head

1 bay-leaf
1½ pints (1 l) water
10 fl oz (300 ml) skimmed milk

Remove the crabmeat from the shells and set it aside for a moment. Put the crab shells with the beheaded but unshelled prawns into a deep saucepan with the peeled, roughly chopped onion and peeled, halved potato. Add the fish heads and bay-leaf. Now pour in the 1½ pints of water. Don't worry that the pan looks an unappetizing mixture at this stage. Bring the water to the boil, reduce to a simmer, cover and cook for 15 minutes. Now remove and discard the fish heads, bay-leaf and crab shells. Remove the potato and set it aside for a moment. Pour everything else into a processor or blender and whizz it to a pulp. Using a ladle, push the soup through a stout metal sieve back into its saucepan: a lot of pulp will be left behind. Mash the cooked potato into the soup, add the milk and reheat the soup gently. (If you prefer a thicker soup, you could add 1½ tablespoons of cornflour creamed in a little water at this stage, and then heat the soup until it thickens.) Divide the crabmeat between 4 bowls and pour the soup on top. Serve immediately.

CHILLED GREEN PEA SOUP
WITH MINT

Fortunately it is still possible to buy excellent frozen peas which are without any added 'flavourings' or hectic green colouring. This is a splendid soup for a warm summer evening. It has a sweet, rich, full flavour.

SERVES 4

1 small onion
1 medium potato
1 pint (600 ml) well-flavoured
    chicken stock
1 lb (450 g) frozen peas
3 tablespoons finely chopped fresh
    mint

5 oz (150 g) plain low-fat yoghurt
Salt and pepper to taste

GARNISH
8 extra mint leaves

Chop the onion, peel and dice the potatoes, and sweat them in a little oil for a few moments until the onion has softened but not coloured. Add the stock and simmer for about 5 minutes, or until the potato is soft. Now add the peas. If they are still frozen, simmer for three minutes; if they are thawed, one minute is enough. Add the mint and simmer the soup for another minute. Liquidize until the soup is smooth. Cool and chill the soup, then beat in the yoghurt. Check seasoning, adding salt and pepper if you wish. Serve in cold dishes with the extra mint leaves floating on top. Hot crusty rolls are a good contrast to the cold soup.

BROCCOLI AND SPINACH SOUP

This is an easy soup with a rich, deep-green colour and excellent flavour. It is a good way of luring a family into eating more leafy dark vegetables.

SERVES 4

2 rashers lean unsmoked bacon
1 large onion
4 oz (120 g) broccoli
2 medium potatoes
1½ pints (1 l) stock or water

8 oz (250 g) frozen spinach or 1 lb (500 g) fresh
Nutmeg
Black pepper

Chop the bacon finely. Put it into a deep pan (preferably non-stick) and let it cook for a moment. It is not necessary to add any fat. Peel the onion and chop it roughly; add it to the bacon. Cover the pan and let the onion and bacon sweat for about 2 minutes. Meanwhile chop the broccoli roughly, including the stalk; peel and chop the potatoes. Add the broccoli and potatoes to the pan, then the spinach, stock, nutmeg and ground black pepper. Bring to a simmer, then cover and cook, barely simmering, for about 20 minutes. Liquidize until the soup is smooth. Check the seasoning, adding salt if you wish, and serve immediately.

ASPARAGUS SOUP

We spend all our holidays in Norfolk, where one of the main local entertainments is picking your own fruit and vegetables. In May and June this means asparagus. Even buying it this way, the best thick stalks are expensive, but the 'thins' are often remarkably cheap. They make a beautifully thick 'creamy' soup – even when, as in this recipe, there is no cream. At other times of the year, you can substitute frozen or even tinned asparagus – but with tinned asparagus, leave out the salt.

SERVES 4

1 onion
1 medium potato

1 celery stalk
8 oz (250 g) asparagus, trimmed

1½ pints (1 l) chicken stock	**Salt and pepper to taste**
6 sprigs fresh parsley	
10 fl oz (300 ml) skimmed milk	**GARNISH**
	Extra parsley sprigs

Slice the onion, peel and dice the potato, chop the celery, trim and chop the asparagus. Brush out a deep saucepan with sunflower oil and stir-fry all the vegetables over a medium heat for about 3 minutes. Add the stock and parsley, bring to a simmer, cover, reduce the heat and cook for about 10 minutes, when the vegetables should be soft. Blend or process the soup and return it to the pan. Add the milk and let it heat through without boiling. Taste the soup and add salt and pepper as necessary. Serve with a few tiny sprigs of parsley floated on top.

GAZPACHO

No cooking is involved in this classic summer soup – just a little liquidizing and chopping.

SERVES 4

2 × 14-oz (450-g) cans Italian tomatoes	**GARNISH**
1 tablespoon good quality olive oil	**Quarter of a cucumber**
2 tablespoons red wine vinegar	**Half a red pepper**
4 garlic cloves	**1 tablespoon chopped fresh parsley**
salt and pepper to taste	
2 tablespoons chopped fresh mint	

Put all the soup ingredients into a processor or blender and liquidize. Dice the cucumber, and de-seed and dice the pepper. If you have time, chill at this stage for an hour. If not, ladle the soup into individual bowls and sprinkle some cucumber, pepper and parsley on each. Drop two ice-cubes into each bowl just before serving with hot crusty bread.

CUCUMBER AND YOGHURT SOUP

If the yoghurt and stock have been sitting in the refrigerator, then they will probably already be cold enough to make an excellent instant chilled soup, with no cooking involved.

SERVES 4

1 cucumber
15 oz (450 g) natural low-fat
  yoghurt
10 fl oz (300 ml) cold chicken stock
Squeeze of garlic purée (or
  3 cloves garlic peeled and
  crushed)

Freshly ground black pepper
Salt to taste
2 tablespoons chopped fresh mint,
  or 1 teaspoon dried
1 tablespoon chopped fresh dill, or
  1 teaspoon dried

Peel the cucumber and chop it roughly. Reserve a little of the herbs for garnish, then blend all the ingredients to produce a smooth purée. Pour into individual bowls and leave to chill again if possible. Just before serving, sprinkle the reserved herbs on top. Serve with hot pitta bread fingers.

CLEAR CHICKEN AND MUSHROOM SOUP

This is a light, elegant soup which can be on the table ten minutes after you first thought of it. It does need good chicken stock.

SERVES 4

1 raw chicken breast
6 oz (175 g) button mushrooms
1½ pints (1 l) strong chicken stock

3 spring onions
Salt and pepper to taste

Skin the chicken, then slice it as finely as possible into thin short strips. Wipe the mushrooms and slice them thinly. Bring the stock to just below boiling point and add the chicken and mushrooms. Poach them for about 5 minutes: the liquid must not boil. Meanwhile, chop the spring onions as finely as possible. Scatter them on to the soup in the last minute of cooking. Check for seasoning: add salt and pepper if you wish. Serve immediately with warmed soft rolls.

MULLIGATAWNY SOUP

There are literally hundreds of different recipes for this Anglo-Indian vegetable and rice soup. This is a quick one, simplified in the interests of speed. If you have time, substitute brown for white rice – but it needs double the cooking time.

SERVES 4

1 large onion	1½–2 pints (1–1.25 l) chicken stock
3 large carrots	1 heaped teaspoon mild curry
2 sticks celery	paste
1 eating apple	3 oz (75 g) any rice
2 cloves mashed garlic	

Fine-chop the onions; dice the carrots, celery and peeled apple. Brush out a large non-stick pan with corn oil and sauté the vegetables and apple with the garlic for about 2 minutes. Add the stock and curry paste, then the rice; cover and simmer for 20 minutes. Blend or sieve half the soup then return it to the pan. Serve immediately.

CELERIAC SOUP WITH DILL

It is surprising that a huge ugly-looking root vegetable like celeriac can have such a delicate flavour. It makes an excellent smooth winter soup.

SERVES 4

1 celeriac (about 12 oz or 350 g)	1 teaspoon dried dill
1 onion	Salt and freshly ground black
1 large potato	pepper to taste
1½ pints (1 l) stock	5 fl oz (150 ml) skimmed milk

Peel the celeriac and cut it into small chunks. Chop the onion roughly. Sauté the celeriac and onion in a little oil for about 5 minutes. Meanwhile, peel and roughly chop the potatoes into small pieces. Add the potato with the stock, dill and seasoning. Simmer until the vegetables are tender. Liquidize or blend the soup and return it to the pan. Add the milk and let the soup heat up again to just below boiling point (about another 2 minutes). Check the seasoning and serve.

MUSHROOM AND POTATO SOUP

Use the dark-gilled flat mushrooms if possible for this soup – they have a better flavour.

SERVES 4

1 onion
2 medium potatoes
8 oz (225 g) mushrooms
1 pint (600 ml) dark stock or water

6 sprigs fresh thyme, or
 ½ teaspoon dried
½ teaspoon sugar
Salt and pepper to taste
5 fl oz (150 ml) skimmed milk

Slice the onion and sauté it over a fairly high heat, stirring constantly, until it becomes dark brown. Peel and roughly chop the potatoes, wipe and slice the mushrooms. Add them to the pan under a lowered heat and let them sweat gently, covered, for about 3 minutes. Add the stock, thyme, sugar and seasoning. Cover and simmer for 20 minutes, or until the vegetables are soft. Add the milk and let it heat through without boiling. Blend and serve with triangles of thick wholemeal toast.

CREAM OF PARSNIP SOUP

Humble root vegetables – parsnips, carrots and potato – are combined here to make a memorable soup: creamy, fragrant, dense and sweet. A good soup for a winter's day and very economical.

SERVES 4

2 large parsnips
2 carrots
1 onion
1 potato
1½ pints (1 l) stock or water

1 bay-leaf
1 tablespoon curry paste or powder

GARNISH
1 tablespoon plain yoghurt

Cut the parsnips and carrots into small chunks. Peel and chop the onion and potato. Put all the vegetables in a large pan and pour on the stock. Add the bay-leaf and the curry paste. Bring the stock to the boil, cover tightly, then simmer for 20 minutes or until the vegetables are soft and beginning to break up. Remove the bay-leaf. Blend, process or sieve and serve immediately with crusty bread. A swirl of yoghurt makes an attractive garnish.

LUKE'S FAVOURITE SOUP

Our older son, Luke, was the classic non-eating toddler, and I the classic worried mother. Eyes glittering with interest at the hysterical reaction it produced in me, he would appear to refuse everything except biscuits, or bread with peanut butter. I eventually discovered that soup was one offering that did not have this effect on him. The lentil soup given here was the breakthrough, and even though he is now a soup connoisseur, and not at all fussy about his food, this one remains his favourite. It is a wholesome, satisfying and filling soup – high in fibre, minerals and vitamins. If you have more time available use whole green lentils instead of the orange ones. Whole lentils have more flavour and more fibre.

SERVES 4 GENEROUSLY

1 onion
1 carrot
1 thin piece lean back bacon, fat removed
1 stick celery
1 medium potato

2 cloves garlic, mashed
1 × 14-oz (450-g) tin tomatoes
4 oz (110 g) orange lentils
1½ pints (1 l) stock or water
1 teaspoon mixed dried herbs

Chop the onion finely, dice the carrot and bacon, and slice the celery and unpeeled potato. Sweat all these chopped ingredients with the mashed garlic in a deep pan brushed out with oil until they are wilted and translucent. Add the stock or water, tomatoes with their juice, lentils and mixed herbs. Bring to a simmer and cook, tightly covered, for 20 minutes, when the lentils and vegetables should be soft. Taste for seasoning, adding salt if you wish. Serve just as it is with warmed wholemeal rolls, or blend to a thick purée.

BEAN AND BACON SOUP

A thick, glowing substantial soup that is almost a meal in itself. Fruit and cheese to follow with this soup makes for a pleasant light meal.

SERVES 4

2 onions
2 cloves garlic
2 rashers lean unsmoked bacon
2 tablespoons tomato purée
4 oz (100 g) rice – an absorbent round-grain pudding rice or arborio is best, but any rice will do

2 sprigs fresh thyme, leaves stripped, or ½ teaspoon dried
2 pints (1.25 l) stock or water
1 × 14-oz (450-g) tin white beans – e.g., cannelini or butter beans

Finely chop the onion, garlic and bacon. Sauté gently without adding any more fat for about 5 minutes. Stir in the tomato purée, the rice, thyme and stock or water. Bring to a simmer, cover and cook gently for about 20 minutes. Drain the tin of beans and rinse them off in cold water. Add them to the soup and stir well. Now transfer half the soup to a liquidizer or processor and blend until it is smooth. Return this blended soup to the pan and let it cook for a further minute. Serve immediately in deep bowls with fresh wholemeal bread.

SNACKS AND STARTERS

The traditional British snack is also, unfortunately, the least desirable food on health grounds: fried eggs and bacon, sausages, hot dogs, hamburgers, chips . . . they are all high in saturated fat and often full of preservatives and other additives too.

This section gives some ideas for healthier alternatives. Most of them are designed for a light lunch or supper dish; a few are meant to be starters for entertaining. I have included several dishes using eggs and cheese. Eggs cook quickly and, personally, I would certainly find it hard to do without them altogether. Four or five a week, the NACNE Report recommended level, is not excessive and will allow for the occasional omelette or pancake. Cheese is another useful quick-cooking ingredient. It appears in these recipes in much smaller quantities than is traditional, and I have also suggested using low-fat and medium-fat cheeses where appropriate.

SPICED POACHED MUSHROOMS
ON WHOLEMEAL TOAST

The traditional way to cook mushrooms on toast involves a frying pan and a lot of fat: without the fat, the mushrooms can turn out dry. This method produces a succulent alternative. We often have this dish as a weekend brunch followed by fruit. One bonus of this recipe is that there is no need to put yellow fat on the toast – the mushrooms come in their own moist sauce.

SERVES 4

8 oz (225 g) mushrooms
1 teaspoon English mustard
  powder
Black pepper
⅛ nutmeg
5 fl oz (150 ml) skimmed milk

1 teaspoon mild curry paste
Wholemeal bread for toast

GARNISH
Parsley sprigs (optional)

119

Wipe the mushrooms. Put them in a non-stick saucepan large enough to take them in two layers at the most. Sprinkle on the mustard, black pepper and grated nutmeg. Measure the skimmed milk into a jug, add the curry paste and stir briefly. Pour the milk over the mushrooms, bring to a simmer and cook very gently, uncovered, for about 10 minutes, turning them occasionally so that they are all well-coated with the liquid. Watch them like a hawk in the last few minutes: skimmed milk burns easily. At the end of ten minutes most of the liquid should have evaporated, leaving tender, moist mushrooms with a little sauce just clinging to them. Time the preparation of the toast to coincide with the last few minutes of cooking the mushrooms. Heap the mushrooms on to the toast, and garnish with a few parsley sprigs if you like.

'HEALTHY' CHEESE ON TOAST

A simple snack made in moments from ingredients most people have in their refrigerators. Unlike traditional cheese on toast, the saturated fat content in this recipe is very low.

SERVES 4

8 large slices wholemeal bread
2 oz (50 g) Cheddar cheese
5 oz (150 g) cottage cheese, Quark
  or other low-fat soft cheese
1 tablespoon plain yoghurt
1 teaspoon English mustard
  powder

Black pepper
Nutmeg

GARNISH
Tomatoes

Put the cheeses, yoghurt and seasonings in a food processor or blender until a smooth, soft paste forms. Add a little skimmed milk if necessary. Heat the grill. Toast the bread on one side. Spread the other with the cheesy paste. Grill until the cheese is bubbling and golden. Serve immediately, garnished with a slice of tomato on each slice of toast.

PITTA BREAD WITH GRILLED CHEESE AND ONIONS

This is a quick, tasty hand-held snack exploiting the enveloping virtues of pitta bread. The soft, mild cheese makes a good foil to the crunchier texture and strong taste of the well-browned onions.

SERVES 4

2 large onions
4 oz (110 g) any soft moist cheese
  (e.g., Camembert, goat's
  cheese, Mozzarella)

4 pitta breads

Slice the onions thinly. Heat a teaspoon of sunflower oil in a non-stick saucepan. Add the onions and stir-fry vigorously for about 4 minutes until the onions have wilted and are pale brown all over. Set aside for a moment. Slice the cheese as thinly as possible. Cut the pitta bread open completely and then in half horizontally. Pre-heat the grill. Set the sliced cheese on the bottom halves of the pitta bread and grill close to the heat until the cheese melts and bubbles. Put the top halves under the grill briefly until they just puff up. Quickly warm the onions again and spread them on top of the cheese. Re-form the pittas and serve immediately.

COTTAGE CHEESE WITH FRUIT

Cottage cheese can make an excellent, simple snack or starter for late summer. The bland taste and texture of the cheese is complemented by the sharp, sweet tastes of the fruit and dressing. The dish is quickly assembled, but it repays careful arrangement on pretty plates.

SERVES 4

1 × 12 oz (350 g) tub of cottage
  cheese
2 nectarines or peaches
4 large, sweet, ripe tomatoes

DRESSING
2 tablespoons safflower oil

1 tablespoon lemon juice
Freshly ground black pepper
A little salt

GARNISH
1 tablespoon finely snipped chives

Scoop out the cottage cheese using two dessertspoons to achieve a good shape. Put two scoops on each plate. Halve and stone the nectarines or peaches, then cut each half into thin segments. Slice the tomatoes finely. Arrange the fruit pleasantly on each plate. Shake the dressing ingredients together. Trickle the dressing over the cheese and fruit. Sprinkle the snipped chives over the cheese. Serve at room temperature.

SOFT CHEESE AND HERB PÂTÉ WITH RAW VEGETABLES

This simple pâté takes only about five minutes to prepare. Let it chill for at least 15 minutes before you serve it with fingers of carrot and celery and florets of cauliflower.

SERVES 4–6

FOR THE PÂTÉ
1 tub (8¾ oz, 250 g) Quark cheese
   (or other low-fat soft cheese)
3 tablespoons finely-chopped fresh
   mixed herbs, e.g., chives, sage,
   parsley, basil
2 cloves mashed garlic
½ teaspoon ground coriander
½ teaspoon lemon juice

RAW VEGETABLES
2 carrots
3 sticks celery
4 oz (110 g) cauliflower
(Or similar quantities of other raw
   seasonal vegetables)

Beat all the pâté ingredients together well with a fork. Turn the mixture into a serving bowl, cover and chill for 15–30 minutes. Scrub and trim the carrots, then cut them into sticks. Cut the celery to match. Trim the cauliflower into florets. Put the pâté bowl in the centre of the serving dish and surround it with neat piles of the vegetables.

MOZZARELLA WITH TOMATO

An absurdly quick and simple first course, often served in Italy. When fresh basil is not in season use coriander or parsley.

SERVES 4

2 Mozzarella cheeses
1 lb (500 g) sweet, very ripe
   tomatoes

DRESSING
2 tablespoons good olive oil

2 teaspoons white wine vinegar
Freshly ground black pepper
A little salt
15 basil leaves

Slice the Mozzarella as thinly as possible and lay it diagonally across a flat serving dish. Slice the tomatoes thinly (you could skin them if you have time) and lay them on either side of the sliced cheese. Shake all the dressing ingredients together and trickle it over the cheese and the tomatoes. Tear the basil leaves into small strips and scatter them all over the dish. Serve at room temperature with French bread.

QUICK PAN PIZZA

The last thing I usually feel like after a hard day's work is messing about with flour in the kitchen. I make an exception for this pizza, which can be made in about 25 minutes from start to finish with store-cupboard ingredients. You don't need yeast or strong flour and there is no kneading or rising: the dough is quickly made from ordinary self-raising flour and olive oil, then gently fried in a pan brushed out with a little olive oil. A simple tomato sauce goes on top, then some grated cheese browned under the grill. We often have this pizza as a quick snack if we are going out again in the evening. The flavour is infinitely superior to that of a bought pizza and it costs a fraction of the price.

SERVES 4

FOR THE DOUGH
8 oz (225 g) wholemeal or white
   self-raising flour
4 fl oz (100 ml) water
2 tablespoons olive oil
1 tablespoon mixed dried herbs
Black pepper

TOPPING
1 onion
small tin tomatoes (7 oz, 200 g)
1 teaspoon dried oregano
Black pepper
Pinch salt
3 oz (75 g) Edam or Gouda cheese

Make the tomato sauce by fine-chopping the onion and sweating it for a few minutes in a saucepan brushed out with oil. Add the tinned tomatoes in their juice, the oregano, black pepper and a pinch of salt. Mash the tomatoes down well, bring to a simmer and cook, uncovered, for 10 minutes. (If you prefer a smooth sauce you could blend it, but this is not really necessary.)

While the sauce is cooking, make the dough by mixing the flour with the water, olive oil, dried herbs and black pepper. Knead it very briefly then roll it into a 10-inch (25-cm) round on a floured board. Neaten the edges. Brush a large non-stick frying pan out with olive oil under a very moderate heat and slide in the dough. Let it cook for about 5 minutes. Lift it out, then brush the pan out with oil again and cook the other side. Don't worry if the base looks a bit unappetizing – it will be covered with sauce.

Pre-heat the grill. Spread the sauce over the cooked pizza, then grate the cheese over it and grill until the cheese is well-browned and bubbling. Serve the pizza warm and cut into wedges.

The same basic recipe can be endlessly elaborated by adding anchovies and olives, tuna or prawns, peppers, fresh herbs, mushrooms, and so on.

PIZZA TOASTS

This is a quickly made lunch or supper snack designed on the same principle as the frozen 'French bread pizzas'.

SERVES 4

1 small (7½-oz, 200-g) tin tomatoes
3 tablespoons tomato purée
1 teaspoon dried oregano or
    1 tablespoon chopped fresh
    marjoram
Black pepper
Salt to taste

1 small round wholemeal 'batch'
    loaf

GARNISH
1 tin anchovies, drained
16 sprigs parsley to garnish

Drain the tomatoes (keep the juice for another dish) and mash them with the purée and dried oregano or fresh marjoram, the pepper and salt to taste. Cut the loaf into 8 thick rounds, trimming off any excessive crust. Toast the bread lightly on both sides. Spread it with the tomato mixture, then sprinkle on the cheese. Grill till the cheese is bubbling and beginning to brown. Garnish each slice with diagonal strips of anchovy and two sprigs of parsley.

LITTLE COURGETTE PATTIES

These delicately spiced savoury patties make an excellent light supper dish. It is worth taking a little time to 'de-gorge' the courgettes by drawing out excess moisture with salt, then rinsing and squeezing them. This gives a much crisper result. Ricotta is the best fresh cheese to use, but any curd cheese will also work well. Coriander gives a more exciting flavour, but if you can't get it, parsley is an acceptable substitute.

SERVES 4:
makes 12 patties

4 young courgettes
Salt
4 oz (100 g) Ricotta, or other light, low-fat fresh cheese
1 tablespoon grated Parmesan cheese
1 large egg

2 oz (50 g) fresh brown breadcrumbs
3 tablespoons finely chopped fresh coriander or parsley
1 teaspoon ground coriander
½ teaspoon garam masala
2 tablespoons plain flour

Stand the colander in the sink. Grate the courgettes into the colander, sprinkle them with salt and leave them for 15 minutes. Meanwhile, prepare the rest of the mixture. Put the Ricotta (or low-fat soft cheese), Parmesan cheese, egg, half the breadcrumbs, the fresh coriander or parsley, ground coriander, garam masala and flour into a mixing bowl. Use a large fork to beat all these together. Rinse the courgettes under cold water to get rid of the salt, then squeeze out as much moisture from them as you can with your hands. Add them to the mixture, beating well again. Form the mixture into 12 neatly shaped patties. Coat each one in the remaining breadcrumbs. Brush out a large non-stick pan with sunflower oil. Cook the patties over a very moderate heat for about 5 minutes each side until they are crisp and well browned.

POACHED EGGS ON A JADE BED

Since we are blessed with semi-open-plan offices, where noise and disturbance are perpetual, for a really concentrated day's work I sometimes retreat home with a colleague. If the work is going well I don't want to stop to do any elaborate cooking for lunch. This sort of dish fits the bill perfectly: it's a rich-tasting green vegetable purée with a poached egg sitting on top. It looks best served in individual brightly coloured shallow dishes. The vegetable purée can be made in advance and reheated in a microwave or, very gently, on top of the stove.

SERVES 4

8 oz (225 g) fresh spinach
2 oz (50 g) broccoli spears
½ head lettuce
8 oz (225 g) frozen peas
Squeeze each of garlic purée and
   mixed herbs purée, or 1 garlic
   clove, mashed, and ½ teaspoon
   mixed dried herbs

Pinch salt
2 eggs
2 teaspoons grated Parmesan
   cheese

Wash and roughly chop the spinach, broccoli and lettuce. Put them into a deep pan with a well-fitting lid, add the peas, garlic purée, mixed herb purée, a pinch of salt and a tablespoon of water. Cover tightly and cook gently for about 6 minutes. Meanwhile, poach the eggs until they are set as you like them. Blend or process the vegetables with their liquid until you have a chunky purée. Taste for seasoning. Spoon half the purée into each serving dish and set an egg on top. Sprinkle some Parmesan cheese over the top of each dish. Serve with triangles of wholemeal toast.

ITALIAN OMELETTE

(Frittata)

I first ate an omelette like this in the simple café of an Italian hilltop village as a teenager, and I've never forgotten the taste. A hunk of freshly baked French bread and a mixed salad is all that is needed to provide a pleasant meal, usually from store-cupboard ingredients. The omelette, unlike the French variety, is cooked slowly and served flat, cut into thick wedges.

SERVES 4

4 onions
5 eggs
2 oz (50 g) grated Parmesan cheese
Freshly ground black pepper

A little salt
1 tablespoon fresh chopped
   parsley
2 tablespoons olive oil

Finely slice the onions. Beat the eggs with a fork, then add the cheese, pepper, salt and parsley. Heat the oil in a frying pan (the 10-inch (25-cm) size is ideal). When it is hot add the onions and cook them until they are golden and just beginning to turn brown. Now lift the onions out and add them to the beaten egg mixture. Raise the heat a little and add the egg mixture to the pan. Turn down the heat immediately and let the omelette cook gently for about 7 minutes. Pre-heat the grill. Inspect the underside of the omelette with a palette knife – it should be firm and golden. Now put the frying pan under the grill until the top of the omelette is just set. Carefully slide a palette knife under the omelette and transfer it to a well-warmed dish. Serve immediately, cut in wedges.

SPANISH TORTILLA

This Spanish potato omelette is closely related to the Italian *frittata* and is cooked in much the same way.

SERVES 4

4 medium onions
3 large potatoes
4 eggs
2 tablespoons skimmed milk

Salt and pepper to taste
1 tablespoon finely chopped fresh
   parsley

Slice the onions finely; cut the potatoes in half, then slice them (do all this in the food processor if you have one). Heat a tablespoon of oil in a lidded non-stick pan: the 10-inch (25-cm) size is ideal. Add the vegetables and cook them slowly, stirring frequently over a low heat, covered, for about 15 minutes, when they should be well browned and soft. Beat the eggs with the milk, salt and pepper. Lift the vegetables out of the pan and add them to the egg mixture. Pour the mixture back into the pan (making sure that the vegetables are well distributed) and let it cook over a low heat for about 7 minutes. When the top is just set, slide the omelette on to a plate, then flop it upside down back into the pan and let the other side brown for about 2 minutes. Sprinkle the top with the parsley. Cut it into wedges and serve it warm with a tomato salad. This omelette can also be served cold.

To adapt this recipe for two people, halve the quantities and cook in an omelette pan. Cut the omelette in half to serve.

PIPERADE

This dish is popular in the Basque country and in Provence. It's really an elaborated form of scrambled eggs and makes a light lunch or supper dish. Use red rather than green peppers – the flavour is sweeter.

SERVES 4

1 medium onion	Black pepper to taste
1 lb (450 g) peppers, preferably red	Salt to taste
1 lb (450 g) sweet, ripe tomatoes	3 eggs
2 cloves garlic, crushed	

Slice the onion finely and stir-fry it in a deep non-stick pan brushed out with oil. Cook until it is wilted but not brown. De-seed and slice the peppers, skin and chop the tomatoes; add them to the pan with the crushed garlic. Cover and cook without colouring on the gentlest possible heat for about 10 minutes, when the peppers should be soft but not mushy. Add salt if you wish. If there is a lot of watery juice, boil it down until you are left with a thick consistency. Remove the pan from the heat. Beat the eggs, then add them to the pan, stirring until everything is well incorporated. Replace the pan over a very gentle heat. When the eggs begin to set, take the pan away from the heat; the eggs will continue to cook. Keep stirring and transfer to a warmed serving dish. Serve immediately with triangles of wholemeal toast.

EGG AND VEGETABLE FLAN

This flan is really a crustless quiche, much less trouble to cook and tastes just as good, if not better, than the traditional pastry version.

It's a pleasant 'Thursday' dish – an easy way of using up odds and ends in the refrigerator.

SERVES 4

2 large onions
2 leeks
6 oz (175 g) broccoli
1 teaspoon sunflower oil
1 oz (25 g) any hard cheese
3 medium-sized eggs

5 fl oz (150 g) skimmed milk
Ground black pepper
Pinch of salt
2 tablespoons finely chopped
  parsley

Pre-heat the oven to Gas Mark 4, 350° F, 180° C.

Peel and finely chop the onions; clean and finely slice the leeks. Chop the broccoli into bite-sized pieces. Heat the oil and sauté the vegetables, stirring frequently to prevent browning. Grate the cheese. Meanwhile, grease a quiche tin or dish very well. Spread the sautéed vegetables evenly over the dish: they should come within ½ inch (1 cm) of the top. Beat the eggs lightly, add the milk, season with ground pepper and a pinch of salt, and stir in the finely chopped parsley. Pour the egg mixture carefully and evenly over the vegetables. Sprinkle the grated cheese over the top. Bake in the centre of the pre-heated oven for 35–40 minutes, when the flan should be springy, well set and golden on top. Serve warm or cold, cut in wedges. Small baked potatoes cooked on skewers in the same oven make a good accompaniment with salad.

POTTED HADDOCK

Traditionally, 'potted' dishes were made with an enormous quantity of butter. A low-fat soft cheese gives an equally good result and only a fraction of the saturated fat. This method of 'jugging' the haddock also gets rid of a lot of the salt. Look for undyed pale haddock.

SERVES 4

8 oz (250 g) smoked haddock
2 spring onions
½ teaspoon mild curry paste
6 oz (175 g) Quark or other low-fat
  soft fresh cheese

1 lemon
4 parsley sprigs

Put the haddock in a large jug and fill the jug with boiling water. After 4 minutes, carefully pour the water away and fill the jug again with fresh boiling water. Leave for another 4 minutes. Meanwhile chop the spring onions roughly. Lift out the haddock, remove any skin or bones and put the fish in a liquidizer or food processor. Add the chopped spring onions, the curry paste, Quark and the juice of half the lemon. Blend or process until smooth. Spoon the mixture into individual dishes, levelling off the tops neatly. Chill until the mixture is firm. Garnish each dish with a parsley sprig and thin slices of the remaining lemon. Serve with wholemeal toast.

MELON, GRAPE AND MINT VINAIGRETTE

This is a refreshing summer starter, when melons are cheap. Serve it in individual glass dishes.

SERVES 4

1 large green or yellow melon
8 oz (225 g) green seedless grapes
1½ tablespoons very finely chopped mint

DRESSING
2 tablespoons olive oil

2 teaspoons fruit or white wine vinegar
Pinch salt

GARNISH
8 extra mint leaves

De-seed the melon. Scoop out balls if you have a melon scoop, otherwise cut it into neat dice. Mix these with the grapes and mint. Blend or shake the dressing ingredients and pour it over the fruit. Chill for at least 15 minutes before serving in individual dishes garnished with the whole mint leaves.

GINGERED GRAPEFRUIT

Our children are traditionally allowed ginger wine heavily diluted with something fizzy and non-alcoholic as a Christmas Day treat. As a result, we often have most of a bottle of ginger wine standing reproachfully in the cupboard for the rest of the year. It's certainly too good to ignore: hence this recipe, which makes a light, refreshing starter.

SERVES 4

1 pink grapefruit	3 tablespoons ginger wine
1 yellow grapefruit	Pinch ground dried ginger
Small bunch green seedless grapes	

Peel and then segment the grapefruit carefully, removing all the pips and membrane. Do this over a bowl, otherwise you will lose a lot of the juice. Halve the grapes and add them to the grapefruit. Spoon the ginger wine over the fruit, stir it well and leave to chill for at least 15 minutes. Serve in individual glass dishes with a mean pinch of ground ginger sprinkled on top.

PEPERONATA

Like most Mediterranean food, this dish is supremely healthy and also has a full, satisfying taste. It is really a sweet pepper and tomato casserole, served cold and decorated with olives.

SERVES 4
as a first course, 2 as a light main course

1 lb (450 g) sweet ripe tomatoes	Black pepper
2 large red peppers	Salt to taste
2 large yellow peppers, or 4 red peppers	
2 cloves garlic, well crushed	GARNISH
	Black olives

Skin the tomatoes by dropping them briefly into boiling water, then slipping the skins off. De-seed and halve the peppers, then cut them into long, thin strips. Brush a deep non-stick pan with olive oil and sauté the crushed garlic until it softens. Now add the peppers, reduce the heat to a minimum, cover tightly and cook very slowly for 10 minutes. Make sure the peppers do not burn – add a little water if necessary. Now roughly chop the tomatoes and add them to the pan with some black pepper and a bare minimum of salt. Cover again and cook very gently for another 5 minutes. Let the dish become cold, then serve on individual plates garnished with black olives. Offer warm French bread on the side.

SEAFOOD SALAD

This crisp salad makes a good-looking green, pink and black starter. Serve it in individual portions with some hot, crusty bread. Buying frozen squid 'tubes' does away with the fiddly preparation of the squid.

SERVES 4

2 prepared squid tubes
1 medium onion
2 cloves garlic
2 tablespoons chopped fresh
  parsley
2 tablespoons water
2 tablespoons white wine
2 oz peeled prawns (defrosted if
  they are frozen)

DRESSING
2 tablespoons olive oil
1 tablespoon lemon juice
Freshly ground black pepper

TO SERVE
4 large, firm lettuce leaves (Iceberg
  is ideal)

GARNISH
8 black olives, stoned

Cut the squid tubes carefully into neat rings. Slice the onion finely, peel and mash the garlic. Brush out a non-stick lidded saucepan with a little oil and sauté the onion and garlic for about 3 minutes. Add the sliced squid, half the parsley, wine and water. Bring to a gentle simmer and cook, tightly covered, for about 8 minutes. Test that the squid are tender. Add the prawns and stir to mix well. Drain the fish (keep the liquid for another dish). Blend or shake the dressing ingredients. Add the dressing while the fish is still warm and toss well. Set aside to cool. Pile on to the lettuce leaves and garnish with the olives and remaining parsley.

CELERIAC RÉMOULADE
WITH SMOKED SALMON

Celeriac looks unattractive in its raw unpeeled state: a bit like a hairy turnip. Peeled, blanched and cut into strips, however, it makes a delicate starter. The classic French sauce for it is made with a mustardy mayonnaise. This is a much healthier version made with yoghurt. The partnership with smoked salmon is perfect: the strong taste and soft texture of the salmon contrasting beautifully with the crunchy texture and delicate celery flavour of the vegetable.

SERVES 4

4 thinly sliced pieces of smoked salmon
1 medium-sized celeriac

DRESSING
5 oz (150 g) plain low-fat yoghurt
1 tablespoon capers, well rinsed and drained
1 teaspoon Dijon mustard

4 sprigs fresh parsley
2 sprigs fresh tarragon (optional)
Juice and zest of a lemon
Freshly milled black pepper
A little salt

GARNISH
4 large black olives
½ lemon

The easiest way to deal with celeriac is to cut it first, unpeeled, into 'rounds' which you drop into a bowl of cold water containing a dash of vinegar or lemon juice. Set another pan of water to boil at the same time. Now peel each round thickly, then slice it into matchstick strips. Drop these into the boiling water for 3–4 minutes. Drain them and 'refresh' them under the cold tap to arrest the cooking process. Pat dry. To make the dressing, blend all the ingredients in a processor or blender. Mix the celeriac with the dressing and let it sit in the refrigerator if you have time. Arrange prettily on individual plates with the salmon. Garnish each plate with a black olive and two wafer-thin slices of lemon.

CUCUMBER AND YOGHURT SALAD
WITH PITTA BREAD

(Tzatziki)

Cucumber and yoghurt salads are popular in many parts of the world. Sometimes, as with this Greek recipe, they are served as starters or dips. In Indian cookery they are served as a balancing 'cool' element with 'hot' curries. This is a light refreshing starter which takes only a few moments to assemble.

SERVES 4

¼–½ cucumber
5 oz (150 g) low-fat natural yoghurt
1 clove garlic, crushed to a pulp
1 dessertspoon finely chopped
    fresh mint, or 1 teaspoon dried
Freshly ground black pepper

A little salt
4 pitta breads

GARNISH
4 extra mint leaves
4 black olives

Dice the cucumber finely (leave the peel on). Tip the yoghurt into a bowl and stir in all the other ingredients. Add the cucumber and mix well. Refrigerate it if you have time. Cut the pitta breads in half and heat them through on both sides under a hot grill until they puff up. Serve the salad on individual flat plates, each one garnished with a mint leaf and a black olive. Offer the pitta bread piping hot from a basket lined with a napkin.

CREAMED AVOCADO

Choose soft, ripe avocados for this classic and quickly made starter, and serve wholemeal toast with it. Avocados contain a lot of fat, but as it is polyunsaturated you can eat them without too much worry.

SERVES 4

2 large, ripe avocados
2 drops Tabasco sauce
Juice of ½ lemon

2 cloves garlic, well mashed
1 teaspoon olive oil
Freshly ground black pepper

Skin and stone the avocados, scraping away as much deep green flesh from the skins as possible. Mash the flesh, using a potato masher, with all the other ingredients. Don't aim for an over-smooth result. Serve immediately: avocados start to go brown as soon as their stones are removed.

AVOCADO WITH PRAWN DRESSING

This is an unusual and economical way of serving that faithful old
standby, avocado with prawns. The stoned avocado is halved, then
sliced, rounded side up, so that it keeps its pear shape. The dressing is
trickled on top.

SERVES 4

4 oz (110 g) prawns in their shells
4 tablespoons low-fat plain yoghurt
1 tablespoon lemon juice
1 teaspoon tomato purée

Pinch salt
2 large ripe avocados
Small bunch fresh chives

Reserve 4 prawns, whole, for garnish. Shell the remainder and purée
them in the blender with the yoghurt, lemon juice and salt until they
form a smooth paste. Halve the avocados, then peel them carefully.
Put each half on an individual flat serving dish, flat side down, and
slice it vertically, retaining the pear shape. Trickle the prawn dressing
over the centre of each pear. Snip the chives over the top and garnish
each plate with a whole prawn.

POULTRY AND MEAT

Most of these recipes are for poultry, as this is the least fatty type of meat. Fortunately it is also the easiest and quickest to cook. Many of the dishes involve the magically transforming and rapid technique of stir-frying (see page 63), where a wok (see page 46) will be a great help. However, they can all be cooked successfully in an ordinary pan too. There are also several recipes for the less fatty types of pork and lamb, and a few for beef.

Spices, herbs and other aromatic ingredients like garlic, ginger, lemon and orange juice are important in this type of cookery, and it is well worth stocking up on them when you are committed to a healthier diet. A little wine helps too – just a dash is often enough to improve the final flavour of a dish tremendously.

AMERICAN CHICKEN WITH MUSTARD

Chicken joints in a savoury breadcrumb casing are simple to cook. In this recipe the mustard gives a tang to the joints without overwhelming them. The secrets of a perfect result are that the joints should be at room temperature before you start, and the breadcrumbs should be as dry as possible (this ensures that they absorb very little fat). This dish is especially good served cold with a salad.

I also give an alternative method of cooking this dish in the oven which takes slightly longer but gives a crisp rather than a soft coating. Children usually prefer this version, as it has more resemblance to 'take-away' chicken, but of course there is no added fat, so it is much healthier.

SERVES 4

1 tablespoon Dijon mustard	1 small egg, very lightly beaten
1 teaspoon English mustard powder	2 tablespoons dried mixed herbs
4 quarter-chicken leg joints, at room temperature	4 oz (110 g) stale or oven-dried wholemeal breadcrumbs

Pan method

Mix the Dijon mustard with the mustard powder. Cut each chicken joint in half at the thigh. Skin them and prick them all over. Rub the mustard paste all over the chicken. Now dip the joints into the lightly beaten egg. Mix the dried herbs with the breadcrumbs and use them to coat each joint. Heat a little oil in a large non-stick lidded sauté pan. Slide in the joints. Let them cook briefly each side for about 2 minutes on a moderately high heat. Now lower the heat and put on the lid. Allow about 5 minutes' cooking each side with the lid on, then another 5 minutes each side with the lid off. Test for 'doneness' by sliding a sharp knife into the fleshiest part of the joint, right up to the bone. When the juices run clear, the chicken is cooked. Serve with a simple puréed vegetable – perhaps parsnips or sprouts (see page 203) – in winter; and in summer with a tomato and basil salad (see page 206) and a sharp chutney (see page 228).

Oven method

Pre-heat the oven to its maximum – Gas Mark 9, 475° F, 240° C. Prepare the coating for the chicken as above. Put the chicken pieces on an oiled baking tray and cook them for 15 minutes in the hottest part of the oven. Now reduce the temperature to Gas Mark 7 (425° F, 220° C), move the joints to a middle shelf and then cook for another 20–30 minutes or until no red juices run from the centre. There is no need to turn the joints over.

FIERY GRILLED CHICKEN

Plain grilled chicken can be dull: here is a simple but 'hot' sauce to perk it up. This also makes an excellent barbecue sauce for people who enjoy a spicy assault on their taste-buds.

SERVES 4

4 chicken joints	½ teaspoon cayenne pepper
	1 teaspoon paprika
SAUCE	1 teaspoon sugar
2 tablespoons tomato purée	½ teaspoon ground cumin
1 tablespoon olive oil	½ teaspoon ground coriander
3 cloves garlic, mashed	½ teaspoon ground ginger
1 tablespoon white wine vinegar	½ teaspoon English mustard

Pre-heat the grill to moderately hot. Brush the skinned chicken joints with the olive oil and set them under the grill to start cooking for about 4 minutes each side while you prepare the sauce. Blend or process all the sauce ingredients to a smooth paste, then brush it on both sides of the joints. Grill for another 10 minutes each side or until the tops are crisp and the joints are cooked. (Brush the joints with the sauce again during the cooking.) Serve with a green salad and warmed pitta bread.

STUFFED CHICKEN BREAST

This elegant supper dish is special enough for a dinner party and easy enough for everyday eating. The stuffing is made from a diced mushroom and parsley mixture and forms a neat wedge in each breast. A non-stick lidded sauté pan is essential for this dish, though you could improvise with a non-stick frying pan tightly covered with foil.

SERVES 4

FOR THE STUFFING
1 onion
1 tablespoon finely chopped fresh
  parsley
4 oz (110 g) dark-gilled mushrooms
A little cayenne pepper

Black pepper
1 lemon
1 tablespoon oil

4 small chicken breasts
2 tablespoons stock or water

First make the stuffing by finely chopping the onion, parsley and mushrooms and mixing them together (this can be done in a food processor, but don't over-process). Add the cayenne, a generous quantity of black pepper, the grated zest of the lemon and half its juice. Brush out the pan with oil and gently sauté the stuffing ingredients for about 6 minutes, uncovered, when they will have softened and halved in bulk. Spread the stuffing out to cool completely.

Skin and bone the chicken breasts if necessary. Carefully cut a large 'pocket' by slicing deeply into the length and breadth of each breast. Pack an equal quantity of the cooled stuffing into each pocket, pushing it in and smoothing it off neatly at the edge.

Brush out the pan with oil again. Slide in the chicken breasts in one layer. Let each side brown well at a high temperature for about a minute. Cover the pan tightly and lower the heat to the minimum. The chicken will now cook in its own steam. Leave it undisturbed for about 10 minutes (time will vary according to thickness).

When the breasts are cooked, transfer them to a warm place for a moment. There should be a small pool of dark cooking liquid in the pan. Add 2 tablespoons of stock or water to this, together with the remaining lemon juice. Boil it down vigorously until there is just enough to put a tablespoon over each breast. The simplest way to serve the meat is just as it is with a little sauce spooned over each. Alternatively, you could slice each breast diagonally into 6 or 7 pieces and fan them out on the plate, again with a little sauce over each. Serve with mange-tout peas, baby carrots and potatoes simmered in their skins.

GRILLED CHICKEN KEBABS

A simple chicken dish in which the meat is tenderized and flavoured by a simple yoghurt and lemon juice marinade.

SERVES 4

1 lb (450 g) skinned boned chicken
5 oz (150 g) plain yoghurt
3 cloves garlic
2 tablespoons fresh chopped mixed herbs, or 1 tablespoon mixed dried herbs

2 tablespoons lemon juice
Black pepper to taste

GARNISH
1 tablespoon chopped parsley
1 lemon

Remove any remaining skin or fat from the chicken and cut it into neat, bite-sized cubes – not too small. Have a mixing bowl ready. Pour in the yoghurt. Add the garlic, herbs, lemon juice and black pepper. Stir the yoghurt mixture well and add the cubed chicken. Chill for at least 15 minutes – longer if possible. When you are ready to cook, pre-heat the grill. Thread the chicken on to skewers, shaking off the excess yoghurt. Grill for about 10 minutes, turning the meat several times so that it cooks on all sides. Garnish with chopped parsley and lemon wedges and serve with rice and a selection of spicy relishes: for instance yoghurt and cucumber (see pages 133–4) and an orange and onion salad (see page 205).

INDIAN-STYLE GRILLED CHICKEN DRUMSTICKS

In India, yoghurt and lemon juice have been traditionally used to tenderize tough, stringy chickens, and an overnight steeping was certainly necessary for the marinade to do its work. With today's tender, plump chickens, prolonged marinating is not really necessary: if you are really short of time, 20 minutes will still give excellent results. This is a subtle, spicy dish. Although it contains fresh chilli it is not 'hot'.

SERVES 4

12 skinned chicken drumsticks

MARINADE
2 cloves garlic
1 small cube ginger, peeled
1 small onion
1 fresh chilli, de-seeded
1 tablespoon chopped fresh
  coriander
1 tablespoon ground coriander

Juice of 1 lemon
Freshly ground black pepper
5 oz (150 g) plain yoghurt
¼ teaspoon salt

GARNISH
A little more chopped fresh
  coriander
1 lemon

Slash the flesh of each drumstick in about 3 places. This allows the marinade to penetrate more easily. Now mix all the marinade ingredients in a food processor or blender and pour the mixture over the chicken. Use your hands to work it well into every piece. Leave the chicken for about 20 minutes. Now heat the grill to its hottest. Lift the chicken out of the marinade (it's not necessary to shake the marinade off completely). Grill the chicken pieces, turning them frequently: about 15 minutes should be enough. They should be well browned outside and just cooked inside. Test them with a skewer: they are ready when the juices run clear. Serve with plenty of rice, garnished with lemon wedges and a little coriander. A yoghurt and cucumber salad (see pages 133–4) makes a pleasant relish with this dish.

CHICKEN QUARTERS WITH LEMON, ROSEMARY AND PARSLEY

I once stayed at an Italian 'hotel' that was little more than a shabby, previously grand nineteenth-century villa, formerly inhabited, so it

was claimed, by Napoleon's sister. The hotel management was un-
touched by any knowledge of the culinary prejudices of foreign
visitors and the excellent food was simplicity itself: a short menu of
innocently local Italian dishes. The garden was full of neglected,
abundantly fruiting lemon trees and wild rosemary. Parsley grew
everywhere, each plant the size of a small shrub. A chicken dish of the
type given here, using some of that garden abundance, was one of the
regulars on the menu.

SERVES 4

4 chicken quarters
2 tablespoons plain white flour
2 lemons
6 fl oz dry white wine
2 cloves garlic, mashed

4 sprigs fresh rosemary
Freshly ground black pepper
1 tablespoon finely chopped fresh
 parsley

Skin the chicken and cut each piece in two at the thigh joint. Dust the
chicken with the flour. Heat a little oil in a non-stick sauté pan and
brown the chicken very well, turning it frequently. Meanwhile, grate
the zest from the lemons (using a zester makes this quicker) and
squeeze the juice. When the chicken pieces are brown, add the lemon
juice, wine, garlic, rosemary sprigs and pepper. Bring to a bare
simmer, cover, and cook for 25 minutes. Test that the meat is cooked.
Transfer the chicken to a warmed serving dish and keep it hot. Add
the parsley to the pan, then boil down the cooking liquid rapidly until
you have just enough to pour a tablespoon over each serving. Remove
the rosemary from the pan before serving with warmed pitta bread
and a tomato salad.

STUFFED CHICKEN THIGHS

In this dish a fragrant, brightly coloured fruit and vegetable stuffing
makes a perfect foil for the chicken thighs. Packets of skinned and
boned chicken thighs are now available from supermarkets and cook
quickly in a very hot oven. Serve with a puréed vegetable and thick
slices of fresh wholemeal bread.

SERVES 4

STUFFING
2 eating apples
2 carrots
1 onion
1 stick celery
2 tablespoons chopped parsley

2 tablespoons tomato purée
Freshly ground black pepper

8 boned, skinned chicken thighs
8 fl oz (200 ml) water or white wine
Salt to taste

Pre-heat the oven to Gas Mark 9, 475° F, 240° C. Make the stuffing first. Grate or roughly process the cored apples, carrot, onion and celery. Brush a non-stick sauté pan with a little oil and put it on to a moderate heat. Put in the prepared vegetables with the chopped parsley, tomato purée and ground black pepper. Cook, stirring constantly, for about 5 minutes. Spread the stuffing on to a plate to cool.

Spread the chicken thighs with the cooled stuffing and roll them up. There is no need to fasten them. Now tuck them tightly, open side down, into a shallow flame- and oven-proof dish just big enough to hold them all. Pour half a wineglass of water round them and cover them loosely with oiled greaseproof paper. Cook on the highest shelf in the pre-heated oven for 12 minutes. Now remove the paper and cook for another 6 minutes to brown the meat. Check that the meat is cooked thoroughly by inserting a skewer right into the meat. Any juices should run clear. Take the cooked chicken out of the dish and set it in a serving dish to keep warm. Pour 8 fl oz (200 ml) of water or white wine into the cooking dish with a little salt, put it over a fierce heat and scrape all the cooking juices into it, stirring well until it reduces and thickens a little. It should be a deep brown colour and speckled with tiny pieces of stuffing. Pour the sauce over the meat and serve immediately.

STEAMED CHICKEN PARCELS

Steamed food is 'healthy' because no added fat is needed. However, it can be bland, so it needs a few sharper or stronger flavours to enhance it. In this recipe a whole meal can be steamed in one pan, thus cutting down on both preparation and cooking time. Add whatever seasonal vegetables you like: good partners to the chicken are new potatoes and broccoli, but young carrots and mange-tout peas would go equally well.

SERVES 4

4 chicken breasts, boned and skinned

STUFFING
1 oz (25 g) fresh wholemeal breadcrumbs
2 fat leeks

1 egg yolk
Salt and freshly ground black pepper
1 tablespoon chopped fresh parsley

Hold the chicken breasts down flat on a chopping board with the palm of your hand. Use a very heavy sharp knife to slice them horizontally so that you have 2 thick escalopes from each breast. Now make the stuffing by mixing the breadcrumbs with the finely chopped leeks and the egg yolk. Spread a little of the stuffing all over one side of each piece of chicken, then roll them up and fasten them with a cocktail stick or toothpick. Put the chicken parcels on a plate and sprinkle them meanly with a little salt and generously with freshly ground black pepper. Steam for 25 minutes. Add the vegetables at the appropriate time. Tiny new potatoes take about 25 minutes, broccoli sprigs about 10 minutes. Sprinkle the chopped parsley over the chicken and spoon a little of the cooking liquor over the food. Serve immediately with a little sharp or spicy chutney handed separately.

CHICKEN WITH BROCCOLI

This is a quick stir-fried chicken dish. Its bright colours, interesting textures and clean taste make it an excellent choice for a speedy supper. It's economical too – a half chicken will feed 4 people.

SERVES 4

1 half-chicken or 2–3 breast fillets
6 oz (175 g) broccoli spears
1 red pepper
4 spring onions

SAUCE
2 teaspoons cornflour
6 fl oz (175 ml) stock

1 tablespoon red currant jelly
1 tablespoon soy sauce
1 tablespoon dry sherry
Garlic purée, or 2 cloves fresh garlic, crushed
1 teaspoon safflower oil (or sunflower or corn oil)

Skin and bone the chicken if necessary. Cut the flesh into neat, evenly shaped, bite-sized pieces. Now prepare the vegetables: cut each broccoli spear vertically into 3 or 4 thin strands; cut the pepper into matchsticks, and the spring onion, on the slant, into half-inch pieces.

To make the sauce, cream the cornflour with a little of the stock, then add the red currant jelly, soy sauce, dry sherry, garlic purée and the rest of the stock. Stir it well.

Put the teaspoonful of safflower oil into the wok or frying pan. Stir-fry the chicken, continually turning it against the hot sides of the pan until it changes colour all over and just begins to brown. Now add the vegetables: broccoli first, stir-frying for a minute; then the pepper, stir-frying for another minute; then the spring onion. Stir-fry for another 30 seconds. Now add the sauce and keep stirring for a minute. Cover the pan and simmer for 2 minutes. Remove the lid and check the consistency of the sauce. If it is too thin, let it bubble to reduce. There should be just enough to cling to the food. Serve piping hot with rice and stir-fried beansprouts (see page 203).

STIR-FRIED CHICKEN WITH LEMON, CORIANDER AND TARRAGON

This simple dish has a wonderfully fragrant aroma and subtle taste: the marriage of lemon, fresh coriander and tarragon with chicken is a happy one. Tarragon dries well, so the dried herb will still give a good flavour if fresh is not available. Fresh parsley can be substituted for the coriander, but the flavour will, of course, be quite different.

SERVES 4

3 large chicken breast fillets
2 cloves garlic
2 large onions
1 tablespoon sunflower oil
2 bay-leaves
2 tablespoons lemon juice
3 fl oz (75 ml) dry white wine
3 fl oz (75 ml) chicken stock
2 teaspoons cornflour creamed in a little water

Black pepper
3 tablespoons finely chopped fresh coriander or 2 tablespoons finely chopped fresh parsley
1 tablespoon finely chopped fresh tarragon or 1 teaspoon dried
Salt to taste

Cut the chicken into neat, bite-sized pieces. Crush the garlic and chop the onion as finely as possible. Heat the sunflower oil in a wok or deep frying pan. Put in the garlic and onion and stir-fry them vigorously until they are soft and well browned. Remove the garlic and onion with a slotted spoon and set them aside for a moment. Now add the chicken pieces with the bay-leaves and stir-fry them over a high heat for about a minute and a half, or until the chicken pieces are browned all over. Add a little more oil if necessary. Return the garlic and onion to the pan with the lemon juice, wine, stock and creamed cornflour. Add the black pepper, bring the pan to simmering point, cover and leave for 2 minutes. Take the lid off the pan and raise the heat. Now let the sauce reduce until it is thick and syrupy. Just before it is ready, add the herbs and stir them in well. Check for seasoning and add a little salt if necessary. Reduce the heat and let the dish simmer for another minute. Remove the bay-leaves and serve piping hot with plain rice and watercress, spinach and lettuce salad (see page 206).

PERSIAN CHICKEN
WITH YOGHURT AND APRICOTS

Some people may count sheep or work out World football elevens while falling asleep, but I compile mental lists of the ten dishes I would take to a desert island. This one is always included. It combines gentle spiciness with fragrance and a hint of sweetness, a combination I find hard to resist. The sauce is rich-tasting and 'creamy', yet entirely healthy. The yoghurt is stabilized with cornflour, so will not separate.

Many of the best Middle Eastern or Indian dishes do seem to take a long time and a major effort to prepare. In spite of the long list of ingredients, this dish can be made from start to finish in about 35 minutes, as it is all cooked on the top of the stove in one pan. The same recipe works perfectly for drumsticks (allow 3 or 4 per person), but they do need to be skinned first and will also take quite a lot longer to cook.

Like all casserole-type dishes, this one is even better refrigerated and re-heated a day later.

SERVES 4

SPICE MIXTURE
1 bay-leaf
½ teaspoon ground cinnamon
½ teaspoon grated nutmeg
½ teaspoon ground cloves
1 teaspoon ground coriander
1 teaspoon ground cumin
¼ teaspoon cayenne
½ teaspoon ground ginger
8 cardamom pods, cracked

5 oz (150 g) plain low-fat yoghurt
1 teaspoon cornflour
5 fl oz (150 ml) chicken stock or
    water

1½ tablespoons ground almonds
2 onions
1 tablespoon sunflower oil
4 skinned and boned chicken
    breasts
2 tablespoons sultanas
8 dried apricots, sliced in half
4 cloves garlic, well crushed
Salt to taste

GARNISH
1 tablespoon finely chopped fresh
    coriander or parsley

Assemble the spice mixture first as this will save time later: just measure all the spices on to one plate. Pour the yoghurt into a large jug, then beat the cornflour into it. Add the stock or water and stir it well.

Peel and slice the onions. Heat a tablespoon of sunflower oil in a large, lidded non-stick sauté pan under a medium heat. Brown the onions well, then remove them for a moment with a slotted spoon. Slice each chicken breast on the slant into two, then, in the same oil, brown them on both sides. Now sprinkle in the spices and turn the chicken rapidly – this should not take longer than about 10 seconds – just enough to fry the spices a little so that they release their essential oils. Working quickly, spoon in the yoghurt mixture a tablespoon at a time, stirring it well as it hits the pan.

Sprinkle in the ground almonds, then return the onions to the pan. Sprinkle in the sultanas, sliced apricot and garlic. Bring the sauce to simmering point, then reduce the heat to a minimum. Cover the pan tightly and simmer for 10 minutes, or until the meat is cooked. If there is too much sauce for your taste, remove the chicken to a serving dish and keep it warm while you boil down the liquid. Check for seasoning, add salt if you wish. Spoon the sauce over the chicken and sprinkle with the chopped coriander or parsley. Serve with plain rice and some chutney.

SWEET AND SOUR CHICKEN

Recipes involving honey and vinegar have a long history in Europe and the Middle East. This one is a quick and simple recipe for grilled chicken breasts. It does not really need salt, but add it if you wish.

SERVES 4

4 chicken breast fillets, skinned

MARINADE
Garlic purée, or 4 cloves fresh
  garlic, well mashed
3 tablespoons wine vinegar or fruit
  vinegar

1 tablespoon honey
2 teaspoons ground coriander
Freshly ground black pepper
1 tablespoon olive oil

Mix the garlic purée, vinegar, honey, coriander, pepper and oil in a dish. Cut the chicken breasts in 2 or 3 pieces horizontally and turn them over in the marinade. Leave them for about 10 minutes. Pre-heat the grill. Grill the breasts on both sides brushing constantly with the remaining marinade. The outsides should be a deep golden brown and the insides just creamy. Serve with a warm steamed fennel salad (see page 212) and hot wholemeal pitta bread.

LAMB KEBABS WITH PITTA BREAD

Lamb is a fatty meat, but the leg is relatively lean. It makes a good light meal grilled on skewers and served with yoghurt and cucumber salad (see pages 133–4), hot pitta bread and a bean salad (see page 209).

SERVES 4

12 oz (350 g) lamb from the leg
1 lemon
½ teaspoon ground cumin
1 clove garlic, mashed

1 tablespoon finely chopped fresh
  coriander
1 teaspoon safflower or sunflower
  oil

Trim the meat, removing all the visible fat. Cut it into 1-inch (2.5-cm) cubes. Squeeze the juice from the lemon all over it with the ground cumin, the garlic, half the fresh-chopped coriander and the oil. Turn the meat well and leave it to marinate for at least 15 minutes (preferably an hour). Heat the grill and thread the meat on to skewers.

Grill, turning frequently, for about 7 minutes. Serve immediately, garnished with the remaining coriander.

MINCED LAMB SHEFTALIA

This is a Greek Cypriot dish which can be made with lamb or pork and is sometimes sold ready-prepared by Cypriot shops in London, usually in a caul or skin like a sausage. Minced or pounded meat dishes are popular in both Greek and Middle Eastern cookery. Pounding the meat was traditionally several hours' work; now it can be reduced to a few minutes with a food processor. This is a spicy, kebab-like dish consisting of a well-processed meat mixture which is shaped into little 'torpedoes' on skewers and then grilled. They can be prepared ahead of time for a barbecue or quickly assembled for a snack meal indoors. The sheftalia are served in warmed pitta 'pockets' with a choice of crunchy salads to pile in with them. If you don't have a food processor, pass the meat at least twice through the finest plate of a mincer.

SERVES 4

8 oz (225 g) lean lamb	2 spring onions
1-inch (2.5-cm) cube fresh ginger	2 cloves garlic, mashed
Small bunch fresh coriander	2 thick slices crustless wholemeal
½ teaspoon ground cumin	bread
1 teaspoon lemon juice	4 pitta breads

Cut any visible fat off the meat, then cut it into rough chunks and drop it into the food processor. Add the grated ginger, coriander, cumin, lemon juice, spring onion and garlic. Dip the bread into cold water, then squeeze it dry and add it to the mixture in the goblet. Process for 2 or 3 minutes, or until you have a smooth paste. Dampen your hands and shape the mixture into 8 'torpedoes', each one round a skewer. Brush each one with a little oil, then grill under a moderate heat for about 10 minutes (or 20 minutes on a barbecue), turning the skewers constantly. When cooked they should be golden brown all over. Keep the sheftalia warm while you heat through the pitta breads and cut them in half, to make 'pockets'.

Serve the meat still on skewers and let people fill the pitta pockets as they like from a variety of prepared salads and dips – e.g., crunchy green salad, coleslaw and a yoghurt and cucumber dressing.

SAUTÉED LAMB'S LIVER WITH RED WINE AND MARJORAM

Lamb's liver is tender and cheap. It is also packed with iron and zinc and is low in fat. This speedy dish is a succulent and satisfying main meal. Set it off with potato cakes (see page 200) and a simple green salad. If you don't have fresh marjoram you could substitute parsley or dried oregano. Cutting the liver while it is still frozen makes it easier to produce wafer-thin slices, but of course fresh liver can be used too.

SERVES 4

12 oz (350 g) frozen lamb's liver
2 tablespoons flour seasoned with black pepper and salt to taste

1½ tablespoons chopped fresh marjoram or ½ teaspoon dried oregano
4 fl oz (100 ml) dark stock
4 fl oz (100 ml) red wine

Cut the liver into wafer-thin ¼-inch slices. Dip it into the seasoned flour so that it is well coated on all sides. Heat a teaspoon of sunflower oil in a non-stick frying pan. Fry the liver for about 3–4 minutes each side until it is crisp and dark on the outside and still slightly pink inside. Set aside in a warm place. In the same pan, add the marjoram or oregano and red wine and stock. Boil fiercely until it is thick, well reduced and syrupy. Pour the sauce over the liver and serve immediately.

LAMB'S KIDNEYS IN RED WINE

Kidneys, like liver, are often despised as 'awful offal' and are usually sold very cheaply. A healthy diet means a varied diet: kidneys are a good source of iron, zinc and vitamin A. Lamb's kidneys are tender and cook very quickly. In this recipe they provide the basis of a rich sauce to serve with plain rice or noodles.

SERVES 4

8 lamb's kidneys
1 onion
2 cloves garlic, crushed
1 tablespoon wholemeal flour
5 fl oz (150 ml) red wine
1 tablespoon tomato purée

2 fl oz (50 ml) water
3 tablespoons finely chopped fresh parsley
1 teaspoon made English mustard
1 tablespoon lemon juice

If you object to the slightly bitter taste of kidneys, soak them in a little milk for about 20 minutes if you have time.

Grate the onion and sauté it in a little oil, then add the mashed garlic. Sprinkle in the flour and stir vigorously to blend it in. Add the red wine, purée, water, half the parsley, the mustard and lemon juice. Stir well again and let the sauce simmer for at least 5 minutes.

Meanwhile, pat the kidneys dry, then slice them thinly, cutting round the cores (discard these). Slip the kidneys into the pan and simmer for about 6 minutes. Serve very hot, sprinkled with the remaining parsley on a bed of spiced rice or plain noodles.

CHICKEN LIVERS
WITH SAGE AND ORANGE

Chicken livers are both cheap and a real fast food. In this recipe they are cooked in an aromatic red wine sauce spiked with sage and orange. Have all the ingredients chopped ready before you start: the livers cook so quickly that there is no time to prepare as you go.

Serve this dish on individual beds of plain rice and offer a green salad on the side, with a simple French dressing.

SERVES 4

1 lb (450 g) chicken livers (thawed, if frozen)
2 bunches spring onions
15 fresh sage leaves or 1½ teaspoons dried sage
1 orange
2 tablespoons plain flour, preferably wholemeal
Salt

Freshly ground black pepper
1 tablespoon olive oil
5 fl oz (150 ml) red wine
3 fl oz (75 ml) stock or water
1 tablespoon soy sauce

GARNISH
1 tablespoon finely chopped fresh parsley

Line a platter with kitchen paper. Trim the livers, removing any traces of green (the bitter-flavoured bile duct), and put them on the platter. Chop the spring onions very finely – include all the green part. Chop the sage leaves finely. Grate the zest from the orange and squeeze the juice. Spread another piece of kitchen paper with the flour and season it lightly with salt and freshly ground black pepper. Dust each chicken liver very lightly with the seasoned flour.

Heat a tablespoon of olive oil in a large, shallow sauté or frying pan. Slide in the chicken livers and cook them on a moderate heat for about a minute and a half each side, or until they have a golden crust. Now, working quickly, add the chopped spring onions, the sage leaves, orange zest, orange juice, red wine, stock or water and soy sauce. Bring the liquid to a simmer. Cook the livers, uncovered, for about 5 minutes, turning them frequently. They are ready when no more blood appears on the surface: they should be firm on the outside and pale pink-brown inside. The sauce should now be reduced and syrupy – give it a few more moments under a high heat if it is still too thin. Serve immediately, garnished with the chopped parsley.

LITTLE TURKEY SCALLOPS WITH ROSEMARY

Turkey breast fillet is now widely available in supermarkets (or of course you can cut your own from a whole bird or part-joint). In this recipe the fillets are sliced wafer thin: 2 fillets will easily feed 4 people. The meat cooks in only 4 minutes and the sauce takes only a minute more. The strongly aromatic flavour of rosemary is a perfect partner to the mild flavour of the turkey. Serve it with potato purée and cabbage and carrot salad (see pages 201, 211).

SERVES 4

2 turkey breast fillets (each about 8 oz or 225 g)
2 to 3 tablespoons plain flour
Black pepper
A little salt
2 tablespoons olive oil
2 tablespoons lemon juice

4 fl oz (100 ml) chicken stock
2 tablespoons finely chopped fresh rosemary, or 1 teaspoon dried

GARNISH
A few extra rosemary sprigs

Each turkey breast has an easily visible tendon running down the middle. Slice the breast in half along this line and pull or cut the tendon out. Cut each half in half again across its width. Now, using a very sharp, slim knife held parallel to the chopping board, cut each piece into wafer-thin slices. Each breast should yield about 12 small scallops.

Shake the flour on to a piece of kitchen paper and grind on plenty of black pepper and a mean amount of salt. Dust each little scallop on both sides with the flour.

Heat the olive oil in a medium-sized non-stick sauté pan over a medium heat. Slide in the turkey slices. Allow about 2 minutes each side; flip them over with a palette knife when they look golden. Cook them in batches if necessary, and keep them warm for a moment.

Now add the lemon juice, stock and rosemary to the pan, mixing it well. Let it bubble for a few seconds, then slip the scallops back into the pan. Simmer for about 10 seconds, then serve immediately, garnishing the dish with a few extra spikes of rosemary.

BREAST FILLET OF DUCK
WITH ORANGE AND CRANBERRY SAUCE

Duck is expensive, but as an occasional treat it is worth cooking well. The skin is exceptionally fatty, and in this recipe most of it is discarded. The duck is roasted quickly in the oven and served with an easily made delicate, fruity sauce which offsets it perfectly. Serve it with jacket potatoes slashed then topped with a rosette of fromage blanc and some green peas. This recipe also works very well with chicken breast.

SERVES 4

4 duck breast fillets	Freshly ground black pepper
2 oranges	1 tablespoon soy sauce
2 lemons	1 teaspoon chopped fresh sage, or
2 tablespoons cranberry sauce	½ teaspoon dried
3 fl oz (75 ml) apple juice	2 teaspoons cornflour
3 fl oz (75 ml) chicken stock	

Pre-heat the oven to Gas Mark 6, 400° F, 200° C, and have a baking tray ready. Cut the skin away from the lean meat. Keep a few strips of the thin part of the skin to lay on top of each breast. Discard the rest. Put the fillets with their strips of skin on the baking tray in the oven to roast for 25 minutes, removing the skin for the last 15 minutes of cooking time.

While the duck is cooking, grate or pare the zest of the oranges and lemons. Squeeze the juice from the pared fruit and add it to the cranberry sauce with the apple juice, stock, pepper, soy sauce, sage and cornflour in a small saucepan. Bring to the boil, then let the sauce simmer and reduce. There should be just enough to put about 1½ tablespoons on each plate.

Check that the duck breasts are cooked. Remove them from the oven and pat them free of fat. Pour off all the fat from the baking dish, scrape the juices into the sauce and heat it again. Slice each breast into neat diagonal slices, then fan the slices out on to individual well-warmed plates. Trickle a little sauce over each serving and bring it to the table immediately.

STIR-FRIED PORK WITH SPRING ONIONS AND CARROTS

The actual cooking of this easy dish takes only a few minutes. As with all Chinese-based stir-fried dishes, the time is taken in careful pre-paration. Cut the ingredients scrupulously to the same size and have everything ready before you begin.

SERVES 4

12 oz (350 g) pork fillet

MARINADE
1 tablespoon soy sauce
1 teaspoon cornflour
1 tablespoon dry sherry
½ teaspoon sugar

½-inch (1-cm) cube fresh ginger
1 clove garlic
2 young carrots
1 green pepper
6 spring onions
2 teaspoons corn oil
5 fl oz (170 ml) stock or water

Slice the pork fillet along its length several times, but keep it in its original shape. Now cut it horizontally into wafer-thin strips. Mix the marinade ingredients and pour them over the pork. Stir well and set aside for 10 minutes.

Meanwhile, peel and grate the ginger and mash the garlic. Cut the carrot into the thinnest possible matchstick strips. Cut the green pepper in half. De-seed it, remove the membranes and cut into tidy matchstick strips. Chop the spring onions into one-inch lengths diagonally. Heat a teaspoon of the corn oil in a wok (or deep frying pan) and add the ginger and garlic, stir-frying for about 30 seconds. Now add the pepper and carrots and stir-fry them, turning vigorously all the time, for 2 minutes. Remove them from the pan and set aside for a moment.

Add the remaining teaspoon of oil to the wok or pan and put in the pork with all its marinade juices. Stir-fry for 2 minutes, then add the cooked vegetables and the stock or water. Reduce the heat, add the spring onions, stir carefully, cover and cook for a further minute.

Serve with plain rice and a chunky, hearty salad or stir-fried courgettes (see page 198).

PORK TENDERLOIN
WITH ORANGE AND MINT

Pork tenderloin is an exceptionally lean cut which lends itself well to fast cooking. In this recipe the meat is partnered by a piquant, lively sauce which includes orange, fresh ginger and mint. The sauce is assembled first; the pork itself takes only about 3 minutes to cook.

SERVES 4

1 pork tenderloin about 1 lb (450 g) in weight

SEASONED FLOUR MIXTURE
1 tablespoon cornflour or plain flour
1 tablespoon ground cumin
1 tablespoon paprika
Freshly ground black pepper

SAUCE MIXTURE
Grated zest of one orange
Juice of two oranges
1 tablespoon finely chopped fresh mint, or 1 teaspoon dried
2 teaspoons soy sauce
1-inch (2-cm) cube fresh ginger, grated, or a pinch of dried ginger
2 garlic cloves, mashed
6 fl oz (175 ml) stock

GARNISH
A few extra leaves of fresh mint (or substitute parsley if fresh mint is not available)

Trim any visible fat from the meat. Slice it, slightly on the diagonal, into wafer-thin rounds. Mix all the seasoned flour ingredients together and use the mixture to dust the meat slices. Set them aside for a moment. Mix all the sauce ingredients together. Heat a non-stick frying pan and brush it with a little sunflower oil. Put in the meat and let it brown briskly on both sides (about a minute each side), then turn down the heat to very low and let the meat cook for another minute.

Transfer to a warmed dish and keep hot. In the same pan, add the sauce, stirring hard to incorporate all the meat juices. Let it bubble and reduce until it becomes thick and syrupy. Slip the meat back into the pan for about 20 seconds under a low heat. Garnish with more fresh mint, if available, or parsley if not. Serve with plain or spiced rice and a green salad.

PORK AND MUSHROOM KEBABS WITH FRESH SAGE AND GINGER

This is a quick and 'healthy' way of serving a lean cut of pork. It is coated with a strong marinade (the intense flavour means the meat does not need to be marinated for a long time), then threaded on to skewers and grilled. Fresh sage makes an ideal partner to pork. Unlike many of the most useful herbs, sage is evergreen and will go on providing leaves through the winter (when the taste is also less strong). In the summer, this is a perfect recipe for outdoor cooking.

Note: flat skewers are easier to handle than round ones: the meat is more likely to stay in place.

SERVES 4

MARINADE
2 × 1-inch (2-cm) cubes fresh ginger
Generous squeeze garlic purée or 3 cloves garlic
10 fresh sage leaves, or 1 teaspoon dried

3 tablespoons lemon juice
2 teaspoons soy sauce
1 tablespoon olive oil

1 lb (450 g) pork tenderloin
4 oz (110 g) button mushrooms

Make the marinade first. Grate the ginger, making sure you leave all the hairy fibres behind. Squeeze the garlic purée into the ginger, then add the sage leaves. Pound them to a paste with the garlic and ginger using a mortar and pestle (or alternatively chop the leaves into the garlic and ginger on a board). Add the lemon juice, soy sauce and olive oil. Transfer the marinade to a bowl.

Trim the meat of all the visible fat. Dice it into bite-sized cubes (not too small, as the meat will shrink) and drop it into the marinade with the button mushrooms. Turn it so that everything is well coated and leave for 10 minutes.

Pre-heat the grill. Thread the meat and mushrooms on to skewers. Grill for about 7 minutes, basting with the remaining marinade and turning frequently. The meat should be well browned on the outside. Serve with plain rice or warmed pitta bread and salad.

CHILLI CON CARNE

Like many another good dish that was originally the province of the poor, chilli con carne has turned affluent. The result is that the balance of meat to other ingredients has altered – so much so that in some recipes it is hard to spot the beans among the lavish quantities of meat. In this quick, simple recipe, the tables are turned. The meat plays second fiddle to the beans, making it both an economical and a tasty dish.

The amount of chilli seasoning suggested here will give a mild result, but if you can tolerate more, you could double or even treble it.

SERVES 4
generously

6 oz (175 g) lean minced beef
1 onion
1 teaspoon chilli seasoning (or to taste)
1 clove garlic, mashed

14-oz (450-g) tin tomatoes
2 tablespoons tomato purée
Black pepper to taste
2 × 14-oz (450-g) tins red kidney beans.

Heat a non-stick saucepan and sauté the meat under moderate heat until it changes colour and the fat runs out. Pour the fat off, or blot it up with kitchen paper. Add the sliced onion and stir-fry it with the chilli seasoning, garlic, chopped tomatoes with their juice, tomato purée and black pepper. Simmer, covered, for about 10 minutes, then uncovered for another 15 minutes. Drain the kidney beans and rinse them well under a cold tap. Add them to the meat mixture and simmer for another minute. Serve with plain rice.

Note: the flavour of this dish is improved by reheating.

SPICY MEATBALLS IN TOMATO SAUCE

Almost every country in the world has a meatball recipe. This is not surprising, as meatballs combine the virtues of being economical, simply made and hospitable to all kinds of interesting flavours. Now, the advent of the food processor means they can also be quickly prepared. The method given here assumes possession of a food processor. (A hand mincer is a good substitute but will obviously take much longer. Pass the meat through the mincer three times and knead the mixture well.)

SERVES 4

1 onion
2 cloves of garlic
8 oz (225 g) good quality minced beef
½ bunch fresh coriander or parsley
1 fresh chilli pepper, de-seeded
2 teaspoons plain yoghurt
4 tablespoons ground rice
1 tablespoon ground coriander
Freshly ground black pepper
A little salt

¼–½ teaspoon cayenne pepper
1 teaspoon paprika

FOR THE TOMATO SAUCE
1 onion
2 cloves garlic
14-oz (450-g) tin Italian tomatoes
1 tablespoon tomato purée
1 tablespoon ground coriander
Salt and pepper to taste

Make the meatballs first. Start by processing the two onions and the garlic finely; set aside half for the tomato sauce. Now add the meat, the coriander or parsley, the fresh de-seeded chilli, the yoghurt, ground rice, seasonings and spices. Process until the mixture has formed a soft, pliable ball round the blade. Dampen your hands and form the mixture into small balls – about the size of a large marble. With practice you can use both hands to make two at once. Heat a little oil in a large non-stick sauté pan and drop the balls into it, shaking the pan gently so that they roll about and become brown on all sides. Let them cook for about 3 minutes under a very low heat. Remove them from the pan and set them aside for a moment.

In the same pan, sauté the remaining onions and garlic which should immediately brown from the meat juices, and add the tomatoes with their juice, the purée and the ground coriander, with salt and pepper to taste. Let the sauce cook over a medium-high heat for 2 minutes, covered. Now transfer the sauce to the processor and process for a few seconds – it should not be entirely smooth. Return both sauce and meatballs to the pan. Bring the sauce to a bare simmer. Cover the pan tightly and cook for 20 minutes. Shake the pan gently, still covered, from time to time. (Taking off the lid would let out too much of the valuable steam which helps cook and tenderize the meatballs.)

Serve with plain noodles or rice and a simple green salad.

STIR-FRIED BEEF WITH MUSHROOMS

The fresh chilli and ginger give this Chinese-inspired dish its pungency and fragrance. All the ingredients can be prepared well in advance and kept, covered, in the refrigerator, ready for last-minute assembly. It is an equally good dish for a family supper or for entertaining friends. The rich, glossy-looking sauce speckled with green onions looks spectacular and needs only some plain boiled rice to set it off.

SERVES 4

1 clove garlic or a squeeze of garlic purée
1-inch (2-cm) cube fresh ginger
1 fresh green or red chilli
4 oz (110 g) dark-gilled mushrooms
6 spring onions
1 piece of sirloin steak, about 12 oz (350 g)

SAUCE MIXTURE
2 teaspoons soy sauce
1 teaspoon cornflour
½ teaspoon sugar
5 fl oz (150 ml) stock or water

1 tablespoon sunflower oil
2 tablespoons finely chopped fresh coriander or parsley

First, prepare all the vegetables. Peel and crush the garlic. Peel and grate the ginger. De-seed and finely chop the fresh chilli. Slice the mushrooms; chop the coriander and spring onions finely. Remove any fat from the beef and slice it into small, neat, evenly sized strips.

Now prepare the liquid for the sauce. Mix the soy sauce, cornflour, sugar, and stock or water. Heat the oil until it is sizzling in a wok or deep frying pan. Put in the crushed garlic and grated ginger and stir-fry for about half a minute. Now add the beef and stir-fry for about one minute. When it looks opaque, add the chilli and continue to stir-fry for another minute, turning the food all the time. Add the mushrooms and stir-fry for another minute. Now add the liquid mixture with the coriander and spring onions. Give another few fast turns, then cover the wok or pan, reduce the heat to a bare simmer and leave it for another minute, until the sauce is thick.

Serve piping hot with plain boiled rice.

PASTA AND RICE

When people are poor, they look for ways of eking out expensive and scarce meat or fish. In Asia and in the Mediterranean, cuisines evolved in which the meat, well-padded with vegetables, was the garnish to the rice or pasta rather than the meat being the centrepiece. As well as filling hungry bellies, this diet also has the virtue of providing the right sort of balance between fats and carbohydrates.

Fortunately for us, there is no penance in following suit. Some of the best food in the world comes from Italy, India and China. Pasta and rice also have the inestimable virtues of being quick to cook and trouble-free to prepare – no peeling, chopping or dicing. We eat pasta at least twice a week, and my general aim is to have the sauce ready in the time it takes for the pasta to cook. I have included several recipes of this type here.

Most cookery books maintain the fiction that their readers will want to cook pasta as a first course. I am assuming that this will only be the case when you want to dine elegantly. For those who are just eating an ordinary supper, pasta is a perfect main dish, and these are the quantities I have catered for in the recipes. You may use brown or white pasta as you please, but brown pasta is really best reserved for strong-tasting sauces.

Rice needs just a little more care than pasta. Brown rice takes twice as long as white to cook. These recipes assume shortage of time, so the cooking times refer to white rice. Brown rice may be substituted in any of them when you have more time.

SPAGHETTI WITH ANCHOVIES AND OLIVES

The popular name of this Roman dish is *Spaghetti alla puttanesca* – 'Harlot's Spaghetti'. It is hot, spicy, quickly made, and goes as well with wholewheat as with white spaghetti. The robust combination of ingredients means that Parmesan cheese is not usually sprinkled on top.

One of the many virtues of this dish is that, apart perhaps from the chillies, most of the ingredients could well be store-cupboard items. Beware of adding any more salt – many of the ingredients already contain it. Don't add salt to the spaghetti water either.

SERVES 4

8 anchovy fillets
3 oz (75 g) large black olives
1 tablespoon capers
2 large fresh chillies
4 garlic cloves, crushed
14-oz (450-g) tin Italian tomatoes
1 teaspoon tomato purée

1 teaspoon dried oregano or 1
   dessertspoon fresh chopped
   marjoram
1 lb (500 g) spaghetti
2 tablespoons fresh parsley, finely
   chopped

Drain the anchovies and drop them into a basin of water to soak. This removes excessive saltiness. Stone the olives and chop them, drain the capers. De-seed the chillies and chop them. Heat the oil and add the chilli with the crushed garlic. Turn them in the heat for a few moments, then add the tomatoes, with their juice, the tomato purée, oregano or marjoram, olives and capers. Raise the heat until the sauce is bubbling, then reduce the heat and let it simmer for about 10 minutes. Start cooking the spaghetti about half way through this stage. When the sauce is well thickened, add the drained anchovies and mash them into the sauce. Drain the spaghetti, return it to the pan, add half the sauce with the parsley and toss. Serve on well-warmed individual deep plates with a little of the remaining sauce on each.

SPAGHETTI WITH MUSHROOM SAUCE

This is a spaghetti dish served with a rich, earthy-looking dark brown and green sauce. The sauce can be made from start to finish while the spaghetti is cooking. Use any mixture of your favourite fresh herbs for the sauces – even fresh parsley on its own is better than dried herbs. I don't think this sauce needs salt, but taste it before serving and add it if you wish.

SERVES 4

1 lb (500 g) spaghetti
2 medium onions
2 cloves garlic
12 oz (350 g) flat mushrooms
5 fl oz (150 ml) chicken stock
1 bunch fresh mixed herbs, e.g.,
  parsley, coriander, lovage,
  thyme

1 bunch spring onions
1 tablespoon low-fat soft cheese
Black pepper and salt to taste

TO SERVE
Parmesan cheese to taste

Put the spaghetti into plenty of boiling water.

Chop the onion and garlic finely and sweat it till just golden, about 5 minutes. Meanwhile roughly chop the mushrooms. Add them to the onions, turning them briskly for a few minutes. Add the chicken stock and simmer for a minute. Finely chop the herbs and spring onions, and add them to the sauce with the low-fat soft cheese. Simmer for another 5 minutes, boiling down the amount of liquid if necessary. Drain the spaghetti, then return it to the pan. Add about half the sauce to the spaghetti, tossing it well with black pepper (and salt if you wish). Serve the spaghetti on heated plates, adding some of the remaining sauce on top of each one. Hand the Parmesan cheese separately.

SPAGHETTI ALLA CARBONARA

I once heard this dish described as 'Italian eggs and bacon', but it is nothing like so greasy a meal as that suggests, especially if, as here, you omit the cream they often add in Italy. Its classic simplicity means that it also makes very fast food.

Spaghetti alla carbonara is usually served as a first course in Italy, but with the quantities increased it also makes an excellent main dish. Following it with a crunchy salad to contrast in texture provides a satisfying meal.

SERVES 4

4 oz (110 g) unsmoked back bacon
3 garlic cloves
1 lb (500 g) spaghetti
3 eggs
6 tablespoons grated Parmesan
  cheese

3 tablespoons skimmed milk
Generous quantity of black pepper
Salt to taste
Extra Parmesan cheese to serve

161

Put the spaghetti in a large pan of rapidly boiling water. It will take anything from 6 to 12 minutes to cook, depending on age and brand. Remove the visible fat from the bacon; dice the lean meat. Heat a non-stick saucepan and put in the bacon without adding any fat. After a few minutes, when enough fat has run out from the bacon, add the whole peeled garlic cloves. Cook, stirring often, until the bacon is crisp. Discard the garlic. Drain the bacon on kitchen paper.

Crack the eggs into a basin and add the cheese, milk, black pepper and salt to taste. Beat this mixture very lightly.

Drain the cooked spaghetti and return it to its pan on a low heat. Add the cooked, garlicky bacon and mix it into the spaghetti for about a minute. Turn off the heat and add the egg and cheese mixture to the spaghetti, tossing it thoroughly. The heat from the spaghetti is all that is needed to cook the egg. Serve immediately on deep, well-warmed plates with extra Parmesan cheese on top.

SPAGHETTI WITH SWEET ONIONS AND MUSHROOMS

This pasta dish rivals Spaghetti alla carbonara in its speed and simplicity. The sauce is basically a huge quantity of onions rendered meltingly sweet by rapid stir-frying in a deep pan with a dash of stock, and a generous quantity of parsley added later. The sauce can be made from start to finish while the spaghetti is cooking.

SERVES 4

1 lb (500 g) spaghetti
2 lb (1 kg) onions
6 oz (175 g) button mushrooms
1 tablespoon ground coriander
6 fl oz (160 ml) good stock
    (preferably brown)

Freshly ground black pepper
4 tablespoons finely chopped fresh
    parsley
Pinch of salt
Parmesan cheese to taste

Put the spaghetti into boiling water. Slice the onions finely (use a food processor if you have one). Cut the mushrooms in half. Choose a deep non-stick pan and heat a tablespoon of olive oil in it over a brisk heat. Add the onions and stir-fry vigorously for about 4 minutes. The onions will change from white to cream to gold. They will be much

162

reduced in bulk. Do not let them burn – keep turning, lifting and stirring. When they are deep gold, add the mushrooms and stir-fry for another minute, then the coriander and stir-fry over a moderate heat for a few seconds. Now add the stock, raise the heat and let the sauce bubble until it is thick and there is only a little liquid left. Grind on plenty of black pepper and add about half the parsley and a pinch of salt to taste. Cook, uncovered, on a low heat for another minute. Drain the cooked spaghetti and return it to the pan. Pour on the sauce and toss well with the heat very low for a few seconds. Serve with the Parmesan cheese and remaining parsley sprinkled on top.

SPAGHETTI WITH MUSSELS

Fresh mussels are an underrated and cheap delicacy in Britain. Tender, sweet, freshly cooked mussels are nothing like the rubbery tasteless blobs that come out of jars in vinegar and brine (though tinned mussels, I admit, are much better if you can find them). Pasta and shellfish always make a happy combination, especially in a really simple sauce like this.

SERVES 4

1 lb (500 g) spaghetti
2 quarts fresh mussels (or a 1-kilo bag)
A little white wine or water: enough to cover the bottom of the pan
3 large onions

3 cloves garlic (crushed) or a generous squeeze of garlic purée
5 tablespoons chopped fresh parsley or coriander
2 teaspoons lemon juice
Freshly ground black pepper

Time the spaghetti to coincide with the sauce being ready. (It will take from 6 to 12 minutes, depending on age and brand.)

Wash the mussels in several changes of water to get rid of their sand and grit. Throw away any that float to the top. Scrape off their hairy beards. Discard any that are open and will not close when sharply tapped. Set them in a large lidded pan in two layers (cook them in batches if necessary). Pour over enough wine or water to come about half an inch up the pan. Bring to the boil, then reduce to a bare simmer, cover and cook for 6 minutes or until the mussels have opened.

Meanwhile, fine-chop the onions and sauté them for about 4 minutes in a teaspoon of olive oil in a non-stick saucepan, stirring them well to prevent sticking. Add the garlic purée in the last minute of cooking. Remove from the heat for a moment.

Strain and reserve the mussel liquor. Discard any mussels that have not opened. Set aside a few whole mussels for garnish. Take the rest out of their shells.

Add 10 fl oz (300 ml) of the liquor to the onions (make it up with water if necessary), then half the parsley, lemon juice, and a generous quantity of black pepper. Bring the sauce to the boil, and keep it boiling hard until it has reduced and thickened a little. Add the mussels at the very last moment – don't let them boil, just heat them enough to warm them through.

Drain the spaghetti, then return it to its pan. Add about half the mussel sauce and toss well. Serve the pasta on well-warmed individual plates with the rest of the sauce, the remaining parsley and the whole mussels on top.

SPAGHETTI WITH CLAM SAUCE

It is true that tinned fish is generally rather salty. However, the flavour is usually excellent, and of course there is also considerable saving in time. Clams are difficult to find fresh, so buying them tinned is often the only way to make this useful sauce.

This pasta dish can be on the table within about 15 minutes from starting. The sauce is made while the spaghetti is cooking.

SERVES 4

1 lb (500 g) spaghetti
2 large onions
2 cloves garlic, mashed
2 teaspoons ground coriander
1 tablespoon plain flour

5 fl oz (150 ml) white wine
10-oz (300 g) tin clams
Freshly ground black pepper
4 tablespoons finely chopped
  coriander

Set the spaghetti to cook in a pan of boiling water. Chop the onions finely. Brush out a non-stick pan with olive oil and sauté the onions until they soften. Add the garlic and ground coriander and cook for a further minute. Sprinkle in the flour, stir it well, then add the wine and half the liquid from the clams. Bring to a simmer and let the sauce thicken and reduce a little. Add some freshly ground black pepper, and three quarters of the finely chopped coriander and cook for a further 2 minutes. At the last moment add the clams. Stir well and let them heat through without boiling. Taste for seasoning: it should not need any more salt as there is plenty in the liquor. Drain the spaghetti. Toss it in half the clam sauce and put the spaghetti in a warmed serving dish with the rest of the sauce spooned on top. Sprinkle with the remaining coriander.

SPAGHETTI BOLOGNESE

Looking back through some 'classic' cookery books, I was surprised to see how much meat was recommended – even quite recently – for this useful and popular dish. One American recipe gave 1½ lbs for four people. Such an enormous amount of beef is undesirable on both health and cost grounds! This recipe uses a very small quantity of lean meat, simmered in a rich sauce of vegetables.

SERVES 4

6 oz (180 g) lean minced beef
2 carrots
2 celery sticks
2 onions
1 garlic clove, mashed
14 oz (450 g) tin tomatoes
2 tablespoons tomato purée
2 sprigs fresh thyme, leaves
    stripped, or ½ teaspoon dried

2 tablespoons finely chopped fresh
    parsley, or 2 teaspoons dried
Black pepper
5 fl oz (150 ml) red wine, stock or
    water
5 fl oz (150 ml) stock
1 lb (500 g) spaghetti
Parmesan cheese to taste

Spread the meat over the base of a non-stick pan and let it cook over a low heat for about 5 minutes without any additional fat. Meanwhile, grate the carrots, celery and onions (use a food processor if you have one). Sweat them with the garlic in another non-stick pan brushed with oil for about 5 minutes until they have softened. Use kitchen paper to blot up the fat from the meat, then add it to the vegetables with the tomatoes, purée, herbs, black pepper and wine, stock or water. Cover tightly and simmer for 15 minutes. Add a little water if the sauce seems too dry.

The sauce can be made in advance and re-heated, or kept just below simmering point for up to an hour. Time the spaghetti to be ready at the same time as the sauce. Check the sauce for seasoning and add salt if you wish. Serve on well-heated deep dishes with the Parmesan cheese handed separately.

PASTA BOWS WITH TOMATO AND MUSHROOM SAUCE

This is a simple, homely pasta dish made from fresh tomatoes and button mushrooms. The extra flavourings can be varied according to what you have in your store-cupboard. If fresh tomatoes are too dear, use the tinned variety, drained. The little ridges of pasta bows hold this kind of sauce beautifully, but you could also use twists or rigatoni instead.

SERVES 4

2 garlic cloves
1 tablespoon olive oil
2 thin slices unsmoked back bacon, fat removed
1 large onion
8 oz (250 g) small button mushrooms
1½ lb (700 g) ripe fresh tomatoes
½ teaspoon sugar
1 teaspoon lemon juice

1 tablespoon ground coriander
Freshly ground black pepper
1 tablespoon dried oregano or marjoram
2 tablespoons tomato purée
1 lb (500 g) pasta bows
Salt to taste
4 tablespoons grated Parmesan cheese

Peel the garlic cloves and let them sweat, without colouring, in the hot olive oil for about 4 minutes in a saucepan. Meanwhile, finely chop the bacon and onion; wipe the mushrooms and slice them finely. Dip the tomatoes into boiling water, then slip off their skins and chop them roughly. Remove the garlic cloves from the oil and discard them. Add the chopped bacon and onion to the oil and sauté them for a minute. Now add the mushrooms, raise the heat and stir-fry everything vigorously, turning constantly, for another 3 minutes, by which time the mushrooms should look golden and be much reduced in bulk. Add the chopped tomatoes with the sugar, lemon juice, coriander, ground pepper, oregano or marjoram and tomato purée; cover and simmer for another 10–15 minutes. The sauce should now be soft and juicy.

Time the pasta so that it is ready (cooking time varies according to size and manufacturer) at the same time as the sauce. Drain the pasta and return it to its pan. Taste the sauce and add salt if necessary, but remember that the cheese is salty. Add half the sauce and half the cheese to the pasta and toss it well. Serve the pasta on individual plates with a little extra sauce and Parmesan on top.

PASTA BOWS WITH SICILIAN SPINACH AND RICOTTA SAUCE

The fresh-tasting, creamy-textured sauce for this dish is made entirely with 'healthy' ingredients. If you cannot find Ricotta easily, use one of the other low-fat curd cheeses instead. This delicate sauce is also excellent with fresh pasta – fetuccine or spaghetti.

SERVES 4

1 lb (500 g) pasta bows
2 large onions
2 lb (1 kg) fresh spinach
1 tablespoon sunflower oil
¼ nutmeg

Pinch salt
Freshly ground black pepper
8 oz (250 g) Ricotta cheese
Grated Parmesan cheese to taste

Time the pasta to be ready at the same time as the sauce (cooking time varies according to size and manufacturer).

Chop the onions finely. Wash the spinach, then roll it up into a cigar shape. Fine-chop the stalks and roughly chop the leaves. Heat the tablespoon of oil in a large saucepan and stir-fry the onions briskly for about 3 minutes, until they are golden. Add the spinach, stirring it well into the onions. Reduce the heat immediately and put the lid on the pan. Cook for about 7 minutes, stirring occasionally. Grate the nutmeg into the pan, add a pinch of salt and plenty of ground black pepper. Turn the heat off. Crumble the Ricotta into the spinach sauce, then stir it in with a fork so that it is well incorporated. Drain the cooked pasta and return it to its pan. Pour the sauce over with a tablespoon of the grated Parmesan and toss the pasta well. Serve on well-heated plates with extra Parmesan sprinkled on top.

FRESH TAGLIATELLE WITH ROMAN DRESSING

Fresh pasta is now available in pasta shops, specialist delicatessens and large supermarkets. The taste is 'juicier' and stronger than that of dried, and it cooks in less than half the time: only 3 to 5 minutes. The sauce for this classic dish is really just an assembly job: the whole dish can be on the table in about 6 minutes.

SERVES 4

4 oz (110 g) cooked lean ham
4 oz (110 g) Parmesan cheese
1½ lb (750 g) fresh tagliatelle
Freshly ground black pepper

8 oz (225 g) frozen petits pois
8 tablespoons low-fat fromage blanc

Put the water on to boil for the pasta. Chop the ham very finely and grate the cheese if it is in a single piece. Boil the tagliatelle until it is *al dente*. Boil the peas for 2 minutes and drain. Drain the tagliatelle and return it to the pan. Add the ground black pepper, cooked peas, chopped ham, half the Parmesan cheese and all the fromage blanc and toss well. Serve on warmed plates with the extra Parmesan sprinkled on top.

TAGLIATELLE WITH COURGETTES

A simple, quick supper dish which also has the virtue of being cheap.

SERVES 4

1½ lb (750 g) young courgettes
1 large onion
1 lb (500 g) mixed green and white tagliatelle
3 cloves garlic, mashed
2 tablespoons white wine (stock or water can be substituted)

½ teaspoon chopped fresh sage, or ¼ teaspoon dried
1 tablespoon chopped fresh parsley
Freshly ground black pepper
A little salt
Parmesan cheese to taste

Wash, top and tail the courgettes. Cut each one into four, lengthways, then finely chop them horizontally. You should end up with a pile of small, neat, triangular pieces. Chop the onion finely. Put the pasta into a large pan of salted water and cook it vigorously (the time varies

– usually not more than 9 minutes, but consult the directions on the packet). Heat the oil in a saucepan and sauté the onion and garlic, stirring frequently. Now add the chopped courgettes and stir-fry for about 4 minutes or until the courgettes are just cooked. Add the wine and let it bubble fiercely for a moment, then turn down the heat and add the chopped sage, parsley, ground black pepper and a little salt.

Drain the cooked pasta and then return it to its saucepan. Add the courgette sauce, then some Parmesan cheese, and serve immediately with more Parmesan handed at the table.

PENNE (PASTA QUILLS) WITH RICOTTA AND PRAWNS

I first ate this dish at the home of the American painter Robin Richmond, who was brought up in Rome and now lives in London. Perhaps these cross-cultural influences are at work on her food, which is always wonderful.

In this dish a standard tomato sauce is thickened with Ricotta, though you can use another low-fat fresh cheese if Ricotta is unavailable. The modest quantity of prawns added at the last moment gives an interesting texture and excellent flavour. A chunky pasta such as penne (the quill-shaped variety) is best for this robust dish, but you could also use spaghetti or tagliatelle. Traditionally, Parmesan cheese is not offered with fish sauces on pasta in Italy, but I feel that this is a rule which it is often a pleasure to break.

SERVES 4

2 medium onions
3 cloves garlic
1 tablespoon olive oil
2 × 14-oz (450-g) tins tomatoes
2 tablespoons tomato purée
1 tablespoon chopped fresh basil, or 1 teaspoon dried
1 sprig fresh thyme, stripped from stalk, or ½ teaspoon dried

Ground pepper to taste
1 teaspoon sugar
1 lb (500 g) penne or other pasta
12 oz (350 g) Ricotta cheese
Grated Parmesan cheese to taste
4 oz (110 g) peeled frozen prawns, thawed

Begin by making the tomato sauce base. Chop the onions very finely and crush the garlic. Heat the oil and sauté the onions and garlic until they are well softened. Add the tomatoes with their juice, the purée, chopped herbs, pepper and sugar. Press the tomatoes gently to break them up, stir well and leave the sauce to cook on a medium heat, uncovered, for about 10 minutes. By this time it should have reduced to a thick, jam-like consistency. Meanwhile, put the pasta on to cook in a pan of boiling water.

Break up the Ricotta gently with a fork. Reduce the heat under the tomato sauce and incorporate the Ricotta into it a little at a time until it is well mixed. Add the Parmesan cheese and the prawns. Stir well, just enough to heat the prawns through. Check the seasoning and add salt if necessary. Drain the pasta and return it to the pan in which it cooked. Pour all the sauce over the pasta and mix it in thoroughly. Serve immediately on well-warmed deep plates. Offer extra Parmesan cheese at the table.

CHICKEN PILAU

This is a straightforward pilau whose spicy ingredients might well be varied according to what you have in the store cupboard. This one is gently flavoured, but you could add cayenne if you like 'hot' tastes. This is a tasty and economical way of using up cooked chicken.

SERVES 4
generously

3 onions

SPICES
1 teaspoon turmeric
1 teaspoon ground cloves
2 teaspoons cumin seeds
2 tablespoons ground coriander
Freshly ground black pepper

12 oz (350 g) basmati rice
4 tablespoons plain yoghurt
16 fl oz (400 ml) chicken stock

2 tablespoons chopped fresh
   coriander or parsley
3 tablespoons raisins
Pinch of salt
1 egg
1 tablespoon flaked almonds
6 oz (160 g) cooked skinless
   chicken

GARNISH
Extra fresh coriander or parsley

Chop one of the onions and fry it in the oil with all the spices for about 3 minutes over a medium heat. Wash the rice and add it to the pot, turning it to coat it well, then the yoghurt, the stock, the chopped fresh coriander or parsley, the raisins and a pinch of salt to taste. Bring to the boil, then reduce to a bare simmer and cover tightly. Cook for 16 minutes. Meanwhile, hard boil the egg; and fry the remaining onions in a teaspoonful of oil in a non-stick pan until they are well browned, stirring them all the time. Remove them from the pan and drain them on kitchen paper. Toast the flaked almonds in the same pan and drain them in the same way. Chop the cooked chicken into bite-sized chunks.

When the rice has been cooking for 16 minutes, carefully fold in the chicken, replace the lid and cook for another 5 minutes. Serve heaped in a mound on a warmed platter garnished with the browned onions, almonds, quartered egg and a little extra coriander or parsley. A tomato salad makes a good side dish.

RICE WITH SQUID AND MUSSELS

This tasty rice dish has no elaborate spices or herbs – its exquisite flavour comes from the sweet, delicate flavour of fresh mussels and squid. Preparing the mussels is fiddly, but the effort is worth it. The mussels are cooked first and their liquor retained to cook and flavour the rice. The excellent bags of Welsh mussels are so cheap that this is a reasonably economic dish for 4 people. Buying the squid ready-prepared in 'tubes' costs a little more, but saves time.

SERVES 4

2 quarts (1 kilo) bag fresh live mussels
10 fl oz (300 ml) of water
1 lb (450 g) prepared squid 'tubes'
12 oz (300 g) basmati or patna rice

3 medium onions
1 bunch parsley
1 bunch spring onions
2 tablespoons sunflower oil
Black pepper

Wash the mussels in several changes of water to get rid of their sand and grit. Throw away any that float to the top. Scrape off their hairy beards. Discard any that are open and will not close when sharply tapped. Heat the water in a large, lidded sauté pan. Put half the cleaned mussels in the pan, bring half the water to the boil, then reduce it to a simmer and put the lid on. Cook the mussels for about 5 minutes or until they open. Do not overcook. Strain the mussels in a fine sieve, retaining the liquor, and repeat the operation with the second half of the batch. Take the mussels out of their shells, leaving about 10 whole to garnish the dish later. Discard any mussels that have not opened. Measure the liquor in a jug and make it up to 16 fl oz (425 ml) if necessary with water.

While the mussels are cooking, prepare the squid by chopping it into fine rings. Wash the rice under the cold tap in a sieve until the water runs clear.

Slice the onions finely and fine-chop the parsley and spring onions, reserving a little of each for the garnish.

Heat the oil in a heavy flame-proof casserole and sauté the onion until it is golden brown. Add the squid, parsley, rice and mussel liquor. Bring the liquid to the boil, cover the casserole tightly (with foil or a tight-fitting lid) and reduce the heat immediately to a bare simmer. Leave it to cook absolutely undisturbed for 16 minutes. By this time all the liquid should be absorbed and the rice should be tender. (Alternatively, the dish may be transferred to a pre-heated oven at Gas Mark 3, 325° F, 170° C, for 25 minutes.) Grind some black pepper over the shelled mussels and fork them through the rice mixture gently but thoroughly. Transfer the food to a heated serving dish and garnish with the remaining mussels, parsley and spring onions.

Serve with peperonata (see pages 131–2).

RICE WITH MONKFISH AND HAKE

Recently we had a young friend living with us who declared that she would eat 'anything' except fish. She explained that she had had an unfortunate encounter with a fishy fish as a three-year-old; since then she had banned fish from her diet. This was a challenge I could not resist. Having successfully softened her up with the occasional fish pâté, I put this dish on the table while offering to cook her an omelette, which I took care to make sound very boring. The attractive pink and green of the rice obviously caught her eye. She refused the omelette and proceeded to have not just one but two helpings of the rice dish!

This is the kind of mixed fish and rice dish which is cooked and eaten all over the world wherever there is a coastline and easy access to rice. It is an economical way of 'stretching' expensive fish and also very healthy: no saturated fat, plenty of unrefined carbohydrate and a full-bodied flavour. I don't think this dish needs salt, but you could add a little to the cooking liquid if you are uncertain.

This dish takes about 45 minutes to prepare and cook, but it is worth the extra trouble.

SERVES 4
generously

1 monkfish tail, about 12 oz (350 g)
1 bay-leaf
5 medium onions
1 tablespoon chopped fresh dill, or 1 teaspoon dried
4 peppercorns
Juice and peel of 1 lemon
1 hake cutlet
12 oz (350 g) cod cutlet

12 oz (350 g) long-grain rice, preferably basmati
1 red pepper
1 tablespoon olive oil
2 teaspoons ground cumin
½ teaspoon ground black pepper
4 spring onions
8 oz (225 g) whole prawns
1 bunch fresh coriander or parsley

Put the monkfish in one piece in a pan with 8 fl oz (200 ml) of water, the bay-leaf, one of the onions cut roughly into 2 or 3 pieces, half the fresh dill (or ½ teaspoon of the dried), the peppercorns, the lemon juice and the lemon zest roughly chopped. Cover the pan, bring to the boil, then reduce the heat immediately till the water is barely trembling. After 4 minutes add the hake and cod, also in one piece, and poach for a further 2 minutes (this part can be done in a microwave). Carefully lift the fish out with a slotted spoon. Strain the liquid and set it aside for a moment. The fish should still be firm and only just opaque – slightly undercooked.

Meanwhile, slice the remaining onions and the de-seeded red pepper finely. Heat the oil in a flame-proof pan (choose one with a tight-fitting lid). Add the onions and red pepper. Stir-fry over a high heat for about 3 minutes, turning vigorously all the time. The onions should be a good golden-brown colour. Add the ground cumin and ground pepper and stir them in for a few seconds. Add the washed rice and the poaching liquid from the fish made up to 16 fl oz (425 ml) with water. Add the remaining dill. Cover the pan tightly, bring to the boil, then cook on the lowest possible heat for about 16 minutes. The rice mixture can also be cooked in the oven (see page 87). It will take 25 minutes in a pre-heated oven at Gas Mark 3, 325° F, 170° C. Finely chop the spring onions.

Cut the fish into bite-sized chunks and add it to the rice, which should be almost cooked with a little liquid left in the pan. Replace the lid and cook a further 3–5 minutes, when all the water should have been absorbed.

Peel half the prawns and reserve the remainder for garnish. At the last moment stir in the prawns just to heat them through. Add the chopped spring onions and coriander, reserving a little of both for garnish, and stir them well into the rice. Transfer the rice mixture to a large shallow dish and garnish with the remaining coriander, spring onions and whole prawns. Serve with a sharp salad of tomatoes dressed with oil and lemon juice, or endive, watercress and orange salad (see page 206).

MUSHROOM PILAU

This is an economical and spicy vegetarian rice dish, simple to assemble and cook as long as you have a good range of basic spices in your store cupboard.

SERVES 4

2 onions
2 cloves garlic
1-in (2.5-cm) cube fresh ginger
1 tablespoon ground coriander
1 tablespoon ground cumin
1 teaspoon ground turmeric
1 tablespoon paprika
6 cardamom pods
2 bay-leaves

1-in (2.5-cm) stick cinnamon
2 tablespoons sultanas or raisins
1 lb (450 g) mushrooms
12 oz (350 g) basmati or patna rice
18 fl oz (750 ml) stock or water
Salt to taste
2 small eggs
1 tablespoon finely chopped fresh
   coriander or parsley

Chop the onion and sauté it in a little oil until it begins to colour. Add the mashed garlic, the grated ginger, all the spices and the sultanas or raisins, stirring vigorously for about a minute. Slice the mushrooms and add them to the pan, then the washed rice. Add the stock or water and salt to taste, bring it to the boil, cover tightly and cook on the lowest possible heat for 20 minutes, when all the liquid should have been absorbed and the rice should be tender. While the rice is cooking, boil the eggs for 10 minutes, plunge them under cold water, shell and quarter them. Fork the rice mixture through gently and transfer to a warmed serving dish. Scatter the chopped coriander on top, add the quartered eggs, and serve with a tomato salad and a spicy chutney.

RED RISOTTO

This thick, warm-looking Italian risotto is studded with broccoli and red pepper, entirely meat-free but very filling. The secret is the hearty tomato sauce which forms the basis of the stock and gives the rice its glowing colour.

SERVES 4

3 medium onions
2 cloves garlic
14-oz (450-g) tin tomatoes
1 teaspoon dried oregano
Freshly ground black pepper
½ teaspoon sugar
2 tablespoons tomato purée

1½–2 pints (1–1.25 l) chicken stock
1 tablespoon olive oil
8 oz (225 g) broccoli
1 red pepper
12 oz (350 g) Italian rice
2 oz (50 g) freshly grated Parmesan
   cheese

Make a basic tomato sauce by sautéing the chopped onions, then adding garlic, tomato, dried oregano and freshly ground black pepper and sugar. Simmer for 3 minutes. Put the tomato purée into a measuring jug and make up the liquid to the 2-pint (1-litre) level by adding the stock. Mix well.

Heat a little olive oil in a deep pan and sauté the broccoli and red pepper for a few minutes. Add the Italian rice and sauté for about a minute – just enough to coat it thoroughly. Now add the tomato stock a ladleful at a time, stirring constantly. Keep adding the stock over a medium heat until the rice is cooked and creamy (about 25 minutes). Add more water if necessary. At the last moment stir in the Parmesan cheese. Serve immediately with a green salad.

PRAWN PILAU

This pleasant, spicy rice dish makes good use of frozen prawns. Generous use of spices means that it should not need salt, but add it if you wish.

SERVES 4

2 large onions
10 oz (275 g) basmati or patna rice
15 fl oz (400 ml) stock
8 oz (225 g) frozen prawns,
  defrosted

SPICES AND FLAVOURINGS
3 cloves garlic
1-in (2-cm) cube ginger
2 green chillies

2 tablespoons finely chopped fresh
  coriander
4 cardamom pods
1-in (2.5-cm) stick cinnamon
1 teaspoon ground cumin seeds
1 teaspoon turmeric

GARNISH
A few extra coriander leaves

Slice the onions finely. Brush out a non-stick pan with a little oil and brown the onions well. Now prepare the spices and flavourings: mash the garlic, grate the ginger, de-seed and chop the chilli. Mix these with the chopped coriander, cracked cardamom pods, whole cinnamon, turmeric, ground cloves and cumin seeds. Remove the onions from the pan and set them aside for a moment. Brush out a heavy, lidded pan with a little oil, add all the spices and flavourings and stir-fry them vigorously for about 10 seconds. Now add the washed rice and half the browned onions and stir everything gently to incorporate it. Add the stock and bring it to the boil. Put the lid on, reduce the heat to a bare minimum and cook undisturbed for 16 minutes. Now add the prawns, forking them through to heat them. Replace the lid and leave the pilau to stand for another 4 minutes. Turn the pilau out on to a warmed platter, heaping it up in the centre. Sprinkle the remaining browned onions on top and add a few whole coriander leaves to garnish. Serve with a tomato and onion salad.

SPICED RICE

This rice is good enough to eat on its own, or you could finish it off with a home-made tomato sauce for a more complete meal. It is also a perfect accompaniment to meat or vegetable dishes made with a moist sauce. It may seem as if there are a lot of ingredients, but if you have a good basic stock of spices, that should not present too much of a problem.

SERVES 4

1 onion
1 green or red chilli
½-inch (1-cm) cube peeled fresh
   ginger
1 clove mashed garlic
1 tablespoon ground coriander
2 teaspoons ground cumin
1 teaspoon ground cloves
4 cardamom pods (just use the
   seeds)

1 teaspoon ground turmeric
1 bay-leaf
12 oz (350 g) rice
18 fl oz (750 ml) stock
3 oz frozen peas

GARNISH
1 tablespoon finely chopped fresh
   coriander or parsley

Slice the onion, chop the chilli and peeled ginger, and remove the cardamom seeds from their pods. Brush out a heavy, lidded pan with oil and sauté the onion, chilli and ginger until the onion begins to colour. Now add the garlic, ground coriander, cumin, cloves, cardamom seeds, turmeric and bay-leaf. Stirring all the time, cook on a gentle heat for another minute. Wash the rice and add it to the pan with the stock. Add salt if you wish, though a spicy dish like this is perfectly all right with little or none. Bring to the boil, cover tightly (drape the lid with foil if necessary) and lower the heat to the bare minimum. Cook, undisturbed, for 20 minutes. Run the peas under a hot tap for a moment to thaw them if they are still frozen. Stir them into the cooked rice and let it stand for 5 minutes. Garnish with the finely chopped coriander and serve.

FISH

Fish and healthier eating make perfect partners. Fish is one of the few foods which is still hunted: it is therefore less likely to be messed about with additives, hormones and preservatives. It contains little saturated fat and offers an enormous range of flavours and textures.

For the cook, fish has two other tremendous advantages. First, unlike meat, it is always tender and never toughens during cooking (the only exception is shellfish). Second, it is astonishingly quick to cook. Even a 3-pound whole fish can be steamed and on the table in less than half an hour. Indeed, the only danger with fish is *over-cooking*.

This section suggests a range of quick and reliable ways of cooking fish. Some of the recipes involve 20 minutes or so in a hot oven; in others the fish is ready in less than 5 minutes. Most of these recipes are very straightforward. Good fish is best complemented by the simplest of added flavourings.

ST CLEMENT'S PLAICE

This method of cooking plaice fillets couldn't be simpler: a swift bath in a marinade of orange and lemon juice followed by a 4-minute session under the grill. Plain steamed or boiled potatoes and a colourful salad of varied lettuces are all this dish needs to accompany it.

SERVES 4

MARINADE
2 large oranges
2 lemons
5 fl oz (150 ml) white wine
1 teaspoon soy sauce

1 tablespoon finely chopped fresh
  parsley
Freshly ground black pepper

8 plaice fillets
2 teaspoons olive oil

Cut a thin sliver from one orange and one lemon, cut each sliver in half and set them aside to garnish. To make the marinade, squeeze the juice from the oranges and lemons and mix it with the wine, soy sauce, chopped parsley and freshly ground black pepper in a shallow dish which will take the fish in one layer. Place the fish skin side up in the marinade and set it aside for 15 or 20 minutes (though it will not come to any harm if you leave it for up to an hour). Use the marinating time to cook any accompanying vegetables or to prepare a salad. Pre-heat the grill to high. Spread foil over the grill-pan – this makes it easier to handle the fish later. Lift the fish out of the marinade and put it skin side down on the foil. Pour the olive oil into a cup and use a pastry brush to paint the fish with it. Grill the fish for 4 minutes, until the top is just flecked with brown. While it is cooking, pour the marinade into a saucepan and let it boil fiercely for a few minutes until it is thick and syrupy. Serve the fish on individual well-warmed plates with a little of the sauce spooned over. Garnish with the slivers of orange and lemon.

GRILLED WHOLE PLAICE

Whole plaice are usually among the cheapest fish you can buy. Look for stiff, bright-looking fish and ask the fishmonger to clean and behead them for you. The flavour of the whole fish is always better than that of the same fish filleted. This simple, speedy and straight-forward way of cooking plaice is one of my favourites.

SERVES 4

4 cleaned plaice with heads and fins removed.

Generous squeeze garlic purée, or 2 large very well-crushed cloves garlic

2 tablespoons olive oil

Freshly ground black pepper

GARNISH
1 tablespoon finely chopped fresh parsley
Lemon wedges

Pre-heat the grill. Pat the plaice dry with kitchen paper, then put them on a sheet of oiled foil, dark-skin side up. Blend the garlic purée well with the oil and black pepper. Brush half of the garlicky oil over the fish. Grill the first side for about 2 minutes. Turn the fish over very carefully (use two fish slices). Brush the white-skin side with the remaining oil. Grill for 3 minutes or until it is faintly brown. Sprinkle with parsley and serve with lemon wedges.

FISH PLAKI

The Greeks have a fool-proof method of cooking firm fish. 'Plaki' means that the fish is cooked in a thick, garlicky tomato sauce with onions. Don't hold back on either the parsley or the garlic.

SERVES 4

About 2 lbs (900 g) of any large, firm fish, e.g., bream or brill; or 4 smaller fish, e.g., grey mullet or snapper
Juice of 1 lemon
2 medium onions
3 large garlic cloves

14-oz (450-g) tin tomatoes
Pinch of salt
Ground black pepper
4 tablespoons chopped fresh parsley
3 tablespoons white wine or water

Pre-heat the oven to Gas Mark 5, 375° F, 190° C. Make sure the fish has been thoroughly scaled and gutted. Rinse it, pat it dry, then squeeze the lemon juice all over the inside and outside. Put it in an oven-proof dish just large enough to hold it. Slice the onions and sauté them for a few moments in the oil. Add the mashed garlic cloves and cook for a few moments more. Don't let them colour. Add the drained tomatoes (keep the juice for another dish) and mash them down. Simmer, uncovered, for about 5 minutes. Now add the salt, pepper and parsley. Cook for a minute longer, mixing well. Turn the heat off and add the wine.

Now pour the sauce over and around the fish. Cover the dish with foil and bake in the pre-heated oven for 40 minutes. Serve with baked potatoes.

COD WITH MUSHROOMS AND BACON

Cod is enhanced if it has strong flavours to partner it. In this dish, bacon, mushrooms and herbs do the trick. This is a good recipe to liven up frozen cod.

SERVES 4

4 flat mushrooms
1 onion

1 tablespoon chopped fresh parsley

1 tablespoon chopped fresh dill, or
½ teaspoon dried
Freshly ground black pepper
5 fl oz (150 ml) white wine or water

4 thinly cut pieces unsmoked back
bacon
4 pieces cod fillet (thawed, if
frozen)

Pre-heat the oven to Gas Mark 4, 350° F, 180° C. Cut off and dice the mushroom stalks. Finely chop the onions and sauté them in a little oil. Add the finely chopped parsley and dill, the diced mushroom stalks, ground black pepper and wine or water. Simmer for 2 minutes.

Choose a shallow oven-proof dish which will just hold the fish. Trim the fat off the bacon and lay the pieces in the bottom of the dish. Put each piece of fish neatly on top of one of the bacon pieces. Now pour the sauce around the fish and put one mushroom cap on top of each fillet, dark side down. Cover the dish tightly with foil and cook in the pre-heated oven for 15 minutes. Lift each piece of fish out carefully with its bacon, topped by a mushroom (serve dark side up) on to well-warmed plates. Put about a spoonful of the herby sauce on each serving and set aside in a warm place. Quickly heat up the remaining sauce and boil it fiercely to reduce it. Check the seasoning and add salt if necessary. Sieve the sauce and pour a little round each fish. Serve with glazed carrots, peas and chunky wholemeal bread to mop up the juices. If you prefer a thicker sauce, it could be thickened at the final stage with a little plain flour, made into a paste with a few drops of cold water.

COD PORTUGUESE STYLE

The cuisine of Portugal is not tremendously exciting, but the Portuguese do have innumerable interesting ways of cooking the cod that frequent their Atlantic waters. This is *the* classic Portuguese cod dish. It is amazingly quick and easy, and very good to eat. It is also an excellent way to use frozen cod – but this must be defrosted first and patted dry, otherwise it gives off far too much liquid.

SERVES 4

1 small (7-oz, 200-g) tin tomatoes
2 cloves garlic, crushed
2 sprigs fresh thyme, leaves
  stripped, or ½ teaspoon dried
2 tablespoons finely chopped fresh
  parsley, or 2 teaspoons dried

5 fl oz (150 ml) wine (preferably
  red, but white will do) or water
Black pepper to taste
4 thick cod fillets

Rub the tomatoes through a sieve into a bowl. Add the crushed garlic, thyme, parsley, wine and black pepper. Stir well. Pat the fish dry and place it in a lidded sauté or heavy frying pan in one layer. Pour the sauce around and over the fish. Bring the sauce to the boil, then immediately reduce the heat so that the sauce barely trembles. Cover and cook for 8–10 minutes, or until the fish is just opaque. Lift the fish out gently with a fish slice on to a warmed serving dish and put it in a warm place for a moment. Raise the heat and boil the sauce down a little until it is thick. Check for seasoning, adding salt if necessary, then pour over the fish. Serve with plain boiled potatoes in their skins and French peas (see page 197).

COD BAKED IN PIQUANT SAUCE

Even at Billingsgate, the great London fish market, apparently overflowing with fish of every shape, size and colour from all over the world, three quarters of what is sold is cod, plaice or haddock. This, apparently, is because we customers are so unadventurous in our choices. However, at least it is always possible to buy cod, and even frozen cod can be very good. The meaty, sweet flavour and delicate texture of cod are enhanced by oven-baking in a rich sauce. This one is a thick tomato-based sauce with parsley, ginger and chilli, which lend flavour that is piquant but not too 'hot'. No fat is added to this dish.

SERVES 4

SAUCE
7-oz (200-g) tin tomatoes
2 × 1-in (2-cm) cubes fresh ginger
1 medium onion
Generous squeeze of garlic purée,
  or 3 cloves fresh garlic, mashed
1 tablespoon tomato purée

1 tablespoon lemon juice
1 tablespoon soy sauce
½ teaspoon chilli powder
2 tablespoons finely chopped fresh
  parsley
4 cod fillets (thawed, if frozen)

Pre-heat the oven to Gas Mark 8, 450° F, 230° C. Discard about half the juice in the tin of tomatoes (keep it for stock). Pass the rest, with the tomatoes, through a sieve into a large saucepan. Now grate the ginger and onion into the tomato, add the garlic, tomato purée, lemon juice, soy sauce, chilli powder and finely chopped parsley and stir well. Add salt if you wish. To save time you may use a processor or blender for the sauce – drop the parsley in whole – but it produces a rather over-smooth texture. Tuck the fish into a shallow oven-proof dish in one layer – choose the size so that the fish pieces just fit.

Bring the sauce to the boil in the pan and let it simmer for about a minute. Now spoon it on to the fish. Cover the top loosely with foil and bake in the pre-heated oven for 20 minutes or until the fish is opaque and flakes easily. Serve with plain boiled potatoes in their skins and green beans.

TROUT WITH GREEN STUFFING

Good-quality farmed trout are readily available all the year round. Their delicate flavour and texture are enhanced by this aromatic and gently flavoured stuffing. The stuffed trout are tucked into a shallow oven-proof dish covered in foil and baked quickly in the oven. The result is a tender, juicy fish with a fragrant stuffing. If you are short of time the fish need not be filleted: the result is still good.

SERVES 4

4 trout, cleaned

FOR THE STUFFING
3 oz (75 g) fresh wholemeal bread
½ packet or ½ bunch watercress
3 teaspoons capers
3 tablespoons lemon juice
3 spring onions

2 tablespoons chopped fresh tarragon, or 2 teaspoons dried
1 stick celery

2 tablespoons white wine
Ground black pepper
Salt

If you have time, remove the backbone from the fish. This gives a larger pocket for the stuffing and makes the fish easier to eat. Leave on the heads and tails. Rinse the fish inside and out and pat them dry. Pre-heat the oven to Gas Mark 8, 450° F, 230° C. Now make the stuffing: blend or process all the stuffing ingredients – the texture should be fairly chunky. Fill each fish, but beware of overpacking the stuffing. Place the fish head to tail in a shallow oven-proof dish that just fits them. Trickle the wine around the fish. Grind on plenty of black pepper and a very sparse sprinkling of salt. Tuck a lightly oiled piece of greaseproof paper over the top of the fish, then cover the dish tightly with foil.

Put the dish in the oven and reduce the heat to Gas Mark 5, 375° F, 190° C. Cook for 20–25 minutes and serve immediately with salad and some chunky granary bread. Green herb sauce (see page 223) is a pleasant and simply made addition. Serve it separately.

TROUT STEAMED
WITH LEMON AND SPRING ONIONS

These trout take only ten minutes to steam, and are beautifully complemented by their spring onion and lemon sauce.

SERVES 4

4 trout, gutted with heads and tails left on	2 lemons
2 spring onions	½ teaspoon sugar
	1 tablespoon soy sauce

Use a sharp, heavy knife to score the flesh of the trout on both sides with 2 or 3 diagonal slashes. Put the fish head to tail on a plate that will just fit inside the steamer. Cut the spring onions into 2-inch (5-cm) sections, then cut these lengthwise into fine threads. Scatter the spring onions over the fish. Now prepare the sauce ingredients. Pare the zest of one lemon and cut it into shreds (or use a lemon zester). Cut 4 slices from the other lemon and reserve them for garnish. Squeeze the juice from the remainder and from the other lemon. Mix the zest and juice with the sugar and soy sauce. Spoon this mixture carefully over and around the fish, making sure that plenty of it goes into the slashes. Cover and steam for 10 minutes.

Serve with the sauce spooned over the fish, garnished with the lemon slices. Plain rice and a stir-fried vegetable dish make pleasant accompaniments.

GRILLED RAINBOW TROUT WITH YOGHURT AND DILL

This is an easy, moist way to cook grilled trout and a lovely way to use the summer herb dill (you could substitute fennel).

SERVES 4

4 rainbow trout, cleaned, with head and tail left on

MARINADE
4 tablespoons plain yoghurt
4 tablespoons finely chopped fresh dill
1½ tablespoons lemon juice

Generous amount freshly ground black pepper
Garlic purée, or 2 cloves garlic, crushed

GARNISH
A few extra fronds of dill
Lemon wedges

Pat the fish dry inside and out. Prepare the yoghurt marinade first. Mix the yoghurt, dill, lemon juice, ground black pepper and garlic until they form a smooth paste. Transfer the fish to a sheet of aluminium foil. Brush a generous amount of the marinade inside the fish and on the skin, keeping some back for basting. Leave for 10 minutes. Pre-heat the grill to moderate: too fierce a heat will scorch the skin while leaving the inside raw. Grill the fish for 6–7 minutes each side (the exact time will depend on the size). Baste it frequently with the remaining marinade. The fish is done when the skin is crisp and the flesh just coming away from the bone. Serve with an extra frond of dill and a lemon wedge on each fish.

TROUT WITH LEMON AND PARSLEY

This is an excellent way to cook trout in a frying pan without adding masses of fat. The simple seasoning is just right for a fish that usually has a generous and well-developed flavour which it is a shame to swamp. The trout emerges with a crisp, green-speckled skin, and the tender flesh inside has a pleasant herby, lemony tang.

SERVES 4

2 lemons
3 tablespoons finely chopped fresh
  coriander or parsley

4 trout, cleaned, with heads and
  tails left on

Grate the lemon zest (or pare it with a lemon zester). Set aside a little of the zest for garnish. Squeeze all the juice. Sprinkle about half the coriander or parsley inside the fish, then brush or spoon about half the lemon juice inside. Brush the remaining juice on the skin, both sides, then pat in the remaining parsley. Brush out a large non-stick frying pan (or 2 smaller pans) with olive or sunflower oil. Let the pan warm up over a very moderate heat, then slide in the fish. Don't crowd them or rush them: if you have only one pan, cook them in batches of 2 and keep the first batch warm while you cook the second. Cook the fish for about 5 minutes each side, covering the pan for the first few minutes (this generates the steam that will help cook the fish quickly). Serve garnished with the reserved lemon zest.

HERRING WITH APPLES, BAKED IN THE OVEN

No one knows better than the Scandinavians how to cook herrings. Now that they are plentiful again in Britain, we can enjoy them too. In this Norwegian-inspired recipe, the herrings are quickly cooked with an apple sauce in a very hot oven. Ask your fishmonger to fillet the fish for you: this will save you time and a messy job. If herrings are not available you could substitute large fresh sardines or small mackerel.

SERVES 4

4 large herrings
3 medium onions
1 tablespoon sunflower oil
4 large apples (preferably
  Bramleys)
½ teaspoon dried sage

Freshly ground black pepper
Salt to taste
1 oz (25 g) wholemeal breadcrumbs
1 oz (25 g) Gouda, Edam or
  Emmenthal cheese, grated

Pre-heat the oven to its maximum (Gas mark 9, 475° F, 340° C). Pat the fish dry and pull out any remaining bones with tweezers. Chop the

186

onions finely and sauté them in a little sunflower oil until they are soft. Meanwhile, peel and core the apples and grate them into an oiled, oval, shallow oven-proof dish. Sprinkle in the dried sage. Put a layer of 4 herring fillets close together in the dish on top of the apples, skin side down. Spoon some onion on to each fillet. Grind plenty of black pepper on top of each one and sprinkle on a little salt. Now put the second batch of fillets on top to form a 'sandwich'. Mix the breadcrumbs with the grated cheese and sprinkle them lightly on top. Bake on the highest shelf of the oven for 15–20 minutes and serve immediately with a puréed vegetable (potatoes, carrots or turnips) and a salad.

HERRING ROLLS WITH MUSTARD

This is another Scandinavian recipe: herring fillets are rolled up with a simple mustard spread and quickly baked in a very hot oven. Ask your fishmonger to fillet the fish. Mustard when cooked loses a lot of its fiery flavour but still gives a pleasant tang to the fish.

SERVES 4

4 herrings, filleted
2 tablespoons English mustard
  powder
5 fl oz (150 ml) apple juice or cider

1 tablespoon chopped fresh
  parsley

GARNISH
1 lemon

Pre-heat the oven to Gas Mark 9, 475° F, 240° C. Inspect the fillets for any remaining bones and pull them out with tweezers. Mix the mustard powder with enough of the apple juice or cider to make a paste. Add the parsley and mix well. Spread the paste over the fish and roll each fillet up from the wider end. Fasten them with cocktail sticks if you like, but this is not essential. Tuck the fish tightly into a shallow oven-proof dish and pour the remaining apple juice or cider around it. Cover lightly with foil and bake on a high shelf for 15 minutes. Remove the foil and bake, uncovered, for a further 5 minutes. Spoon a little of the cooking liquid over the fish, garnish with lemon slices and serve with steamed carrots and steamed broccoli.

SPICED HERRING FILLETS

Herrings are cheap and cook quickly. In this recipe they are filleted, coated with a pleasantly spiced breadcrumb mixture, then 'dry-fried'. Ask the fishmonger to fillet the herrings for you. This recipe also works well for mackerel or sardines.

SERVES 4

2 tablespoons plain flour
1 tablespoon paprika
1 tablespoon ground coriander
Salt and freshly ground black
  pepper to taste
1 egg

BREADCRUMB MIXTURE
2 slices day-old crustless
  wholemeal bread
2 tablespoons chopped parsley
1 clove garlic, crushed
Grated rind of 1 lemon

GARNISH
1 lemon, quartered

Prepare the flour mixture first. Mix the flour, paprika, coriander, salt and pepper in a shallow dish. In a second dish beat the egg lightly. In a third dish prepare the breadcrumb mixture by grating or processing the breadcrumbs and adding the parsley, garlic and lemon rind. Keep back a little of the parsley for garnish.

Trim the herring fillets, wash them and pat them dry. Remove any remaining bones with tweezers. Dip each fillet into the flour mixture, then into the egg, then into the breadcrumbs. Brush out a large non-stick pan with corn oil and cook the fillets for about 4 or 5 minutes each side. Keep the first batch on a warmed plate while you cook the second batch. Garnish with the remaining parsley and the lemon quarters. Serve with a fruit sauce (e.g., plum – see page 224), wholemeal bread and a tomato salad.

MARINATED GRILLED SARDINES

The Italian restaurateur and writer Antonio Carluccio once jokingly remarked that sardines must have some magical life-preserving property, as this would explain the extraordinary longevity of the southern Italian fishermen who eat virtually nothing else. This joke may turn out to have some scientific basis: all oily fish are now thought to be especially valuable for keeping arteries healthy. Sardines are now widely available at fishmongers, shops and in supermarkets. They have usually been frozen, but the flavour and texture are still excellent and of course they are also cheap. This Italian way of cooking them could not be simpler or more delicious.

SERVES 4

MARINADE
3 tablespoons olive oil
1 tablespoon lemon juice
Freshly ground black pepper

8 large or 16 medium sardines

GARNISH
Lemon wedges
1 small onion thinly sliced into
  rings

Prepare the marinade by mixing the three ingredients together. Gut the fish neatly: slit the belly near the head and scoop out the insides, leaving the head and tail intact. Rinse inside the fish and pat dry. If the fish are large, score the flesh diagonally with a very sharp knife twice on each side; *don't* do this if they are small. Put the sardines in a shallow dish large enough to take all of them in a single layer. Brush the marinade all over them, inside and out, and leave them for 20 minutes. Pre-heat the grill, then oil the rack. Now grill the fish: they should be about 3 inches away from a moderate heat. For large fish about 3–4 minutes each side should be enough; small ones will take about 2 minutes a side. Handle them carefully when you turn them over. Serve garnished with the lemon wedges and raw onion rings. A generous quantity of tomato salad, preferably made from Italian 'beef' tomatoes, goes well with this dish.

SPICED SARDINES

A simple, gently spiced recipe for sardines. The heads of the fish may be left on or removed, as you prefer.

SERVES 4

8 sardines (fresh or defrosted)
3 tablespoons wholemeal flour
1 teaspoon ground cumin

¼ teaspoon cayenne pepper
Freshly ground black pepper
1 lemon

189

Gut the sardines (you slit the belly near the head and scoop out the insides), leaving heads and tails intact. Rinse them and pat them dry. Put the wholemeal flour in a shallow bowl, add the ground spices and mix them well together. Brush out a non-stick pan with oil and heat it gently. Dip the fish in the flour mixture, then cook them for about 4 minutes each side. Squeeze a little lemon juice over each fish and serve with stir-fried vegetables or a salad and some bread.

CHINESE-STYLE STEAMED WHOLE FISH

A steamed whole fish looks spectacular, cooks quickly and can taste wonderful. In this Chinese dish the fish is slashed, then flavoured with pungent vegetables and steamed in a simple sauce. It is worth taking a little trouble to cut the vegetables into fine, thread-like strips: this way they cook quickly and look beautiful. Serve the fish with plain rice.

SERVES 4

1 sea-bass, about 2 lb (900 g) in
    weight
½-in (1-cm) cube fresh ginger
4 spring onions
2 small sweet pickled gherkins
2 carrots
1 courgette

SAUCE
2 tablespoons soy sauce
3 tablespoons dry sherry
2 teaspoons sugar

The fish should be scaled and cleaned. Leave the head and tail on but snip off the fins. Pat the fish dry. Using a very sharp knife, make 3 or 4 deep diagonal slashes on each side. This allows the flavouring and steam to permeate the fish. Put it on a shallow dish that will fit into your steamer. Peel the ginger root and cut it into thread-like strips. Cut the spring onions into 2-inch (5-cm) lengths and then into fine threads. Cut the gherkins, carrots and courgette into fine threads. Mix these vegetables together and then press them lightly all over the top of the fish.

    Now put water in the steamer and bring it to the boil. Mix all the sauce ingredients together. Drizzle the sauce carefully all over the fish, making sure that plenty goes into the slashes and some runs underneath and around the fish. Cover the steamer tightly and steam the fish for about 20 minutes. Serve immediately.

GREEN-WRAPPED RED MULLET

Red mullet has one of the most satisfying combinations of taste and texture of all fish. Its light, rosy-red skin also gives it a visual head-start. However, it has to be admitted that it is a bony fish and can be awkward to eat: offering diners a separate plate for the bones makes it easier.

Red mullet must be scaled thoroughly. The liver is considered a delicacy and is usually left in, but if you are unfamiliar with the anatomy of the fish and can't recognize the liver, then just clean it and rinse it out in the usual way.

In this recipe, cooked without any added fat, the fish are wrapped in a jacket of green leaves to retain their moisture (spinach here, but lettuce or cabbage can also be used), the cavities are stuffed with a few aromatic herbs of your choice and the fish are ready to eat after 15 minutes in the oven.

SERVES 4

8 red mullet
Handful of any fresh aromatic
  herb, e.g., chives, parsley

8 large spinach leaves
1 lemon

Pre-heat the oven to Gas Mark 6, 400° F, 200° C. Clean and scale the fish. Snip off the fins, but leave heads and tails on. Stuff each cavity with some herbs – they need not be chopped, as they are not meant to be eaten.

Trim off any stalks, then dip the spinach leaves into a bowl of boiling water, just long enough to make them wilt a little so that they are flexible enough to fold round the fish. Trim off any stalks. Squeeze the juice from the lemon over the fish, then wrap each one neatly round the middle with a spinach leaf. Lay the fish head to tail in an oven-proof dish. Cover the top loosely with a piece of foil and bake for 15 minutes. Serve warm with plenty of thickly sliced wholemeal bread and a bean and cucumber salad (see page 209).

MONKFISH TAILS GRILLED WITH LEMON AND DILL

Monkfish has a firm texture and full-bodied flavour – an ideal fish for grilling. Look out for small monkfish tails on market stalls or in the 'bargain' section at your fishmonger's. These tails are not quite so developed in flavour, but much, much cheaper!

SERVES 4

4 small or 2 large monkfish tails

Freshly ground black pepper

MARINADE
3 tablespoons olive oil
Juice of 2 lemons
2 tablespoons chopped fresh dill,
  or 1 tablespoon dried

GARNISH
1 lemon, sliced
Extra fresh dill or parsley

Pull off any remaining skin on the monkfish. Mix all the marinade ingredients in a shallow bowl big enough to take all the fish in a single layer. Place the fish in the dish and rub the marinade in lightly. Leave it for 10 minutes, turning a few times. Meanwhile, pre-heat the grill to medium. Prepare an aluminium 'tray' for the fish from double foil crimped at all the edges and put this on your grill pan. Lay the fish on the foil, bottom side up. Grill for 5 minutes, using the remaining marinade to brush the fish frequently. Turn the fish over and grill the other side, brushing frequently again, for another 6–8 minutes, depending on the thickness of the fish. The fish is ready when it begins to fall away from the central bone and the interior has turned from pale pink to cream. The top should be golden but not brown.

Serve with the juices from the foil spooned carefully on top. Garnish with the extra lemon and fresh dill or parsley. Serve with a salad of halved cherry tomatoes and spring onions. Plain fresh wholemeal bread goes well with this dish, or spiced rice (see page 176) if you have time.

GRILLED SPICED SALMON

British salmon is a world-class delicacy and is delightful straight-forwardly poached or grilled. If you want something just a little more elaborate, this recipe offers a lightly spiced alternative. Tarragon makes a particularly happy combination with the delicate flavour of the salmon.

SERVES 4

4 salmon cutlets	2 teaspoons lemon juice
Black pepper	1 teaspoon olive oil
Garlic purée, or 2 cloves garlic, crushed	1 teaspoon paprika
4 generous sprigs fresh tarragon, or ½ teaspoon dried	½ onion

Pat the fish dry with kitchen paper and grind some black pepper on to both sides. Squeeze the garlic purée into a mortar, then add the tarragon, lemon juice, olive oil, paprika and very finely chopped onion. Pound this mixture with the pestle until it is smooth. (Alternatively, put the garlic on to a chopping board with the tarragon and onion on top and keep chopping until everything is smoothly pulverized. Scrape into a small bowl, then add the paprika, olive oil and lemon juice.) Brush or press this paste into all surfaces of the salmon, including the skin, and set the cutlets aside for 10 minutes. Pre-heat the grill to moderate. Grill the fish for 3–5 minutes each side, depending on thickness. The salmon is ready the moment it has changed colour all through. The upper side should be lightly browned. Serve with salad and new potatoes simmered in their skins.

SALMON WITH CHIVES

When we were children, my mother occasionally used to cook fish, usually plaice fillets, between two plates over a large saucepan. It was regarded as a special treat, reserved for times when we were convalescing from some childhood illness. It is a perfect, quick and gentle method of cooking fish like salmon.

SERVES 4

4 salmon fillets or cutlets	GARNISH
1 tablespoon fresh-snipped chives	Lemon wedges
Freshly ground black pepper	

You will need a large serving plate, big enough to take all 4 pieces of fish in a single layer. Arrange the fish on it and sprinkle on the chives and the black pepper. Pour about an inch of water into a sauté pan which is just a little smaller than the plate. Set the plate on top of the pan and bring the water to the boil. Cover the plate with a large saucepan lid or another plate that fits snugly round the fish. The salmon will now cook in its own vaporized juices. Depending on the thickness of the fish, this will take from 5 to 7 minutes. Garnish with lemon wedges and serve immediately with green herb sauce (see page 223), potato purée and green salad with herbs (see page 208).

SWEET AND SOUR PRAWNS
WITH MUSHROOMS

This is a quick, simple and tangy dish that can be assembled in moments. A wok is the easiest pan to use, but a large, deep frying pan will do. Be careful not to overdo the cooking of the prawns – frozen pink prawns are already cooked and only need heating through. Over-vigorous cooking will produce shrunken prawns with no taste at all. Frozen prawns are always better if they are thawed and patted dry before cooking (use a microwave if you have one). For this recipe, if you *have* to use them frozen, add them half-way through the cooking of the sauce, but reduce the amount of liquid or stock, as they will exude a lot of water.

SERVES 4

4 spring onions
4 cloves garlic
1 red pepper
4 oz small button mushrooms
1 teaspoon sunflower oil
8 oz (450 g) frozen peeled prawns,
    thawed and patted dry

SAUCE
2 teaspoons cornflour

3 fl oz stock or water
1 tablespoon soy sauce
1 tablespoon tomato purée
1 tablespoon white wine vinegar
2 teaspoons sugar

GARNISH
A few fresh coriander leaves

Cut the spring onions diagonally into 1-inch strips. Mash the garlic to a pulp. De-seed the pepper, trim away the membranes and slice the

194

flesh into short, fine matchstick strips. Cut the button mushrooms in halves. Blend all the sauce ingredients together using a wire whisk.

Heat a tablespoon of sunflower oil in the wok or pan and stir-fry the spring onions and garlic for about 10 seconds. Add the pepper and the mushrooms and stir-fry, turning vigorously all the time, for another 30 seconds. Add all the sauce ingredients; bring the mixture to boiling point, then reduce the heat immediately. Simmer gently until the sauce looks fairly thick and glossy. Tip in the defrosted prawns, mix thoroughly, simmer very gently for another minute and serve immediately, garnished with the fresh coriander leaves. Plain rice and a steamed or stir-fried vegetable go well with this dish.

FISH PIE

Most fish pie recipes suggest a mashed-potato topping. I have always found that the potato and the fish seem to end up blended into an unattractive mush. In this recipe the pie has a thick topping of sliced potato. The fish itself is cooked in a simple sauce with plenty of parsley and leeks for flavouring.

SERVES 4

2 medium potatoes
6 fl oz (170 ml) skimmed milk
1 tablespoon cornflour
2 bay-leaves
2 young leeks
Salt to taste

3 haddock or cod fillets
Freshly ground black pepper
Salt
3 tablespoons finely chopped fresh
    parsley

Put the peeled potatoes into a pan of boiling water and let them simmer for about 7 minutes. Blend a little of the milk with the cornflour, add the bay-leaves and the rest of the milk and simmer for a few minutes until the mixture thickens. Wash the leeks and shred them as finely as possible.

Pre-heat the oven to Gas Mark 7, 425° F, 220° C. Cut each fillet into 3 or 4 pieces and put them in a shallow oven-proof dish. Sprinkle each layer of fish with freshly ground black pepper, a mean pinch of salt, the chopped parsley and chopped leeks. Spoon the sauce over the fish and leeks. Slice the half-cooked potatoes as thinly as possible and lay them on top of the fish. Brush the potatoes with a little oil and put the dish in the oven, on the top shelf, for 15–20 minutes. If the potatoes are not well-browned, flash the dish under the grill for a few moments. Serve with chunky wholemeal bread to mop up the juices.

FISH CAKES

Real fish cakes bear no resemblance in taste, colour or texture to those sawdusty rounds with dyed breadcrumb coating beloved of fish and chip shops. You can use any fish, but kippers make excellent fish cakes, as long as you cook them by the 'jugging' method described here (otherwise they are too salty). These little fish cakes make a good family supper dish.

SERVES 4

1 lb (450 g) potatoes
2 tablespoons plain low-fat yoghurt
12 oz (350 g) undyed kipper fillets
1 large onion

3 tablespoons finely chopped fresh parsley
Freshly ground black pepper
½ teaspoon paprika

Peel the potatoes and simmer them until they are cooked. Drain them and mash them with the yoghurt. While the potatoes are cooking, put the kippers in a large jug, pour boiling water on them and leave them for 4 minutes. Pour the water away, then pour fresh boiling water on top. Leave the kippers for another 4 minutes, then drain them. Skin and flake the fish. Chop the onion as finely as possible. Use a large fork to mix the mashed potato with the flaked fish, onion, parsley, freshly ground black pepper and paprika. Knead the mixture briefly, then form it into 8 individual fish cakes. Smear a non-stick pan with sunflower oil and heat it. Fry the fishcakes under a very moderate heat for about 4 minutes each side. Serve with grilled tomatoes and wholemeal bread.

VEGETABLES AND SALADS

Most people, I am sure, do not usually need recipes for vegetables. Fresh seasonal vegetables are best simmered briefly in a minute amount of boiling water or plainly steamed. However, I give a few suggestions here for slightly more unusual methods of cooking familiar vegetables, for when you want to do something a little out of the ordinary.

Salads are the perfect way of eating plenty of raw fresh food. We have a salad with almost every meal, partly because they are so simple and quick to prepare, partly because the colours, textures and tastes can make such a pleasing complement to the main course. I always have a screw-top jar of basic dressing in my refrigerator, but some salads call for dressings of different types: a thick yoghurt-based coating for potatoes or fennel, an orange juice or cider vinegar dressing for salads containing fruit, and so on.

FRENCH PEAS

Out of habit, I always have huge bags of frozen peas in my freezer. This dates from the days when peas were the only vegetable my children would eat. It may be heresy, but I actually find frozen peas very good, especially 'petits pois'. In my view they compare favourably to the often woody and elderly podded peas so briefly available in shops during the summer, quite apart from the awful chore of shelling them. In this recipe I have adapted a French classic which mixes peas and lettuce.

SERVES 4

8 oz (225 g) frozen petits pois
Bunch spring onions
½ teaspoon sugar

1 Webb's lettuce
Small knob of polyunsaturated
  margarine

Plunge the peas into a little boiling water and cook them for 4 minutes with the sliced spring onions and sugar. Remove and discard any very

197

coarse outer lettuce leaves. Slice the remaining lettuce, but not too finely – you should aim to produce inch-wide 'ribbons'. Drain the peas and return them to the pan with the lettuce and the margarine. Cover and shake the pan over the lowest possible heat for a further 2 minutes. The lettuce should be wilted but not soggy. Serve immediately – the dish should not sit around for long.

SWEDE, CARROT AND TURNIP PURÉE

All three of these root vegetables are naturally sweet and nutty; they combine beautifully in this purée.

SERVES 4

12 oz (350 g) swede
4 oz (110 g) turnip
8 oz (225 g) carrots

1 oz (25 g) polyunsaturated
  margarine
¼ nutmeg
Freshly ground black pepper

Peel the swede and turnip, scrub the carrots but do not peel them. Cut all the vegetables into thin slices. Plunge them into just enough water to cover them, put a lid on the pan and simmer until they are very tender – about 7 minutes. Drain (but reserve the cooking water for stock or soup). Add the margarine, nutmeg and pepper. Mash the vegetables finely with a potato masher, or process very briefly. Return the purée to the pan and drive off any wateriness over a little heat, stirring all the time to prevent burning. Check for seasoning. This purée will bear making in advance and reheating in a microwave, or will keep warm (covered) in an oven without spoiling.

STIR-FRIED COURGETTES

Tender young courgettes have a delicate flavour which is enhanced perfectly by stir-frying.

SERVES 4

4 young courgettes
1 small onion
1 clove garlic, crushed

Sliver of fresh ginger
1 tablespoon soy sauce

Cut the courgettes into 5 or 6 pieces lengthways, then into 3 pieces horizontally, to produce thin slices. Slice the onion very finely. Heat a little oil in a wok or deep pan. Add the garlic and ginger and let it sizzle for a moment. Now put in the courgettes and onions. Stir-fry vigorously for about 3 minutes. (This produces a crisp texture – let them cook for a few minutes longer if you prefer a softer result.) Add the soy sauce and keep turning the courgettes until all the liquid has evaporated. Serve immediately.

CELERY WITH MOZZARELLA

This simply cooked celery makes an excellent partner for grilled fish or chicken dishes.

SERVES 4

½ head celery
1 Mozzarella cheese

Freshly ground black pepper

Trim the leaves from the celery and reserve them. Chop the stalks into 2-inch lengths. Put them into a heavy non-stick pan with a tight-fitting lid. Add about an inch (2.5 cm) of water, bring to a simmer, turn down the heat to low, cover and cook for about 15 minutes or until the celery is tender. Meanwhile, slice the Mozzarella cheese as thinly as possible and chop the celery leaves finely. Pre-heat the grill. Drain the celery and put it into a flame-proof serving dish. Grind on some pepper, cover the celery with thin cheese slices and brown under the grill. Scatter chopped celery leaves on top and serve immediately.

SCALLOPED JACKET POTATOES

This is a dish that everyone loves: it combines all the flavour of jacket potatoes and the crispness of chips, without any of the health hazards of chips. Just a dessertspoon of any good quality oil is enough to cook 4 baking potatoes.

SERVES 4

4 medium-large potatoes   Freshly ground black pepper
1 dessertspoon olive oil

Pre-heat the oven to its maximum. Have ready two baking trays, preferably non-stick. Wash the potatoes and pat them dry. Cut them into paper-thin, evenly sized rounds. Lay these in rows on the trays, each slice slightly overlapping the next. Paint the cut surfaces of the potatoes with the oil, using a pastry brush, then grind on some black pepper. Put the tray on the highest shelf of the oven for 15–20 minutes. Keep an eye on the potatoes at the end of the cooking time, as they brown quickly. They should be golden-brown on the outside and just tender inside. Potatoes cooked this way have a good flavour without needing salt, but you could sprinkle a little on if your palate still craves salty tastes!

POTATO CAKES

These puffy little cakes are an interesting way of using up left-over potato. They make a specially good accompaniment to cold chicken or stuffed vegetables.

SERVES 4,
makes 8 cakes

1 lb (450 g) cold mashed potato   1 tablespoon mixed fresh herbs,
3 tablespoons skimmed milk   finely chopped, or 1 teaspoon
1 small egg yolk   dried
¼ nutmeg   3 tablespoons cornflour
Freshly ground black pepper

Mash the cold potato with the milk and egg yolk until you have a smooth, soft mixture. Add more milk if necessary. Grate the nutmeg on to the potato, grind over some pepper and add the mixed herbs. Mix these seasonings in well with a fork. Now work the cornflour into the mixture and knead it briefly. Shake a little extra cornflour on to the work surface, then flatten the potato mixture on to it in a roughly round shape about ½ inch (1 cm) deep. Use a scone-cutter to make 8 round shapes, or just shape them by hand. Brush out a non-stick pan with a little sunflower oil. Gently lift the potato cakes into the pan using a palette knife and cook them over a low heat until they are golden – about 3 minutes each side.

POTATO PURÉE

This is a simple 'healthy' variant on a British classic.

SERVES 4

1½ lb (700 g) potatoes	Ground black pepper
A little salt	1 tablespoon plain yoghurt
1 tablespoon skimmed milk	Nutmeg

Peel the potatoes thinly using a swivel-blade peeler. Cut them into even, medium-sized pieces. Put them into a little boiling water with salt to taste and cook until tender. Drain them. Return them to their pan with the milk over a very low heat. Mash them with a potato masher, then remove the pan from the heat. Add the ground black pepper. Beat in the yoghurt with a large fork until the potatoes are very smooth. Turn into a heated serving dish and grate some nutmeg over the top.

MUSHROOMS IN BEER

Button mushrooms are available all the year round, but are often despised for their lack of flavour. This recipe makes the most of their firm consistency and adds a thick, piquant sauce.

SERVES 4

8 oz (225 g) button mushrooms	2 tablespoons tomato purée
1 large onion	4 fl oz (100 ml) beer
2 tablespoons chopped mixed fresh herbs, or 1 tablespoon dried	Pinch salt
	Freshly ground black pepper

Cut the mushrooms in half; slice the onion thinly. Heat a teaspoon of oil in a non-stick saucepan and stir-fry the vegetables for 3 minutes.

Now add the remaining ingredients. Bring to a simmer, cover and cook for 10 minutes. Remove the lid and boil hard to reduce the sauce to a thick liquid which should just cling to the mushrooms.

STIR-FRIED MANGE-TOUT PEAS AND CARROTS

Bright, colourful vegetables with plenty of crunch make a perfect contrast to soft-textured dishes like steamed fish.

SERVES 4

8 oz (225 g) mange-tout peas
4 carrots
1 teaspoon sunflower oil

Top and tail the peas. Scrub, top and tail the carrots, then cut them into neat matchsticks. Heat a teaspoon of sunflower oil in a wok or deep non-stick pan. Stir-fry the carrots for 2½ minutes, then add the peas and stir-fry for another minute. Serve immediately.

STIR-FRIED CABBAGE

This has to be the most speedy possible way to cook cabbage – and the end-product one of the most delectable ways to eat it.

SERVES 4

12 oz (350 g) white cabbage
1 teaspoon oil
Pinch of sugar

Pinch of salt
Freshly ground black pepper
Seeds from 6 cardamom pods

Shred the cabbage as finely as possible (use the grating plate of the food processor if you have one). Put the cabbage and all the other ingredients into a medium-sized non-stick saucepan. Turn the heat up high and stir-fry the cabbage, turning it constantly, for about 3 minutes. It is ready when it has wilted and has golden-brown speckles all over. Serve immediately.

PUREE OF BRUSSELS SPROUTS

Sprouts still have an unpalatable reputation through being served in a sad, waterlogged state. But this recipe often appeals to avowed sprout-haters who, oddly enough, do not seem able to identify the taste when sprouts are served this way.

SERVES 4

12 oz (350 g) Brussels sprouts
A little salt
Juice of half a lemon

Cook the sprouts in a minimum of lightly salted water over a low heat for about 15 minutes or until they are tender. Drain them well. Use a processor or blender to liquidize them to a chunky purée with the lemon juice. Return the purée to the pan and let it dry out a little, stirring constantly on a very low heat. This purée can be made in advance and re-heated in a microwave or steamer.

STIR-FRIED BEANSPROUTS

This ridiculously cheap vegetable is packed with good things. It makes an excellent salad ingredient, but can also be stir-fried to make a hot vegetable dish in only a few moments. Soggy beansprouts are a sad sight and should be avoided. Certainly only the freshest and crispest are suitable for stir-frying. This recipe makes a good accompaniment to other stir-fried dishes.

SERVES 4

½-inch (1-cm) cube fresh ginger
1 clove garlic
4 spring onions

1 teaspoon sunflower oil
12 oz (350 g) fresh beansprouts
1 tablespoon soy sauce

Peel and grate the ginger. Peel and mash the garlic. Chop the spring onions finely.

Heat a teaspoon of oil in a wok or deep frying pan. When it is almost smoking, add the ginger and garlic and turn them vigorously for 30 seconds. Now slide in the beansprouts and stir-fry them vigorously against the hot sides of the wok for 2 minutes only. Pour on the soy sauce, add the spring onions and stir-fry for another 30 seconds. Serve immediately on a heated dish.

KIDNEY BEAN HOT POT

This vegetarian dish is a genuine 'hot pot' in that it draws shamelessly from the cuisines of many different countries. However, it is a hearty, simple and satisfying dish, mildly spiced with herbs and cumin.

SERVES 4

2 medium onions	1 bay-leaf
1 stick celery	3 tablespoons chopped parsley
2 medium carrots	Black pepper to taste
1 small tin tomatoes	½ teaspoon sugar
1 tablespoon tomato purée	7-oz (200-g) tin red kidney beans
1 tablespoon ground cumin	7-oz (200-g) tin white kidney beans
1 tablespoon fresh chopped tarragon, or 1 teaspoon dried	5 fl oz red or white wine or stock

Chop the onions finely. Heat a little oil in a non-stick pan and sauté the onions until they are well-browned and soft. Meanwhile, chop the celery into half-inch slices and the carrots into fine matchsticks. Sauté all the vegetables for another 2 minutes, turning them all the time. Add the tomatoes, the purée, the ground cumin, tarragon, bay-leaf, parsley (reserving a little for garnish), ground pepper and sugar. Simmer without a lid for 10 minutes until the sauce has thickened and the vegetables have softened. Now add the well-drained and rinsed beans and stir everything together well. Add the wine, cover and cook for another 5 minutes. Serve garnished with the remaining parsley in well-warmed individual deep plates with chunky wholemeal bread.

LENTIL CURRY

(Dhal)

Lentils must be one of the cheapest and most nourishing foods in the world. In India they are eaten daily by many vegetarians with a dish of plain rice. Subtly seasoned and quickly cooked, they go well with any 'dry' spicy food such as tandoori chicken or spiced kebabs. This recipe uses red split lentils: the whole variety has more fibre and flavour, but will take about twice as long to cook.

SERVES 4

4 oz (110 g) red split lentils	1 teaspoon ground cumin
Squeeze garlic purée	1½ pints(1 l) water
½ teaspoon turmeric	Juice of 1 lemon
½ teaspoon ground fenugreek	1 large onion

Put the lentils in a large pan with the garlic, turmeric, fenugreek, cumin and water. Bring to the boil and then reduce the heat to a simmer, leaving the pan uncovered. Cook for about 20 minutes, or until the lentils are soft but not too mushy. While the lentils are cooking, heat a little oil in a non-stick pan. Slice the onions finely, then sauté them gently for about 4 minutes. Now raise the heat to high and brown the onions well, stirring all the time.

Use a potato masher to press down the lentils until they have broken up a little. If there is a lot of water left, boil it off briskly until the mixture is thick but not too dry. Add the lemon juice. Re-heat the onions if necessary. Transfer the dhal to a serving dish and scatter the browned onions on top.

ORANGE AND ONION SALAD

The sweet, refreshing taste of this salad is a pleasant contrast to any spicy dish.

SERVES 4

2 large oranges	2 teaspoons finely chopped
2 small onions or shallots	fresh tarragon
	2 teaspoons tarragon vinegar

Peel the oranges and slice them finely into rounds. Remove all the pips. Slice the onions into thin rings. Arrange the oranges on a platter with the onions on top. Scatter over the tarragon and then the vinegar. Chill for 15 minutes before serving if you have time.

ENDIVE, WATERCRESS AND ORANGE SALAD

SERVES 4

1 large head endive
1 orange
¼ cucumber
1 bunch washed watercress

DRESSING
1 tablespoon olive oil

1 teaspoon lemon juice
A little Dijon mustard
Black pepper
Salt to taste

Slice the endive and cut the orange into segments, discarding the membranes. Leave the cucumber unpeeled and cut it into matchsticks. Tear the watercress into small fronds. Mix the salad ingredients in a bowl. Blend or shake the dressing ingredients together, pour over the salad and toss well.

WATERCRESS, SPINACH AND LETTUCE SALAD

The slightly 'peppery' taste of watercress goes well with the juicy texture of young spinach leaves.

1 bunch watercress
8 young spinach leaves
½ an English lettuce
1 carton mustard and cress

DRESSING
2 tablespoons olive oil
2 teaspoons lemon juice
Pinch salt
Freshly ground black pepper
½ teaspoon Dijon mustard

Trim the stalks of the watercress and chop it coarsely. Trim off the spinach stalks; roll the leaves into a cigar shape and chop them. Tear the larger lettuce leaves into smaller pieces. Arrange the leaves in the serving dish; snip off the mustard and cress and scatter it on top. Blend or shake the dressing ingredients together and trickle over the salad. Serve immediately.

TOMATO AND BASIL SALAD

A simple, classic Italian treat that is good enough for a first course on its own in the summer.

SERVES 4

4 large 'marmande' or beef tomatoes	1 tablespoon chopped fresh parsley
Salt to taste	2 teaspoons red wine vinegar
1 tablespoon chopped fresh basil	1½ tablespoons olive oil

Dip the tomatoes for a few seconds into boiling water and slip off their skins. Slice them very finely and arrange them in a line across a large plate – the slices should not overlap too much. Sprinkle very meanly with salt. Pound the basil with the oil and vinegar so that it makes a green paste. Put a thin line of the paste on each line of tomatoes. Serve immediately.

CRUNCHY GREEN SALAD
WITH LEMON DRESSING

An excellent salad for summer, when fresh herbs are plentiful.

SERVES 4

¼ Iceberg lettuce	DRESSING
2 sticks celery	2 tablespoons olive oil
1 spear chicory	Grated rind and juice of two lemons
1 bunch watercress	1 garlic clove, crushed
1 teaspoon each of fresh chopped marjoram, parsley and chives	Salt and freshly ground black pepper to taste

Shred the lettuce, slice the celery finely, slice the chicory into rounds and chop the watercress coarsely. Mix the salad in a serving dish, then sprinkle the mixed fresh herbs on top. Blend or shake the dressing ingredients together. Trickle the dressing generously over the salad, then toss it.

GREEN AND RED LEAVES

The range of lettuces and chicories now available (see pages 89, 90) is widening all the time. Their tastes and textures are quite different from each other, while the colours are subtly varied, making a beautiful and glossy-looking salad.

SERVES 4

¼ small head raddicchio
4 sprigs endive (both yellow and green stems)
½ head Little Gem lettuce
½ an English lettuce

DRESSING
2 tablespoons olive oil
1 teaspoon lemon juice
Pinch sugar
1 clove garlic, squeezed
Salt and pepper to taste

Wash and dry the leaves, and tear them into slightly smaller pieces. Mix the dressing ingredients well. Put the leaves in the serving bowl, pour the dressing over and toss well. Serve immediately.

GREEN SALAD WITH HERBS

Even a boring old English lettuce can turn into something special in the height of the summer if your garden offers you a good selection of fresh herbs. If your budget doesn't run to the fiendishly expensive walnut oil, use olive or safflower oil instead.

SERVES 4

1 English lettuce

HERBS
1 dessertspoon each of a selection of chopped fresh herbs: choose from parsley, coriander, chervil, chives, sorrel, rocket, basil
1 teaspoon each (chopped) of 2 from: sage, thyme, dill, fennel, tarragon, mint

DRESSING
2 tablespoons walnut oil
2 teaspoons lemon juice
½ teaspoon English mustard
1 clove crushed garlic
Pinch salt
Pinch sugar
Freshly ground black pepper

The lettuce leaves should be completely dry: after washing, spin them well or pat them dry. Tear the large leaves gently into smaller pieces. Scatter the herbs over the leaves. Blend or shake the dressing ingredients together and trickle over the leaves.

NEW POTATO SALAD
WITH YOGHURT DRESSING

Potato salad is nearly always served with mayonnaise, which, if it is made authentically, is full of fat. This low-fat dressing is a tart and pleasing alternative.

SERVES 4

2 lbs (900 g) potatoes

DRESSING
3 tablespoons low-fat natural
   yoghurt
½ teaspoon English mustard
   powder

1 tablespoon white wine vinegar
Salt and pepper to taste

GARNISH
1 tablespoon finely chopped chives

Scrub the potatoes, leaving their skins intact. Steam them (or simmer in a very little water) for 20 minutes, or until they are cooked through. Let them cool a little. Meanwhile, combine all the dressing ingredients in a blender. While the potatoes are still warm, slice them, toss them in the dressing, cover and chill. Scatter with the chopped chives just before serving.

BEAN AND CUCUMBER SALAD

It's true that tinned red, white and green beans usually have both salt and sugar added to them. However, for the health-conscious cook in a hurry, their advantages often outweigh their disadvantages. This salad can be assembled in moments. Add some cottage cheese, a tomato salad and fresh wholemeal bread, and it is good enough to eat on its own as a light lunch.

SERVES 4

14-oz (450-g) tin green flageolet
   beans
½ cucumber
1 tablespoon chopped fresh mint,
   or 1 teaspoon dried

DRESSING
2 tablespoons safflower oil
2 teaspoons dill vinegar or lemon
   juice
1 clove garlic, crushed

Rinse the beans well under fiercely running cold water. Pat them dry. Dice the unpeeled cucumber. Mix the beans, cucumber and mint.

Blend or shake all the dressing ingredients together (there is no need to add salt) and add to the bean mixture, turning it well. Made with fresh mint, the salad can be served immediately if you are short of time. However, it improves if it is chilled a little and allowed to stand for at least 15 minutes, and this is essential if dried mint is used.

RED, WHITE AND BLACK SALAD

A pretty salad made from white cabbage, onion, red peppers and olives.

SERVES 4

6 oz (175 g) white cabbage	DRESSING
1 small onion	3 tablespoons safflower oil
1 red pepper	1 tablespoon white wine vinegar
6 black olives	Pinch of salt
1 tablespoon finely chopped fresh	Crushed garlic clove
coriander or parsley	Freshly ground black pepper

Slice the cabbage very finely. Slice the onion into thin rounds. De-seed the pepper, remove the membrane and chop the pepper into fine thread-like strips. Stone the olives and cut them in half. Mix all the vegetables, adding the coriander or parsley. Blend or shake all the dressing ingredients together, pour over the vegetables and toss well. Dot the olives on top and serve.

WALDORF SALAD

A crunchy sweet-sour American salad, served here with a low-fat dressing. It is ideal to eat with cold chicken or baked potatoes.

SERVES 4

1 oz (25 g) walnut halves	DRESSING
4 oz (110 g) green grapes	2 tablespoons low-fat natural
3 celery sticks	yoghurt
1 green eating apple	2 teaspoons mayonnaise
1 oz sultanas	1 teaspoon finely chopped fresh
	mint
	2 teaspoons lemon juice

210

Break up the walnuts into small pieces. Halve the grapes. Chop the celery. Core the apples (do not peel them) and slice them neatly. Cut the slices in half again. Rinse the sultanas in a little boiling water to soften them, then pat them dry. Blend the dressing ingredients together. Combine the dressing and all the other ingredients, tossing well. Serve immediately.

CABBAGE AND CARROT SALAD

A raw vegetable salad like this is full of fibre, vitamins and minerals: the dressing is a lower-fat version of the traditional mayonnaise.

SERVES 4

5 oz (150 g) white cabbage
1 carrot
1 small onion
1 tablespoon finely chopped fresh
  parsley

DRESSING
2 tablespoons plain low-fat yoghurt
2 teaspoons mayonnaise
¼ teaspoon Dijon mustard

Shred the cabbage (use the slats of a grater, or a food processor); grate the carrot and onion. Mix all the vegetables and add the parsley. Blend all the dressing ingredients together and pour over the salad; toss very thoroughly. Cover and refrigerate for at least half an hour so that the flavours can develop and the vegetables soften just a little.

WINTER SALAD

An easy, quick, robust salad like this makes a perfect and colourful partner for risottos, baked potatoes, pulse dishes and cold meat.

SERVES 4

1 tablespoon sultanas or raisins
2 large carrots
½ small red cabbage
2 spring onions

DRESSING
1½ tablespoons sunflower oil
2 teaspoons lemon juice
Dijon mustard, salt and pepper to
  taste

Put the sultanas or raisins into a cup of boiling water and leave them to steep for 5 minutes. This plumps them up. Grate the carrot and very finely slice or grate the red cabbage. (Use the grating plate of the food processor if you have one.) Chop the spring onions as finely as possible (include all the green part). Drain the dried fruit and pat it dry. Mix all the ingredients together, make and add the dressing and mix well again.

FENNEL SALAD

Traditionally, this crunchy, aniseed-flavoured vegetable is served raw with a garlicky mayonnaise. For this salad it is lightly steamed, then served with a thick, lemony yoghurt dressing speckled with parsley and spring onion.

SERVES 4

2 fennel bulbs

DRESSING
6 tablespoons plain low-fat yoghurt
2 teaspoons lemon juice
Squeeze of garlic purée, or 2
   cloves garlic, well mashed
Pinch of salt

Freshly ground black pepper
2 teaspoons English mustard
   powder
1 tablespoon finely chopped
   parsley
2 spring onions, finely sliced

Put some water on to boil in the steamer. Cut away the bases of the fennel, slice it as thinly as possible and put it in the steamer for 5 minutes. Meanwhile, make the dressing by putting all the ingredients into a blender or processor. (It is hard to achieve the thick emulsion by hand.) Let the steamed fennel cool a little. When it is still just warm, pour the dressing over it, add the parsley and sliced onions and toss well. This salad may be eaten warm or cold.

BEANSPROUT AND RED PEPPER SALAD

This is a crunchy light salad with a high vitamin content.

SERVES 4

8 oz (225 g) fresh beansprouts
1 red pepper
3 spring onions

DRESSING
2 tablespoons sunflower oil
1 tablespoon cider vinegar

¼ teaspoon Dijon mustard
1 teaspoon runny honey

Chop the beansprouts coarsely. De-seed the pepper and remove all the membrane. Cut it in half vertically, then into matchstick strips. Cut the spring onions into fine threads. Combine all the vegetables in a bowl. Blend the dressing ingredients together, pour over the salad and toss well. Chill for 10 minutes before serving.

RED AND YELLOW PEPPER SALAD

When there is a glut of peppers in late summer, even the red and yellow varieties are often temptingly cheap. They make a salad with startlingly bright colours: a good first course or an excellent side salad. To serve it as a side salad mix the two colours of peppers together with the capers and olives on one flat dish.

SERVES 4

2 red peppers
2 yellow peppers
1 tablespoon capers, well rinsed to
    remove brine and vinegar
8 pitted black olives

DRESSING
2 tablespoons olive oil
2 teaspoons white wine vinegar
¼ teaspoon Dijon mustard
Pinch sugar

Pre-heat the grill to its hottest level. Cut each pepper in half. Trim off the stalk and membranes and remove the seeds. Put each pepper cut side down on the grill tray just as it is. Grill until the skin is blackened all over – about 10 minutes. Remove the peppers with tongs and plunge them into cold water. Now rub off all the skin – it should come away easily. Using a very sharp knife, cut the peppers vertically into thin matchstick strips. Pile them on a flat dish, keeping the two colours separate. Scatter the well-washed capers over them. Shake the dressing ingredients together and carefully dribble it over the peppers. Cover and refrigerate until you are ready to serve. Transfer the peppers to individual serving plates and decorate with a few black olives. Serve with warm crusty French bread.

PUDDINGS

We rarely bother with puddings or desserts on weekdays unless we are entertaining. Even then we might well finish the meal as we normally do, with a choice of fresh seasonal fruit. This section gives some ideas for simple puddings you can make when you have the time to go to a little more trouble.

GREEN FRUIT SALAD

This fruit salad looks cool and has a pleasant, subtly gingery taste.

SERVES 4

1-in (2.5-cm) cube fresh ginger
4 fl oz (100 ml) apple juice
4 fl oz (100 ml) orange juice, freshly
   squeezed if possible
A few sprigs mint

½ sweet, green-fleshed melon
1 kiwi fruit
Small bunch green grapes

DECORATION
Mint leaves

Peel and grate the ginger. Add it to the two juices in a pan with the mint leaves. Bring the liquid to the boil, then remove it from the heat and let it stand for 15 minutes to allow the ginger and mint to infuse. Meanwhile ball or neatly cut the melon, peel and cut the kiwi fruit into slices, de-pip the grapes and cut them in half. Transfer the fruit to a glass serving dish. Strain the juice over the fruit, adding any extra melon left behind in the shell. Turn the fruit gently. Chill for at least 15 minutes. Decorate with mint leaves and serve with strained yoghurt.

CITRUS FRUIT SALAD

This is a simple, refreshing fruit salad. Leaving it to marinate for a while improves the flavour.

SERVES 4

2 oranges (blood oranges if they
  are in season)
2 pink grapefruit

1 ugli fruit
A little sugar (optional)
Apple juice

Remove the zest from one of the oranges, blanch it in boiling water for
a minute, cool it down with cold water, then cut it into strips and set it
to one side.

Peel all the fruit and segment it so that you remove all the
membranes. Pile it into a glass dish, sprinkling on a little sugar and
then just enough apple juice to moisten the fruit. Scatter on the strips
of orange zest. Chill if possible before serving.

RASPBERRY SURPRISE

A low-fat, glamorous-looking pudding, very easily assembled in
contrasting layers of colour and needing no extra sugar.

SERVES 4

1 orange
1 banana
About 20 green grapes
1 tablespoon any sweet fruit juice,
  e.g., mango, apple

8 oz (225 g) raspberries (if frozen,
  defrosted)
8 oz (225 g) low-fat fromage blanc
  or thick Greek yoghurt

Dice the orange and banana. De-pip the grapes and cut them in half.
Pour the fruit juice over the fruit and mix it well. Rub the raspberries
through a sieve so that you produce a thick purée. Divide the diced
fruit between four glass bowls. Spoon fromage blanc on top, then
carefully pour a layer of raspberry purée over that. Serve immediately.

FROMAGE BLANC
WITH MOLASSES AND ALMONDS

This pudding must be one of the swiftest possible. Yes, of course
molasses is just sugar under another guise, but a little goes a very long

way. The dark, smoky-sweet taste makes a wonderful contrast to the creamy-smooth blandness of the fromage blanc.

SERVES 4

1 oz (25 g) slivered almonds
8 oz (225 g) fromage blanc (best if chilled)

4 teaspoons pure cane molasses

Put the almonds on a little foil under the grill and brown them well. Heap the fromage blanc into pretty glass bowls. Run a teaspoon under a very hot tap or heat it on a naked gas flame – using a hot spoon helps to control the molasses. Put one teaspoon of molasses on top of the fromage blanc in each bowl, then sprinkle each one thickly with the browned almonds. Serve immediately.

RED FRUIT SALAD

The spectacular red soft fruit of summer make an unrivalled fruit salad. Serve it with fromage blanc – cream would definitely be overpowering!

SERVES 4

8 oz (225 g) strawberries
12 oz (350 g) red currants
12 oz (350 g) raspberries
8 oz (225 g) black cherries

4 oz (110 g) black currants or early blackberries
A little sugar
Apple juice

Slice the strawberries and de-stalk the red currants. Layer the fruit in a glass bowl, sprinkling a very little sugar meanly as you go. Trickle a little apple juice over the fruit – no more than 5 fl oz (150 ml). Leave the fruit to stand at room temperature for about 20 minutes.

MELON WITH BLACKBERRY SAUCE

My local market in North London is open on Sundays and in late summer often has 'undersized' melons just a little too small (and maybe a little too ripe?) for the supermarkets, which are sold off very cheaply. They make a superb swift fruit salad filled with a purée – perhaps made with produce from a neighbouring stall offering bargains in soft fruit not quite perfect enough to be sold at Saturday's much higher price.

SERVES 4

2 small well-chilled Ogen or
  Charentais melons
½ lb (250 g) blackberries (or you
  could substitute strawberries or
  raspberries)

1 tablespoon any favourite liqueur
  or sweet 'fruit' wine, e.g., peach
  or apple

Cut the melons in half and de-seed them. Scoop out just a little more of the flesh and add it to the blackberries and the liqueur. Blend and then sieve the fruit and liqueur to make a purée. Set the melons on serving dishes. Pour the purée into the 'well' in the centre of each melon. Serve immediately.

PEACHES IN RASPBERRY SAUCE

Peaches and nectarines are available for several months in the summer, and are often ridiculously cheap at the end of the season. This special dessert makes the most of their beautiful flavour. It is simple to make.

SERVES 4

6 large peaches or nectarines
8 fresh basil leaves (optional)

8 oz (225 g) fresh or defrosted
  frozen raspberries
2 teaspoons castor sugar

Put the peaches in a saucepan big enough to hold them in a single layer. Cover them with boiling water, add the basil leaves – reserve 4 for decoration – and let them stand for 5 minutes. Remove them with a slotted spoon and slip their skins off. Rub the raspberries through a sieve to obtain a purée. Sprinkle the castor sugar on the purée and stir gently. Slice the cooled peaches evenly. Pour a little of the sauce into the centre of each plate. Now place the peach slices overlapping each other on the sauce. Decorate each serving with a basil leaf.

FRUIT IN A MANGO PUDDLE

Some of the great chefs of 'nouvelle cuisine' began the custom of serving sauce as a puddle on the plate, with other food placed on top. One of the happier examples of this fashion is the use of mango as a deliciously sweet orange purée on which other sweet seasonal fruit is arranged. Fresh mangoes are expensive and may be hard to find, but dried mango is much cheaper and often easier to track down in supermarkets and health food shops. It can be reconstituted very quickly.

SERVES 4

1 fresh mango (or 2 oz (50 g) dried mango with 5 fl oz (150 ml) apple or orange juice and 2 fl oz (50 ml) water)

Any choice seasonal fruit: e.g., 4 figs, 2 bananas, 16 grapes

Peel and stone the fresh mango and pass it through a sieve to make a purée. (If you are using dried mango, reconstitute it by simmering it, covered, with the apple juice and water for 15 minutes, or 5 minutes in a microwave. Blend or process with the liquid until you get a smooth purée. Thin it down with more juice if it is too thick – it should be a thin pouring sauce.) Spread a little of the purée on each plate. Slice the figs, bananas and grapes and arrange them attractively on the purée.

APPLE AND LEMON YOGHURT

A tart, refreshing, simple dessert, very quickly made.

SERVES 4

12 oz (350 g) plain low-fat yoghurt
1 lemon
3 dessert apples

1 tablespoon castor sugar
1 tablespoon flaked almonds

Beat the yoghurt with a whisk until it feels thick and creamy. Cut 2 wafer-thin slices from the lemon and set them aside. Grate all the remaining lemon zest and also put it aside. Squeeze the juice from half the lemon (keep the other half for another dish). Peel the apples thinly, then grate them into the yoghurt. Add the lemon juice and the castor sugar and stir well. Chill, if you have time. Toast the almonds on foil under the grill. Just before serving, cut the lemon slices into two. Pile the yoghurt mixture into individual glass dishes and decorate with the almonds, lemon zest and lemon slices.

PINEAPPLE BOUQUETS

This is a pretty way to serve fruit. Ideally look for the small pineapples that are often sold off cheaply because they look undersized. This way everyone can have one 'bouquet'.

SERVES 4

2 small pineapples
1 pink grapefruit

2 kiwi fruit
2 tablespoons apple juice

Cut the pineapples in half vertically, leaving the leafy section intact. Run a sharp knife all round the flesh and scoop it out. Have a bowl ready and chop the flesh carefully into evenly sized pieces, saving as much of the juice as you can. Peel the grapefruit and segment it, removing all the pithy membranes. Add this fruit to the pineapple and gently turn it all together. Pile the fruit back into the pineapple shells. Now peel and slice the kiwi fruit and slot in the slices to jut at angles between the grapefruit and pineapple pieces. Trickle the apple juice over the fruit and chill before serving.

PINEAPPLE COMPOTE

It is sometimes whispered that tinned pineapple tastes better than fresh. A really ripe, juicy fresh pineapple is one of the best fruits there is and need fear no rivalry from tins. Sadly, however, the fruit on sale in Britain is not always in prime condition: you may discover its immaturity and sourness with dismay after you've got it home. This recipe transforms such pineapple into a delightful dessert by adding some of the flavour and sweetness lacking in the raw fruit.

SERVES 4

3–4 thick pineapple slices
8 fl oz (225 ml) unsweetened fruit
  juice, preferably pineapple
2 teaspoons runny honey

2 teaspoons rosewater (optional)
1 teaspoon arrowroot
12 black grapes

Trim the pineapple and cut out the woody centres. Cut the pineapple into chunks. If the centres are not too hard, dice them; otherwise, discard them. Put the pineapple in a stainless steel or non-stick pan with the juice, honey and rosewater. Simmer, covered, for 10 minutes. Lift out the pineapple and arrange it in glass sundae dishes. Boil down the juice until you have about 5 fl oz (100 ml) left. Cream the arrowroot with a little water and add it to the juice. Boil until the sauce is thickened and transparent, then pour it over the fruit. Chill, then stud with the black grapes for decoration.

WALNUT-STUFFED FIGS IN RED WINE

The distinguished cookery writer Claudia Roden first introduced me to the Middle Eastern custom of stuffing dried fruit with nuts, then simmering it in wine. This is a variant on one of her recipes. You could substitute orange or apple juice for the wine, but the colour of the juice would not be so good.

SERVES 4

12 dried figs
24 walnut halves
½ teaspoon ground cinnamon
6 fl oz (160 ml) red wine

TO SERVE
Thick yoghurt

Slice the figs in half lengthwise (from the stalk). Tuck a piece of walnut tightly into each half fig. Put the figs gently into a saucepan and sprinkle them with the cinnamon, then cover them with the wine. Bring to a simmer, cover tightly and cook for 10 minutes. Serve warm in little china dishes with some chilled thick yoghurt on top.

BAKED GLAZED APPLES

My father, like many men of his generation, is deeply conservative about his food, maintaining all the while with transparent untruth that he is 'not fussy'. Offer him a fruit salad and he feels cheated of a 'proper pudding'. Only something cooked will do. This baked apple dish fits the bill and is ideal for an occasion when the oven is already on for the main course.

SERVES 4

1 orange
4 Bramley apples
3 tablespoons washed sultanas
1 tablespoon brown sugar

TO SERVE
Thick yoghurt

Pre-heat the oven to Gas Mark 7, 425° F, 220° C. Pare or grate the zest from the orange and squeeze its juice. Peel and core the apples. Slice them thinly. Lay the apple slices, generously scattered with sultanas and sprinkled with the orange juice and zest, in a pint oven-proof and flame-proof gratin dish. Bake, uncovered, for 15–20 minutes, or until the apples are just soft. Pre-heat the grill. Sprinkle the apples with brown sugar and flash under the grill until the sugar melts and forms a brown crust. Serve immediately with thick yoghurt.

STUFFED BAKED PEARS

The best eating pear is the superb sweet William, best enjoyed raw, but other pears often benefit from cooking. Use this recipe for firm pears like Conference – plentiful, cheap and often a little tasteless without some help.

SERVES 4

4 large or 8 small firm pears
2 tablespoons washed sultanas
3 tablespoons walnuts
4 fl oz (100 ml) apple (or other fruit) juice

1 tablespoon brown sugar

TO SERVE
Fromage blanc or thick yoghurt

Pre-heat the oven to Gas Mark 5, 375° F, 190° C. Peel the pears, halve and core them. Chop the sultanas and walnuts finely, or process them briefly. Fill the hollows in the pears with this mixture. Tuck the filled pears into a shallow flame-proof and oven-proof gratin dish and pour the apple juice around the fruit. Cover with foil and bake for 20 minutes, basting occasionally. Pre-heat the grill. When the pears are tender, sprinkle the brown sugar over the top and flash under the grill until it melts. Serve with fromage blanc or thick yoghurt.

BAKED BANANAS

En papillote – 'in an envelope' – is a healthy way to cook. How convenient of bananas to come with their own ready-made 'envelopes', tough enough to use for baking. This is an unbelievably simple way of making an easy pudding which most people, children especially, relish. It produces a tender, sweet, moist fruit with an intensified flavour. Choose the small bananas – that way you can look generous by giving each diner two.

SERVES 4

8 small bananas
1 lemon
Sprinkling of brown sugar

TO SERVE
Fromage blanc

Pre-heat the oven to Gas Mark 4, 350° F, 180° C. Put the bananas on a baking tray just as they are and bake for 15 minutes. The skins will look black and highly unappetizing. Slit them carefully and roll the bananas gently on to individual flat serving plates. Use half the lemon to squeeze over the fruit. Sprinkle meanly with brown sugar. Cut the remaining lemon half into small wedges and serve with the bananas and some well-chilled fromage blanc.

USEFUL EXTRAS

People sometimes think that 'healthy' food means never having a sauce or relish with food. Not at all. But the sauces need to be made on a different principle from the classic French sauce, which is based on butter, flour, egg yolks and cream. The newer type of 'healthy' sauce made from natural stock, or vegetable or fruit purées, is one of the few lasting legacies of the *nouvelle cuisine* fashion of the Seventies, and is likely to be around for much longer.

Good stock is vital for sauces and soups, so I give several easy recipes here for variations on the basic themes of meat, fish and vegetable stock.

Also included in this section are a 'healthier' version of chutney, a tasty spiced oil to add zest to grilled food, and a couple of pleasantly unusual mueslis that may encourage you to make your own experiments with different mixtures of grains, fruits, nuts and seeds.

GREEN HERB SAUCE

I am a hopeless gardener, but I do try to keep a good herb patch in my little London garden. Even if I were to neglect it totally the sorrel would continue to spring up bravely every year, and it seems to flourish whatever the summer weather. In fact any selection of favourite or available fresh herbs will work in this useful and fat-free cold sauce for fish or cold meat, but sorrel is especially good.

A good handful fresh green herbs: e.g., 10 sorrel leaves, 10 sprigs coriander, 4 sprigs parsley, 20 mint leaves, 3 sprigs tarragon, 3 sprigs dill

6 tablespoons low-fat fromage blanc or plain yoghurt
2 teaspoons dill or tarragon vinegar (or white wine vinegar)

Put the herbs into a heat-proof jug and pour boiling water on them. Let them stand for 30 seconds, drain them and run a cold tap over them. Squeeze them dry. Put them with the fromage blanc or yoghurt and the vinegar into a blender or processor. Blend until you have achieved a green speckled sauce. Chill for at least 10 minutes.

ROSY RED SAUCE

This light, refreshing cold sauce is excellent with grilled fish.

1 medium onion	½ teaspoon sugar
8 oz (225 g) sweet ripe tomatoes	2 tablespoons white wine vinegar
1 small red pepper	½ teaspoon dried oregano

Chop the onion finely and stir-fry it for a few moments in a deep pan brushed out with a little oil, until the onion is softened. Add the halved tomatoes, the de-seeded pepper roughly chopped, the sugar, white wine vinegar and dried oregano. Bring to a simmer, cover and cook gently for 15 minutes. Push the sauce through a sieve – skins and pips are unpleasant in this kind of sauce. Turn into a serving bowl and chill in the refrigerator.

GOOSEBERRY AND APPLE SAUCE

A tart sauce is always an interesting contrast with oily fish such as mackerel or herring.

8 oz (225 g) dessert gooseberries	½ teaspoon sugar
1 Bramley apple, cored and	Pinch ground ginger
roughly chopped	2 tablespoons water

Put all the ingredients in a pan, bring to a bare simmer, cover and cook until the fruit is very soft. Push through a sieve, pour into a serving dish and serve chilled.

PLUM SAUCE

Sharp fruit sauces are especially useful for grilled oily fish. This sauce goes well with the herring fillets on page 188 and with the spiced sardines on pages 189–90.

8 oz (225 g) fresh plums
Dash white wine vinegar

½ teaspoon sugar
Freshly ground black pepper

Stone the plums. Simmer them in a little water until they are soft. Drain them and discard the juice. Pass the flesh through a sieve. Add the wine vinegar and sugar. Serve cold.

'HOT' DIPPING SAUCE

A fiery sauce is often a good partner to a fairly plain grilled or stir-fried dish and is also good with blander fish. It is easy to assemble in advance while the main dish is cooking.

2 tablespoons tomato purée
2 tablespoons lemon juice
Squeeze garlic purée, or 1 garlic
    clove, well mashed
½ teaspoon cayenne pepper

½ teaspoon mustard
½ teaspoon ground ginger
1 tablespoon water
Salt and pepper to taste

Beat or blend all the ingredients together to make a thin sauce. Pour individual portions into tiny saucers or dishes. The idea is that diners dip their food into their own sauce dishes.

BROWN BEEF OR CHICKEN STOCK

Brown stock is best for dark sauces, for some soups and for gravies. The flavour the real thing produces is infinitely superior to that of either additive-rich 'gravy granules' or a stock cube. It is fiddly to make, but the trouble is well worth it. I have a gigantic stock-making session every now and then and store the results in the freezer.

1 tablespoon sunflower oil
1 lb (450 g) broken-up raw beef
    marrow bones, or a raw chicken
    carcass broken up into about
    4 pieces
2 onions, skins left on

2 carrots
1 bay-leaf
6 peppercorns
Sprig fresh thyme
3 parsley stalks
2½ pints (1.5 l) water

Pre-heat the oven to its maximum. Heat the oil in a deep flame-proof casserole or a good, solid, clean roasting tin. Turn the bones vigorously until they are well browned. Now put them just as they are into the very hot oven on a high shelf for 30 minutes, or until they are turning dark brown. Meanwhile chop the vegetables. Now add them to the pan, turning them in the oil. Leave the pan in the oven for another 15 minutes, or until the vegetables are also well browned. Now add the other ingredients, bring to a simmer, half cover and cook gently for another 2 hours. It is best to do this on top of the stove, but it can also be done in the oven by reducing the temperature to medium-low. Skim frequently and scrape all the brown juices off the side and bottom of the pan. The liquid should reduce by about a third.

Strain, cool and refrigerate. Skim off the fat. This stock will keep for 2–3 days in a refrigerator or up to 6 months frozen.

Note

The simmering stage of this stock can be carried out in a pressure cooker. Don't overfill the cooker (refer to the instruction book for guidance). Pressure-cook for 40 minutes, then cook and store as before.

FISH STOCK

Fish stock makes a world of difference to fish soups and to fish dishes made with rice. Don't use oily or smoked fish trimmings, but otherwise any fish bits can be used. Most fishmongers will give you or sell for a few pence the requisite heads, tails, bones or shells. The only other rule is not to let this stock cook for more than 20 minutes – after that a sour taste can creep in.

About 12 oz (350 g) fish heads, tails, flesh or bones	**1 bay-leaf**
1 onion	**10 peppercorns**
1 carrot	**Sprig fresh thyme**
	1½ pints (1 l) water

Put all the ingredients into a pan and simmer them, skimming frequently. Strain after 20 minutes. Boil the stock down if you wish, to concentrate its flavour. Use within a day or freeze for up to 6 months.

CHICKEN GIBLET STOCK

Never throw away chicken giblets. They make a good quick stock and you can give the cooked liver to the cat.

Chicken giblets
1 onion, halved but not peeled
½ carrot

1 bay-leaf
1 pint (600 ml) water

Put all the ingredients in a lidded saucepan. Cover tightly and simmer for 30 minutes or pressure-cook for 10 minutes. Skim off any scum. Strain and use for sauces or soups within a day, or freeze for later.

CLEAR WHITE STOCK

This useful basic stock will set to a firm jelly and can be kept refrigerated for about 6 days, or frozen. A cooked chicken carcass can also be used, but the flavour will not be as strong.

1 raw chicken carcass
2 onions
1 carrot
2 celery stalks
2 bay-leaves

10 peppercorns
10 whole coriander seeds
Sprig fresh thyme
2 fresh sage leaves
2½ pints (1.5 l) water

Put all the ingredients into a deep pan (break up the carcass a little with a cleaver). Bring to a simmer, half cover, and cook for about 2 hours, letting the liquid reduce a little (or pressure-cook for 40 minutes). Skim frequently. Strain the stock and let it cool. Remove the layer of fat at the top.

VEGETABLE STOCK

This is a useful cheap stock for soups, or an all-purpose stock when you have a vegetarian coming to dinner.

2 large onions
3 carrots
2 sticks celery with leaves
10 whole peppercorns
10 whole coriander seeds

2 bay-leaves
2 parsley stalks
1 sprig thyme
1½ pints (1 l) water

227

Halve but do not peel the onions. Roughly chop the carrots and celery. Add all the seasonings, pour on the water, cover tightly and simmer for 1½ hours. Strain and store in the refrigerator for 2–3 days, or in the freezer for up to 6 months.

SULTANA AND APRICOT CHUTNEY

Many traditional chutney recipes contain a lot of sugar and salt, which of course are preservatives. This recipe is a useful alternative; it contains only about a quarter of the usual amount of sugar and no salt. It will keep for at least four months, but you can use it straight away.

MAKES 2 × 1-LB JARS

6 oz (180 g) sultanas
4 oz (110 g) dried apricots
2 Bramley apples
1 onion
1-in cube fresh ginger

1 teaspoon whole coriander seed
1 heaped teaspoon chilli powder
4 oz (110 g) sugar
15 fl oz (400 ml) cider vinegar

Wash the sultanas and apricots. Chop the apricots roughly; chop the apples (don't peel them) and onion finely. Slice the ginger. Put these and all the other ingredients into a large uncovered pan, bring to the boil and then simmer, covered, for 15 minutes, then very gently, uncovered, for another 15 minutes, by which time the chutney should be thick (it will thicken more on cooling). Pot in clean, dry, warmed jars, stirring well to disperse air pockets. Seal with plastic-lined metal tops.

SPICED OIL FOR GRILLING

Using flavoured oils is an excellent way of adding interest to otherwise plainly grilled fish or meat. Brush it on thinly.

7 cardamom pods, cracked
1 teaspoon coriander seeds, crushed
3 dried chillies
5 black peppercorns

½ teaspoon mustard seeds
5 fl oz (150 ml) sunflower or safflower oil
3 cloves garlic, crushed

Scrupulously wash a jam jar with a lid and dry it very carefully. Drop in all the spices, then pour the oil on top. Store for a week before using. Use within 2 months.

TROPICAL FRUIT MUESLI

Dried mango, pineapple and other tropical fruits are now easily bought from health food shops and even from some supermarkets. They can be used to make an excellent alternative to traditional muesli. You must soak this muesli in skimmed milk overnight or for at least an hour before eating it: the dried fruit will otherwise be too hard to eat. Just cover.

1 lb (450 g) porridge oats
⅛ cup pine nuts
½ cup hazelnuts
1 cup lexia or other raisins

½ cup dried mango
½ cup dried pineapple or papaya
½ cup dried peaches
½ cup dried bananas

Muesli is best made in quantity and stored in a large glass jar or lidded plastic container. Put the oats in first. Snip the dried fruit into smaller pieces. Add all the fruit and nuts to the oats and shake well. Serve with skimmed milk – an overnight soak in it improves the flavour. To soak, just cover the muesli with milk; add more before eating it if it seems too stodgy.

GREEN AND GOLD MUESLI

This is a pleasant version of the classic Swiss fruit and nut dish. Make a week's supply in advance and store it in a glass jar.

1 lb (450 g) porridge oats
1 cup rye flakes
1 cup dried apricots, snipped into
    smaller pieces

1 cup lexia or other raisins
½ cup green pumpkin seeds
1 cup hazelnuts
½ cup raw cashews

Mix all the ingredients together. Serve each portion with skimmed milk or yoghurt.

ENTERTAINING

When you are tentatively groping after a healthier lifestyle it is easy to revert to the bad old ways when entertaining. The assumption seems to be that guests will expect the roast pork with crackling, and apple pie with cream, and that in any case these things are a treat. I have found that both these assumptions are false. I feed visitors 'healthy' food because if I believe in it at all, which of course I do, then it would seem absolutely wrong not to give my guests the best I can offer. I have discovered that many people seem amazed to be told that what they have eaten is 'healthy'; perhaps the best backhanded compliment a cook can receive in such circumstances is, 'You'd never know it was healthy!' Personally, I no longer regard great dollops of cream, sugar and fatty meat as a 'treat'. Such meals are torture to me and my body suffers for days afterwards with the heavy, bloated feeling I remember so well from the past. I certainly do not want to inflict such pain on my guests!

I give here four suggested menus for dinner parties around the year. I am asuming that you will have bread on the table throughout the first two courses. I assume, too, that you will want to spoil and flatter your guests with at least some slightly more expensive ingredients than you would normally buy for yourselves.

Spring

Carrot and coriander soup

Chinese-style steamed whole fish
Plain rice
Watercress, spinach and lettuce salad

Walnut-stuffed figs with thickened yoghurt

Summer

Chilled green pea soup

Fiery grilled chicken
New potatoes in yoghurt dressing
Green and red leaves
Tomato and basil salad

Red fruit salad
with
fromage blanc

Autumn

Seafood salad

Pork tenderloin with orange and mint
Potato purée
Stir-fried cabbage

Melon with blackberry sauce

Winter

Fish chowder

Breast fillet of duck
with
orange and cranberry sauce
Baked potatoes
French peas

Baked glazed apples with thick yoghurt

EVERYDAY EATING

If healthier eating is to be of any benefit, then it must become part of our everyday lives. Here is a suggested eating pattern for two weeks of family meals. I have assumed that weekday lunches are eaten at school or work. I also assume that bread will automatically appear on the dining table at every meal.

WINTER/SPRING

Weekdays

	Breakfast	**Supper**
Monday	Green and gold muesli with skimmed milk	Stir-fried chicken with broccoli Stir-fried bean-sprouts Plain rice Fresh fruit
Tuesday	Wholemeal toast Fresh fruit	St Clement's plaice Potato cakes Green and red leaves Green fruit salad
Wednesday	Tropical fruit muesli with skimmed milk	Pasta bows with tomato and mushroom sauce Baked glazed apples
Thursday	Shredded wheat with skimmed milk and a little sugar	Deep green soup with lentils Herring rolls with mustard Chicory, watercress and orange salad
Friday	Wholemeal toast Yoghurt with molasses	Red risotto Crunchy green salad with lemon dressing Fruit in a mango puddle

Weekend

	Breakfast	Lunch	Supper
Saturday	Green and gold muesli with skimmed milk	Luke's favourite soup Wholemeal rolls Fresh fruit	Fish plaki Steamed potatoes Stir-fried courgettes Fresh fruit
Sunday	Poached egg on wholemeal toast	American chicken with mustard Baked potatoes Winter salad Baked bananas	Quick-pan pizza Red and white bean salad Gingered grapefruit

SUMMER/AUTUMN

Weekdays

	Breakfast	Supper
Monday	Fresh soft fruit with yoghurt Wholemeal toast	Minced lamb sheftalia Chicory, watercress and orange salad Pitta bread Fresh fruit
Tuesday	Green and gold muesli with skimmed milk	Rice with monkfish and hake Tomato and basil salad Peaches in raspberry sauce
Wednesday	Wholemeal toast Lightly stewed fresh plums	Celery soup Pasta bows with spinach and Ricotta sauce Fresh fruit
Thursday	Tropical fruit muesli with skimmed milk	Stir-fried chicken with lemon and tarragon Spiced rice Fromage blanc with molasses

	Breakfast	**Supper**
Friday	Soaked dried fruit with fromage blanc	Salmon with chives New potatoes Green salad with herbs Raspberry surprise

Weekend

	Breakfast	**Lunch**	**Supper**
Saturday	Boiled egg with wholemeal toast Fresh fruit	Spiced poached mushrooms on wholemeal toast Citrus fruit salad	Stir-fried pork with spring onions Plain rice Tomato salad with basil Fresh fruit
Sunday	Green and gold muesli with skimmed milk	Gazpacho Stuffed chicken breast New potatoes Mange-tout peas Baby carrots	Lamb's kidneys in red wine Plain noodles Pineapple compote

INDEX

FOR THE BEST IN PAPERBACKS, LOOK FOR THE 🐧

In every corner of the world, on every subject under the sun, Penguin represents quality and variety – the very best in publishing today.

For complete information about books available from Penguin – including Pelicans, Puffins, Peregrines and Penguin Classics – and how to order them, write to us at the appropriate address below. Please note that for copyright reasons the selection of books varies from country to country.

In the United Kingdom: For a complete list of books available from Penguin in the U.K., please write to *Dept E.P., Penguin Books Ltd, Harmondsworth, Middlesex, UB7 0DA*

In the United States: For a complete list of books available from Penguin in the U.S., please write to *Dept BA, Penguin, 299 Murray Hill Parkway, East Rutherford, New Jersey 07073*

In Canada: For a complete list of books available from Penguin in Canada, please write to *Penguin Books Canada Ltd, 2801 John Street, Markham, Ontario L3R 1B4*

In Australia: For a complete list of books available from Penguin in Australia, please write to the *Marketing Department, Penguin Books Australia Ltd, P.O. Box 257, Ringwood, Victoria 3134*

In New Zealand: For a complete list of books available from Penguin in New Zealand, please write to the *Marketing Department, Penguin Books (NZ) Ltd, Private Bag, Takapuna, Auckland 9*

In India: For a complete list of books available from Penguin, please write to *Penguin Overseas Ltd, 706 Eros Apartments, 56 Nehru Place, New Delhi, 110019*

In Holland: For a complete list of books available from Penguin in Holland, please write to *Penguin Books Nederland B.V., Postbus 195, NL–1380AD Weesp, Netherlands*

In Germany: For a complete list of books available from Penguin, please write to *Penguin Books Ltd, Friedrichstrasse 10 – 12, D–6000 Frankfurt Main 1, Federal Republic of Germany*

In Spain: For a complete list of books available from Penguin in Spain, please write to *Longman Penguin España, Calle San Nicolas 15, E–28013 Madrid, Spain*

A New Book of Middle Eastern Food   Claudia Roden

'It has permanent value' – Paul Levy in the *Literary Review*. 'Beautifully written, interesting and evocative' – Josceline Dimbleby in the *Sunday Telegraph*. This revised and updated edition of *A Book of Middle Eastern Food* contains many new recipes and much more lore and anecdote of the region.

The Pleasure of Vegetables   Elizabeth Ayrton

'Every dish in this beautifully written book seems possible to make and gorgeous to eat' – *Good Housekeeping*

French Provincial Cooking   Elizabeth David

'One could cook for a lifetime on this book alone' – *Observer*

Jane Grigson's Fruit Book

Fruit is colourful, refreshing and life-enhancing; this book shows how it can also be absolutely delicious in meringues or compotes, soups or pies.

A Taste of American Food   Clare Walker

Far from being just a junk food culture, American cuisine is the most diverse in the world. Swedish, Jewish, Creole and countless other kinds of food have been adapted to the new environment; this book gives some of the most delicious recipes.

Leaves from Our Tuscan Kitchen   Janet Ross and Michael Waterfield

A revised and updated version of a great cookery classic, this splendid book contains some of the most unusual and tasty vegetable recipes in the world.

THE PENGUIN COOKERY LIBRARY – A SELECTION

The Best of Eliza Acton   Selected and Edited by Elizabeth Ray
With an Introduction by Elizabeth David

First published in 1845, Eliza Acton's *Modern Cookery for Private Families*, of which this is a selection, is a true classic which everyone interested in cookery will treasure.

Easy to Entertain   Patricia Lousada

Easy to Entertain hands you the magic key to entertaining without days of panic or last minute butterflies. The magic lies in cooking each course ahead, so that you can enjoy yourself along with your guests.

French Provincial Cooking   Elizabeth David

'It is difficult to think of any home that can do without Elizabeth David's *French Provincial Cooking* . . . One could cook for a lifetime on the book alone' – *Observer*

The National Trust Book of Traditional Puddings   Sara Paston-Williams

'My favourite cookbook of the year. Engagingly written . . . this manages to be both scholarly and practical, elegant without pretension' – *Sunday Times*

The New Book of Middle Eastern Food   Claudia Roden

'This is one of those rare cookery books that is a work of cultural anthropology and Mrs Roden's standards of scholarship are so high as to ensure that it has permanent value' – Paul Levy in the *Observer*

PENGUIN HEALTH

Audrey Eyton's F-Plus   Audrey Eyton

'Your short-cut to the most sensational diet of the century' – *Daily Express*

Caring Well for an Older Person   Muir Gray and Heather McKenzie

Wide-ranging and practical, with a list of useful addresses and contacts, this book will prove invaluable for anyone professionally concerned with the elderly or with an elderly relative to care for.

Baby and Child   Penelope Leach

A beautifully illustrated and comprehensive handbook on the first five years of life. 'It stands head and shoulders above anything else available at the moment' – Mary Kenny in the *Spectator*

Woman's Experience of Sex   Sheila Kitzinger

Fully illustrated with photographs and line drawings, this book explores the riches of women's sexuality at every stage of life. 'A book which any mother could confidently pass on to her daughter – and her partner too' – *Sunday Times*

Food Additives   Erik Millstone

Eat, drink and be worried? Erik Millstone's hard-hitting book contains powerful evidence about the massive risks being taken with the health of consumers. It takes the lid off the food we eat and takes the lid off the food industry.

Pregnancy and Diet   Rachel Holme

It *is* possible to eat well and healthily when pregnant while avoiding excessive calories; this book, with suggested foods, a sample diet-plan of menus and advice on nutrition, shows how.

Medicines: A Guide for Everybody   Peter Parish

This fifth edition of a comprehensive survey of all the medicines available over the counter or on prescription offers clear guidance for the ordinary reader as well as invaluable information for those involved in health care.

Pregnancy and Childbirth   Sheila Kitzinger

A complete and up-to-date guide to physical and emotional preparation for pregnancy – a must for all prospective parents.

The Penguin Encyclopaedia of Nutrition   John Yudkin

This book cuts through all the myths about food and diets to present the real facts clearly and simply. 'Everyone should buy one' – *Nutrition News and Notes*

The Parents' A to Z   Penelope Leach

For anyone with a child of 6 months, 6 years or 16 years, this guide to all the little problems involved in their health, growth and happiness will prove reassuring and helpful.

Jane Fonda's Workout Book

Help yourself to better looks, superb fitness and a whole new approach to health and beauty with this world-famous and fully illustrated programme of diet and exercise advice.

Alternative Medicine   Andrew Stanway

Dr Stanway provides an objective and practical guide to thirty-two alternative forms of therapy – from Acupuncture and the Alexander Technique to Macrobiotics and Yoga.

PENGUIN HEALTH

A Complete Guide to Therapy   Joel Kovel

The options open to anyone seeking psychiatric help are both numerous and confusing. Dr Kovel cuts through the many myths and misunderstandings surrounding today's therapy and explores the pros and cons of various types of therapies.

Pregnancy   Dr Jonathan Scher and Carol Dix

Containing the most up-to-date information on pregnancy – the effects of stress, sexual intercourse, drugs, diet, late maternity and genetic disorders – this book is an invaluable and reassuring guide for prospective parents.

Yoga   Ernest Wood

'It has been asked whether in yoga there is something for everybody. The answer is "yes"'   Ernest Wood.

Depression   Ross Mitchell

Depression is one of the most common contemporary problems. But what exactly do we mean by the term? In this invaluable book Ross Mitchell looks at depression as a mood, as an experience, as an attitude to life and as an illness.

Vogue Natural Health and Beauty   Bronwen Meredith

Health foods, yoga, spas, recipes, natural remedies and beauty preparations are all included in this superb, fully illustrated guide and companion to the bestselling *Vogue Body and Beauty Book*.

Care of the Dying   Richard Lamerton

It is never true that 'nothing more can be done' for the dying. This book shows us how to face death without pain, with humanity, with dignity and in peace.